LAGGING
PRODUCTIVITY
GROWTH

Contributors

Hugh J. Arnold, Management Studies, University of Toronto
Orley Ashenfelter, Industrial Relations Section, Princeton University
Donald J. Daly, Administrative Studies, York University
Martin G. Evans, Management Studies, University of Toronto
Randall K. Filer, Department of Economics, Brandeis University
Robert J. House, Management Studies, University of Toronto
Charles Hulten, The Urban Institute
John W. Kendrick, Department of Economics, The George Washington
  University
John B. Kervin, Centre for Industrial Relations, University of Toronto
Harvey Leibenstein, Harvard University
Shlomo Maital, Woodrow Wilson School of Public and International
  Affairs, Princeton University, and Technion-Israel Institute of Tech-
  nology
Jerome A. Mark, Bureau of Labor Statistics, U.S. Department of Labor
Noah M. Meltz, Centre for Industrial Relations, University of Toronto
Mieko Nishimizu, Woodrow Wilson School of Public and International
  Affairs, Princeton University
John R. Norsworthy, Bureau of Labor Statistics, U.S. Department of
  Labor
Sylvia Ostry, O.E.C.D.
P.S. Rao, Economic Council of Canada
Albert Rees, Sloan Foundation
Frank Reid, Center for Industrial Relations, University of Toronto
John Vanderkamp, Department of Economics, University of Guelph
Leonard Waverman, Institute for Policy Analysis, University of Toronto

LAGGING PRODUCTIVITY GROWTH

Causes and Remedies

Edited by

Shlomo Maital
Woodrow Wilson School of Public and International Affairs, Princeton University, and Faculty of Industrial Engineering and Management, Technion—Israel Institute of Technology

Noah M. Meltz
Center for Industrial Relations, University of Toronto.

This book was prepared in part for the Employment and Training Administration, U.S. Department of Labor, under research and development grant No. P.O. 20-34-79-33. Since contractors conducting research and development projects under government sponsorship are encouraged to express their own judgments freely, this book does not necessarily represent the official opinion or policy of the Department of Labor. The contractor is solely responsible for the contents of this book.

Ballinger Publishing Company • Cambridge, Massachusetts
A Subsidiary of Harper & Row, Publishers, Inc.

International Standard Book Number: 0−88410−689−6

Library of Congress Catalog Card Number: 80−17415

Printed in the United States of America

Library of Congress Cataloging in Publication Data

Main entry under title:

Lagging productivity growth.

  Papers from a colloquium held in Toronto, Canada, May 23−25, 1979.
  Bibliography: p.
  Includes index.
  1. Industrial productivity—Congresses.
  2. Industrial productivity—United States—Congresses.
  3. Industrial productivity—Canada—Congresses.
  I. Maital, Shlomo. II. Meltz, Noah M.
  HD56.L33   338′.06   80−17415
  ISBN 0−88410−689−6

To the Memory of Yochanan Peter Comay
1939-1973

Contents

List of Figures   ix

List of Tables   xi

Preface   xv

Acknowledgments   xvii

INTRODUCTION On Interpreting Productivity Change
Albert Rees   1

PART I: Trends   7

CHAPTER 1 Productivity Trends in the United States
John W. Kendrick   9
Comment: Jerome A. Mark and John R. Norsworthy   31

CHAPTER 2 Productivity Trends in Canada
Sylvia Ostry and P.S. Rao   39
Comment: Noah M. Meltz   76

PART II: Causes and Effects   83

**CHAPTER 3 The Importance of Productivity Change in the
Economic Growth of Nine Industrialized Countries**
Charles R. Hulten and Mieko Nishimizu   85
Comment: Orley Ashenfelter and Frank Reid   101

**CHAPTER 4 The Downturn in Productivity Growth: A New
Look at its Nature and Causes**
Randall K. Filer   109
Comment: Leonard Waverman   124

PART III: New Approaches   129

CHAPTER 5 Productivity: A Psychological Perspective
Hugh J. Arnold, Martin G. Evans and Robert J. House   131
Comment: John Kervin and Shlomo Maital   187

CHAPTER 6 X-Efficiency, Intrafirm Behavior, and Growth
Harvey Leibenstein   199
Comment: Donald J. Daly   217

PART IV: Remedies   221

**CHAPTER 7 Remedies for Increasing Productivity Levels in
Canada**
Donald J. Daly   223
Comment: John Vanderkamp and Mieko Nishimizu   240

**CHAPTER 8 Remedies for the Productivity Slowdown in
the United States**
John W. Kendrick   247

SUMMARY and CONCLUSIONS
Shlomo Maital and Noah M. Meltz   265

BIBLIOGRAPHY   275

INDEX   295
About the Editors   301
Participants   303

List of Figures

3-1	Per Capita Output as a Function of Capital-Labor Ratio	87
3-2	Change in per Capita Output as a Function of the Change in K/L and Technical Change	105
4-1	Annual Rates of Gross Labor Productivity Growth: 1948-77	112
5-1	Conceptual Framework	135
5-2	The Conflict Model of Decisionmaking	146
5-3	Diagrammatic Representation of the Difference Between Efficacy Expectations and Outcome Expectations	177
5-4	Consequences of Organizational Decisionmaking	192
6-1	The Nature of the Choice of Effort Problem	203
6-2	Management and Employee Options	206
6-3	Management and Employee Options	207
6-4	Payoff Matrix	209
6-5	Payoff Matrix	210
6-6	Effort Level Choice	211
6-7	Structure of Lexicographic Ordering	212

List of Tables

1-1 Average Annual Percentage Rates of Change for Real Gross Product, Factor Inputs and Productivity Ratios, U.S. Domestic Business Economy 12

1-2 Average Annual Percentage Rates of Change in Total Tangible Factor Productivity for U.S. Domestic Economy 12

1-3 Average Annual Percentage Rates of Change in Real Product, Factor Inputs, and Productivity Ratios for U.S. Private Domestic Business Economy 14

1-4 Average Annual Percentage Rates of Change of Total Tangible Factor Productivity by Industry Group 15

1-5 Components of Price Changes in U.S. Nonfinancial Corporate Sector 18

1-6 Changes in Unit Factor Costs and Product Prices by Major Industry Group 20

1-7 Matrix of Correlation Coefficients (Rates of Change in Total Factor Productivity and in Product Prices Versus Rates of Change in Associated Variables) 23

1-8 Sources of Growth in Real Gross Product 26

1-9 Average Annual Rates of Change 34

1-10 Average Annual Growth Rates of Capital Stock, Nonfarm Business Sector, for Direct and Translog Aggregation of Equipment, Structures, Land, and Inventories 36

1-11 Effect of Net Capital Stock and Other Factors on Labor Productivity Growth in Nonfarm Business Sector 36

2-1 Output per Man-Hour in Manufacturing 42

2-2 Average Annual Percentage Change in Inputs and Outputs 42

2-3   Aggregate Labor Productivity Growth and Interindustry Shifts   45

2-4   Average Annual Percentage Change in Inputs and Outputs:
       Manufacturing Industries   45

2-5   Average Annual Percentage Change in Inputs and Outputs:
       Primary Industries   45

2-6   Average Annual Percentage Change in Inputs and Outputs:
       Service Industries   47

2-7   Average Annual Percentage Change in Inputs and Outputs:
       Construction Industries   47

2-8   Energy Use in Canadian Manufacturing   53

2-9   Demographic Changes in Canada   55

2-10 Variations in Output per Worker (Standardized for Industrial
       Structure: 1970-73)   57

2-11 Average Annual Growth in Labor Productivity   58

2-12 Selected Productivity Equations (Gross Output) Manufacturing
       Industries: 1957-74, Dependent Variable ln Q/L   69

2-13 Selected Productivity Equations (Gross Output) Nonmanufactur-
       ing Industries: 1957-74, Dependent Variable ln Q/L   74

2-14 Ranking of Average Annual Growth in Labor Productivity by
       Industry Sector in Canada   77

2-15 Percent Distribution of Output and Employment by Industry
       Sector in Canada   78

2-16 Average Annual Percentage Change in Inputs and Outputs by
       Industry Sector in Canada   79

3-1   Average Annual Growth Rates of Intertemporal Output, Input,
       and the Dynamic Residual   94

3-2   Intertemporal View of the Importance of Productivity   95

3-3   Average Annual Growth Rates of Real Product, Real Factor
       Inputs, and Total Factor Productivity   96

3-4   Conventional View of the Sources of Growth   97

3-5   The Long-Run Fisherian Rates of Technical Change   100

3-6   Rate of Economic Growth Due to Productivity Change   107

4-1   Annual Rates of Gross Labor Productivity Growth   110

4-2   Regression Results with Change in Gross Labor Productivity
       as Dependent Variable   116

4-3   Effort Component of Labor Supply   121

5-1   The Seven Major Criteria for Vigilant Information Processing   145

5-2   Competitive Information Desired   152

5-3   Information Sources   153

5-4   Sources of Intelligence   154

6-1   Comparison of X-Efficiency Theory with Neoclassical Theory   201

7–1   Comparisons of Gross Domestic Product   227

7–2   Contribution to Differences Between Canada and the United
        States in Net National Income per Person Employed   227

7–3   Land Area and Mineral Production per Person Employed   230

8–1   Total Gross Investment in Relation to Gross Product and
        Sectoral Disposable Income, U. S. Domestic Economy   264

Preface

The purpose of this volume is to examine the decline in productivity growth, its causes, and some possible remedies. It is comprised of eight studies, and contains two noteworthy features. First, developments affecting productivity and its growth rate are explored for both Canada and the United States. The two countries' similar industrial structures and their highly interrelated economies enhance the value of contrasts and comparisons. Parallel examinations reveal that up to the early 1970s Canada did not experience the drop in productivity growth that afflicted the United States. Second, perspectives on productivity from fields other than economics are included. In the past, debate and discussion of productivity has tended to remain within the borders of economics. This book includes both psychological and sociological viewpoints. Specifically, the contribution of management to productivity, as set out by organizational behavior, is extensively surveyed.

There are four parts: Trends, Causes and Effects, New Approaches, and Remedies. Each part contains two chapters and most chapters include both a primary presentation and comments. The comments are intended to deepen understanding of the material and highlight special points of interest.

The introductory chapter is an overview provided by Albert Rees, who sets out the main issues, notes our achievements to date, and outlines current, unsolved problems. Part I addresses itself to long-term trends and factors underlying productivity growth in the United States and Canada.

Part II goes beyond the macroeconomic examination of American and Canadian experience in two respects. Chapter 3 assesses the importance of productivity gains in economic growth for nine industrialized countries (Canada, France, West Germany, Italy, Japan, Korea, the Netherlands, the United Kingdom, and the United States). Chapter 4 uses a multiple regression approach to account for productivity change by such factors as research and development spending, energy prices and the proportion of women in the work force.

Microeconomic and noneconomic factors are the focus of Part III. Chapter 5 provides a survey of the literature on organizational behavior as it relates to productivity, particularly for the individual firm. It shows how management practices affect the motivation of individual members of organizations and their ability to perform their roles effectively.

Chapter 6 examines the relation between utilization of inputs and motivation, as a new application of X-efficiency theory.

Part IV is devoted to remedies for lagging productivity. Chapter 7 addresses the question of how to raise the level of Canada's productivity. It notes that although productivity has been rising faster in Canada than in the United States, there still remains a 7 to 14 percent gap. Author Donald Daly emphasizes changes in government policy, but stresses the necessity of active support from the private sector. Chapter 8 presents prescriptions for counteracting the slowdown in productivity gains for the United States. John Kendrick, the author, urges policies that could, he argues, restore the 3 percent annual growth rate in productivity.

A concluding chapter summarizes the eight papers and outlines areas demanding further research and analysis.

Acknowledgments

Is productivity research productive? Should resources be allocated for bringing productivity researchers together to discuss trends, dissect causes, debate remedies? Two years ago we both felt strongly that these questions deserved affirmative answers and some positive action. We quickly learned that many scholars shared that belief and, in the colloquium on lagging productivity growth held in Toronto May 23-25, 1979, expressed it in their papers, comments, and participation. This volume is the fruit of that gathering.

Equally important, several institutions shared our view and came forward with generous offers of financial support. They are: in Canada, Department of Labor, Economic Council of Canada, Ontario Ministry of Labor, Ontario Economic Council, General Motors of Canada Ltd., and Center for Industrial Relations, University of Toronto; in the United States, Department of Labor and Industrial Relations Section, Princeton University. Partial support for the preparation of this volume came from the Sloan Grant for Applied Microeconomic Research.

For the organizational abilities of Deborah Campbell and Agnes Pearson, much in evidence in both the colloquium and these proceedings, we express our thanks and admiration. Our editor, Carol Franco, and copy editor, Patricia Vigderman, helped bring an untidy manuscript to print with skill and good humor.

Shlomo Maital
Noah M. Meltz

Introduction

On Interpreting
Productivity Change

Albert Rees

It is increasingly clear that the rate of growth of productivity in North America has been falling. In the United States in the period 1948 to 1965 estimated output per hour in the private business sector grew at more than 3 percent a year; from 1965 to 1973 it grew at more than 2 percent a year; and from 1973 to 1978 at less than 1 percent a year. (Economic Report of the President, 1979:68) From 1967 to 1977, output per hour in manufacturing grew at a slower rate in the United States and in Canada than in any major Western European country except the United Kingdom, and at a much slower rate than in Japan. The same slowdown in productivity growth can be seen in measures of multifactor productivity, and so can the relatively poor performance of North America. A study by Christensen, Cummings, and Jorgenson shows the United States last and Canada next-to-last among nine industrial countries in the growth of multifactor productivity from 1960 to 1973 (Christensen, Cummings, and Jorgenson 1977).

Why is this disappointing growth of productivity important? I would answer first that it is important because productivity is the main source of improvement in our standard of living.

Productivity is defined as a ratio of output to one or more inputs. When output per unit of input rises, it is possible for some people to consume more without others consuming less, or even in principle for everyone to consume more. On the other hand, if output rises not because of rising productivity, but only because more inputs are being used to product it, then all of the added output is needed merely to compensate the suppliers of the additional units of input at their old rates of compensation. For example, when productivity is constant workers

1

receive higher real incomes only if they work more hours, or if relative factor prices shift in their favor. However, this last possibility is merely a redistribution of income—one group gets more only to the extent that another group gets less.

This example suggests a second reason why the growth of productivity is important—it helps to mediate social conflict. When productivity rises, there is a social dividend to be distributed. This distribution lubricates the clashes between competing economic groups. When productivity fails to rise, the struggle over income shares may become more intense. The principal reason why Karl Marx was wrong about the inevitability of violent class conflict in capitalist societies is that he failed to foresee the growth of productivity and the consequent tremendous rise in the standard of living of the working class. In a capitalistic society in which productivity does not rise over a long period, he may yet be proved right.

In the United States in recent years there has been much comment on the growing power of economic interest groups in political decisionmaking. Perhaps the increased strength and militance of such groups is related to the lag in productivity growth.

It has also been suggested that when productivity growth decelerates, as it has recently, political and economic bargaining over income shares can contribute to inflation. This will happen if some of the bargaining groups seek to keep their real incomes growing at a rate corresponding to the old rate of growth of productivity—a rate that is no longer sustainable. If an accommodating monetary and fiscal policy is willing to finance these excessive claims to income, the result will be higher prices. Inflation will erode the real value of the claims so that in the aggregate they can be met by actual real output. In the process, claims that were advanced as real claims produce largely nominal gains, and must be advanced again or scaled down.

Just as productivity growth can ease the conflicts between claimants to real income, it can also make less painful the choices between producing more goods and services for consumers and producing other things that contribute to social welfare. Using factor inputs to abate air, water, or noise pollution, to improve worker health and safety, or to conserve vanishing species of plants and animals will reduce measured productivity. The added inputs used in these activities will appear in the denominator of the productivity ratio, but the unmeasured outputs will not appear in the numerator. The more efficient we are in using factor inputs to produce measured conventional outputs of final goods and services, the more easily we can afford to use some of our inputs in other ways that enhance welfare.

It is sometimes argued that it is wrong to limit the output portion of the productivity ratio to conventional goods and services—that the numerator of the ratio should instead be a global measure of welfare. Proposals of this sort must cope with the great subjectivity that is necessarily involved in valuing unmarketed outputs and outcomes such as clean air and good health. The proposals must also specify how to get independent measures of inputs and outputs in such activities as child care by unpaid parents. We are not now close to agreement on how best to do these things, and may never be. I would therefore regard proposals to measure productivity in terms of efficiency in achieving global welfare as at best premature and at worst inherently unfeasible.

Because the concept of productivity is important in understanding the rise in living standards, the distribution of income, and some of the proximate causes of inflation, it would be highly desirable if this concept were well understood by the communications media and the public. Unfortunately, it is not.

Our official productivity statistics measure output per unit of labor input and are therefore called measures of labor productivity. When labor productivity levels off or declines, this is sometimes taken as evidence that workers are not working as hard as they used to, and it is said that "we must all get back to work again." This is, of course, a non sequitur. Declining productivity might reflect less effort by workers, but it could equally well reflect the influence of a host of other forces. If we were to learn that cars now get fewer miles to a gallon of gasoline than they used to, we would not jump to the conclusion that the quality of gasoline had deteriorated; yet this is the same kind of unwarranted inference from a single-input productivity measure. Anything that affects output can affect output per unit of labor input, and this includes many forces other than work effort. There is some evidence that workers do not work as hard as they used to, but my point is that we need to examine such independent evidence—we cannot infer a change in effort from the behavior of productivity alone.

I have been speaking as though the lag in productivity growth were a real phenomenon and not a statistical artifact. Given the very substantial errors in the measurement of productivity, we cannot be absolutely certain that this is so. However, I have spent a good deal of time in the past two years examining the measurement of productivity. In the process, I have become convinced that it is highly unlikely that the apparent lag is merely the result of statistical error.

For the apparent lag in productivity growth to arise from measurement error, two conditions must be fulfilled. First, the error must bias the measure of productivity growth downward. Second, the error must be substantially larger in the last decade than it was in the two preceding ones. The first of these conditions has probably been met, but the second is not at all likely.

For example, on the input side the measure of hours of labor in the

United States is hours paid for rather than hours spent at the workplace. The difference between the two measures consists of paid leave, which is largely paid vacations, holidays, and sick leave. Since workers do not produce output when they are not at the workplace, the growth of paid leave biases the rate of change of productivity downward. However, paid leave time has been increasing ever since World War II, and probably increased most rapidly early in the postwar period. Thus this source of measurement error probably does not contribute at all to the recent lag in productivity growth.

Similarly, it has been shown by some statistical evidence based on small samples of worker time diaries that workers while at the workplace now spend more time than they used to not actually working, but taking coffee breaks and otherwise consuming leisure on the job. However, we do not know anything about the long-term trend in such behavior. Unless the change began quite recently, it would not contribute to the lag in measured productivity growth.

On the output side, measurement error occurs when we fail to record improvement in the quality of products or services and therefore report spurious increases in their prices. These biased price measures are then used to deflate measures of the current dollar value of output, thus understating the rise in real output and in real productivity. There is substantial evidence that errors of this kind occur, but also some evidence that they now occur less frequently than they used to. The whole postwar productivity trend may therefore be understated without any overstatement of the amount of the recent lag. We cannot be certain that the lag is real, but examination of the most obvious sources of measurement error suggests that it is.

What are the sources of productivity change? In commenting on this topic, I do not mean to steal the thunder of those who will discuss it in more detail, but rather I hope to set the stage for them.

Many different factors play a role in productivity change, and the relations between them are highly complex. There is no unique way of partitioning productivity change among these interrelated sources, and the results of any analysis therefore depend heavily on the assumptions it makes. This is not to deny that growth accounting is valuable, but merely to suggest that it is still an art rather than a science, and that we should be tolerant of divergent approaches and results.

Let me give a few examples of the difficulties involved. In the United States in the past decade, there have been two important kinds of change in labor inputs. One is that teenagers and women now form a much larger part of the workforce, and on average these new workers have less experience than adult men. The second is that workers now have more years of schooling than they used to. The first of these changes reduces output per unweighted unit of labor input, the second increases it. If we combine the two effects using base-period earnings weights, we find that overall labor quality has been rising more rapidly recently than in preceding periods, and is therefore not on balance a source of the lag in productivity growth. However, some recent research suggests that the rise in years of schooling has been accompanied by a decline in the marginal return to schooling in production (Freeman 1976). If this is correct, we would get different results if we used current earnings weights rather than historical weights.

Moreover, the effects of changes in the composition of labor inputs may vary with time. Suppose we add to the workforce many new workers with little experience and much schooling. In the short run, their lack of experience could be the more important characteristic and the average quality of labor input would be reduced. But given time, their lack of experience will be overcome and the average quality of labor input will rise again, perhaps above the initial level.

We should also keep in mind that with real forces, as with measurement errors, not every force that lowers productivity contributes to the recent lag in productivity growth. To do so, a productivity-reducing force must be becoming more important. For example, we all know of certain restrictive work practices that reduce productivity in enterprises whose workers are organized by craft unions. An example that became conspicuous recently is the overmanning of pressrooms in the New York newspapers. Such practices are generally of very long standing. There is little systematic evidence on their extent, much less any statistical measure of it. However, what unsystematic evidence one can gather all suggests that in the United States these practices are decreasing in importance. In some cases management is succeeding in eliminating or moderating restrictive work practices through collective bargaining; the extent of collective bargaining in some of the affected industries is decreasing; and employment in some of these industries has been declining. Thus restrictive work practices do not help to explain the productivity lag—on the contrary, their erosion makes it even harder to explain.

Measuring the quality of labor inputs, hard as it is, is a fairly straightforward task compared to the analysis of some other sources of growth. The growth of knowledge, surely the most basic source of growth in productivity, is usually estimated as a residual or, more accurately, as part of a residual. We sometimes find large differences in such residuals between the United States and Canada. However, a large difference in useful knowledge is implausible between two economies whose technology, enterprises, and other institutions are similar and that have a lively exchange of information and people.

Worse yet, in recent years the residuals in growth-accounting studies have turned negative. If we continue to interpret them as measuring largely the growth of knowledge, then we would have to conclude that knowledge useful in production has been decreasing. Knowledge of some sorts may indeed be decreasing in the sense of being less widely diffused —perhaps fewer people know how to shoe a horse than did in 1900—but there cannot be much useful knowledge that is altogether lost.

When we try to sort out the contributions of research and development and capital formation to productivity growth, we are again plagued by the importance of interactions and the lack of broadly based estimates of the return to investment in research and development and of the time lags between outlays and returns. In the United States spending on research and development as a percentage of gross national product has been declining since the mid-1960s, though some of the decline is in defense-related research (Economic Report of the President, 1979:70). Perhaps more of current research is directed toward very long range objectives, such as energy from nuclear fusion, which probably will not reach the point of practical application in this century.

There has also been a decline in the rate of growth of capital in the nonfarm business sector in the United States since 1973 (Norsworthy and Harper 1979). Two of the sources of this may be our tax laws, which bias investment toward owner-occupied housing, and our depreciation accounting procedures, which may lead us to tax the return on capital too heavily when plant and equipment prices are rising. Neither of these conditions is new, but both may become more important when there is rapid inflation, including inflation in land prices, house prices, and the cost of capital equipment.

I have not yet begun to exhaust the list of candidates for the role of culprit in the great productivity lag. There is the increase in expenditures on conservation, pollution control, and worker health and safety, which I mentioned earlier in another context. There is the more general increase in government regulation affecting the cost of doing business. There is the sharp rise in the price of energy in the 1970s, which shifts the focus of research and development efforts and new investment away from saving labor and toward saving energy inputs. As Ezra Solomon has put it, we have redirected our efforts from saving drops of sweat to saving drops of oil. There is the decline in the rate of transfer of labor from agriculture to other industries as the remaining pool of less productive farm labor grows smaller.

Thus when we seek to sort out the causes of the lag in productivity growth, we each know some of the causes, but our lists will not all be the same, and we will not all give the same importance to the various items on them. And somehow all of the causes taken together still seem inadequate to explain the change—there is a mystery here still to be solved. There is therefore lots of room for further research; enough to keep us all very busy.

✳ *Part 1*

Trends

 *Chapter 1*

Productivity Trends
In the United States
John W. Kendrick

INTRODUCTION

The slowdown in productivity growth of the U.S. business economy since the mid-1960s is viewed first in the historical perspective provided by estimates that go back to 1800. The gradual acceleration in rates of productivity growth is traced across a number of periods, culminating in the golden era of the first two decades following World War II. The subsequent deceleration is documented, with due allowance for the fact that the terminal year of this study, 1978, is not yet the peak year of the current economic expansion.

We then look at the period since 1948 more intensively in terms of the different trends in productivity by industry groups. In addition to trends, the variations in rates of change of productivity across subperiods bounded by cycle peak years are discussed. For the business economy as a whole, we also note the typical pattern of productivity change in cycle expansions and contractions, and its role in the explanation of fluctuations.

In the next section, the role of productivity growth in offsetting rising nominal factor prices with respect to unit labor costs and product prices is reviewed. For the nonfinancial corporate sector, strong productivity growth offset more than half the rise in factor prices during 1948–66, with unit costs and product prices rising by less than 2 percent a year, on average. This contrasts with the period after 1966, when slower productivity advance and accelerating factor prices were associated with a much higher inflation rate. Because of the negative correlation between relative changes in productivity and in prices and between relative changes in prices and in output (outside of the extractive and service sectors), there was a significant positive correlation between relative changes in productivity and in output. This was reinforced by the effect of relative scale economies on productivity.

The final section contains the findings regarding causes of productivity advance. First, a Denison-type growth-accounting exercise is used to explain changes in productivity in the U.S. business economy 1948–66, 1966–73, and 1973–78. This makes it possible to explain the deceleration in productivity growth across the three subperiods in terms of the explanatory variables specified in the model.

The primary productivity measure used in the work underlying this paper is based on the concept of total tangible factor productivity (TFP), as developed in earlier work by the author (Kendrick 1974). Briefly, TFP is the ratio of real gross product to a weighted average of labor and capital inputs. The weights are based on factor shares of gross national income in successive periods. Labor input is measured in terms of hours worked or paid for, and capital input is assumed to move proportionately to the real gross stocks of tangible capital—land, structures, equipment, and inventories. Since each of the factor inputs is not internally weighted, the productivity ratios are affected by relative shifts of labor and of capital among industries with differing average rates of remuneration, as well as by changes in age mix. Since the capital estimates are not adjusted for rates of utilization of capacity, the productivity measures are also affected by changing utilization rates.

In addition to TFP, some of the tables show the "partial productivity" ratios (output/labor and output/capital) separately. The reconciliation item between changes in TFP and in the more conventional "labor productivity" measure is the rate of substitution of capital for labor, that is, the rate of change in capital per labor hour, reduced by the relative weight of capital.

PRODUCTIVITY DEVELOPMENTS IN THE U.S. BUSINESS ECONOMY

The description and analysis of productivity movements in this paper are confined to the major sectors and industry groupings of the U.S. domestic business economy. Independent output and input estimates are not generally available for household, private nonprofit institutions, governments, or the foreign business sector. But the domestic business sector is responsible for about 85 percent of gross national product in recent decades, according to the official Department of Commerce estimates. So the trends in the business sector give a fair picture of what has been happening in the economy as a whole, although fragmentary evidence suggests that productivity in the nonbusiness sectors rises less rapidly than it does in the business sector.

Trends for Major Periods Since 1800

Table 1-1 provides a broad historical perspective of trend-rates of growth in TFP, and its contribution to growth of real product and real product per capita in the U.S. business economy.[1] The table tells its own story, but the main features may be summarized briefly. Between 1800 and 1890, TFP grew slowly—at an average annual rate of 0.3 percent, according to the estimates of Abramovitz and David . Since real gross product grew at an average of 4.1 percent and population by 2.8 percent a year, it is clear that most of the increase in real income per capita was due to the growth of factor inputs per capita, particularly capital (including land).

My estimates of a 1.7 percent rate of growth of TFP between 1889 and 1919 represent a sharp acceleration over the earlier period. During this thirty-year period TFP accounted for almost half of the 3.9 percent growth rate and for the major portion of the 2.1 percent a year average increase in real product per capita.

There was further acceleration in the rate of increase of TFP in the period 1919-48, despite the depressing influence on economic growth of the stagnation of the 1930s. The high-water mark of TFP growth, an average annual rate of 2.8 percent, was reached in the 1948-66 period. It accounted for more than all of the increase in real product per capita, since total factor input rose less than the 1.5 percent average rate of population growth. Compared with the nineteenth century, the growth of total input had decelerated considerably more than population growth. But the growth of real product per capita at a 2.4 percent average annual rate was significantly higher than in the nineteenth century because of the notable acceleration of productivity growth.

Finally, in the period 1966-78, the rate of productivity growth fell by more than one-half. Despite a faster growth of factor inputs, mainly labor, and a slowing of population growth, the increase in real product per capita slackened somewhat. The trends for this period are distorted a little by the fact that the ratio of actual to potential GNP was .973 in 1978, according to estimates of the Council of Economic Advisers. But even if the ratio had been 1.00, the growth rate of real product would have been only 0.2 percentage points greater than the 3.1 shown in the table for 1966-78, and the rate of TFP growth about 0.1 percentage point greater.

Table 1-2 shows rates of change of TFP in the major industry groupings of the business economy for three periods between 1889 and

Table 1–1. Average Annual Percentage Rates of Change for Real Gross Product, Factor Inputs and Productivity Ratios, U.S. Domestic Business Economy

	1800–55	1855–90	1889–1919	1919–48	1948–66	1966–78
Real gross product	4.2	4.0	3.9	3.0	3.9	3.1
Population	3.1	2.4	1.8	1.2	1.6	0.9
Real product per capita	1.1	1.6	2.1	1.8	2.3	2.2
Tangible factor input						
Total	3.9	3.6	2.2	0.8	1.0	1.8
Labor	3.7	2.8	1.8	0.6	0.4	1.4
Capital	4.3	4.6	3.1	1.2	2.4	2.6
Productivity ratios						
Total factor productivity	0.3	0.3	1.7	2.2	2.9	1.3
Labor	0.5	1.1	2.0	2.4	3.5	1.7
Capital	-0.1	-0.6	0.7	1.8	1.5	0.5

Source: 1800–1890 based on Abramovitz and David (1973: Tables 1 and 2); 1889–1948 from Kendrick (1961); 1948–1978 from Kendrick and Grossman (forthcoming).

Table 1–2. Average Annual Percentage Rates of Change in Total Tangible Factor Productivity for U.S. Domestic Economy

	1889–1919	1919–1948	1948–1973
Private domestic economy	1.7	2.2	2.5
Farm	0.2	1.7	3.3
Nonfarm	1.5	1.9	2.1
Mining	1.6	2.3	2.4
Contract construction	n.a.	n.a.	0.9
Manufacturing	0.7	2.9	2.3
Transportation	2.4	4.0	2.6
Communications	2.2	1.7	4.2
Electric and gas utilities	3.8	4.6	3.9
Trade	0.8	1.5	2.3
Finance, insurance, real estate	—	—	2.0
Services	2.2[a]	1.0[a]	1.7

Source: Kendrick (1961); estimates since 1948 revised and extended by the author.
[a]Output per unit of labor input for finance, insurance, real estate, and services combined.
n.a.—not available.

1973. (The last period ends with 1973, the most recent business cycle peak year, since industry estimates of real product and productivity were not available for 1978 at the time of the writing.) Note that TFP in the farm sector accelerated much more over the three periods than did nonfarm TFP. Between 1889 and 1919, the 0.2 percent average annual rate of increase was well below that of TFP in the nonfarm economy, and below its own rate of increase between 1800 and 1890—which, according to Robert Gallman (1972) averaged about 0.5 percent a year. From 1919 to 1948, the growth was close to that for the entire business economy; pronounced acceleration began only after 1937. The 3.2 percent increase in the final quarter-century was well above average, although, as we shall see in the next section, deceleration set in after 1969.

Within the nonfarm sector, TFP in mining also showed a marked acceleration over the three periods; although here, too, deceleration has occurred in recent years. Manufacturing TFP registered less than 1 percent a year average growth in the 1889–1919 period, reflecting in part a rapid build-up of capital. In the subsequent period the 2.9 percent gain was above-average, but in the final period 2.3 percent was a bit below average. The regulated groups—rail and nonrail transportation, communications, and public utilities—generally showed above average productivity gains in all three periods. In contrast, the services sector (trade, finance, insurance and real estate, and private agencies) generally increased productivity at rates below the average for the business economy—although measurement problems may impart some downward bias to growth estimates for parts of this sector. Contract construction also exhibited below-average TFP performance, although here too the output estimates are subject to a considerable margin of error.

Productivity Movement Since 1948

In Table 1–3, the growth rates of real gross product, factor inputs, and the productivity ratios since 1948 are shown for subperiods bounded by business cycle peak years (except for 1978, a nonpeak year). There is considerable variation in the rates of change of the several variables across the subperiods within the thirty-year period. Variations in rates of change in productivity and in output correlate positively to the extent that the latter are also related to changes in rates of utilization of capacity, and reflect differing opportunities for economies of scale. Thus, the strong surges of economic growth from 1948 to 1953 and 1960 to 1966 were associated with increases in TFP of nearly 3.5 percent a year, on average. Conversely, slower growth in real product during the 1953–60 subperiod was associated with TFP advances of little more than 2 percent. But the retardation in productivity growth after 1966 was much

Table 1–3. Average Annual Percentage Rates of Change in Real Product, Factor Inputs and Productivity Ratios for U.S. Private Domestic Business Economy

	Real Gross Product	Factor Inputs			Productivity Ratios		
		Total	Labor	Capital	Total	Labor	Capital
1948–78	3.6	1.3	0.8	2.5	2.3	2.8	1.1
1948–66	3.9	1.0	0.4	2.4	2.9	3.5	1.5
1966–78	3.1	1.8	1.4	2.6	1.3	1.7	0.5
1948–53	4.4	0.9	0.3	2.6	3.4	4.1	1.8
1953–57	2.9	0.8	—	2.6	2.1	2.9	0.3
1957–60	2.4	0.3	–0.3	1.8	2.1	2.7	0.6
1960–66	5.1	1.6	1.2	2.4	3.4	3.9	2.7
1966–69	3.5	2.0	1.4	3.1	1.5	2.1	0.4
1969–73	3.6	1.8	1.3	2.7	1.8	2.3	0.9
1973–78	2.5	1.7	1.4	2.2	0.8	1.1	0.3

greater than can be attributed to slowing growth in real product. From 1966 to 1973, the rate of economic growth was well above that in the later 1950s, but the productivity gains were significantly less. And although the growth of real product between 1973 and 1978 was about the same as from 1957 to 1960, the rate of increase in TFP was less than half as great. Obviously, there are variables other than volume changes that help explain the retardation, as discussed below.

Rates of change in TFP for the period 1948–73 are shown for major business sectors and manfacturing industries in Table 1–4. The dispersion in rates of change is greater in the subperiods than over the whole period, of course. In the latter, rates within the manufacturing sector range from 0.6 percent a year for primary metals up to almost 4 percent for electrical machinery. Among the nonmanufacturing sectors rates range from less than 1 percent in contract construction up to 4.2 percent for communications. Finer industry detail would show even greater dispersion.

Although no industry showed a drop in productivity over the whole period, a number did experience declines in one or more subperiods. There were quite a few minuses in the final subperiod 1973–76, particularly in cyclical industries, reflecting still incomplete recovery from the 1973–75 contraction by 1976.

The patterns of productivity change of some industries across the subperiods differ substantially from that of the business economy as a

Industry Group

Industry Group	1948–73	1948–53	1953–57	1957–60	1960–66	1966–69	1969–73	1973–76
Business economy	2.5	3.4	2.0	2.1	3.4	1.5	1.8	0.7
Farm	3.3	5.4	2.7	3.8	2.3	3.2	3.3	1.1
Manufacturing	2.3	2.9	1.0	1.1	3.9	0.9	2.7	0.1
Food	2.8	3.3	2.5	1.1	4.0	1.1	2.8	3.8
Tobacco	2.7	1.1	3.5	4.8	2.0	3.6	3.0	1.1
Textiles	3.3	0.8	3.6	1.9	8.2	0.1	2.7	0.7
Apparel	2.5	2.8	1.4	1.2	2.0	0.8	5.5	2.5
Lumber	3.8	0.4	5.7	1.5	7.2	1.6	4.9	-4.7
Furniture	1.9	2.2	2.7	0.1	2.7	2.0	1.0	0.8
Paper	2.7	3.7	-0.4	1.7	2.8	2.7	5.3	-3.5
Printing and publishing	1.9	2.2	2.8	0.6	3.1	0.2	0.7	-1.0
Chemicals	3.6	1.8	4.3	2.5	5.0	2.9	4.7	-0.8
Petroleum	2.5	1.8	0.6	5.4	4.1	0	2.3	-1.7
Rubber	2.1	2.1	-2.3	5.7	3.6	3.2	1.4	-1.5
Leather	1.1	-2.0	0.7	3.0	3.1	-0.3	2.1	1.2
Stone, clay, and glass	1.6	2.4	0.1	1.1	2.4	0.8	1.7	-0.9
Primary metals	0.6	3.2	-1.5	-4.1	3.3	-3.1	1.8	-3.9
Fabricated metals	1.5	1.4	0.3	2.0	2.6	1.5	0.9	-0.9
Nonelectrical machinery	1.3	2.5	-1.1	1.1	2.6	-0.2	2.3	-0.5
Electrical machinery	3.9	4.4	2.0	2.6	1.2	2.9	3.7	1.6
Transportation equipment	2.6	3.2	1.5	3.3	4.2	-0.5	2.7	3.0
Instruments	2.5	4.6	0.6	3.0	3.5	3.1	-0.4	0.1
Miscellaneous	2.8	4.0	3.3	2.6	1.6	3.1	2.8	1.6
Mining	2.4	4.1	2.2	0.6	4.6	1.7	-0.7	-4.6
Contract construction	0.9	2.6	1.8	4.2	2.0	-0.3	-5.0	1.8
Railroads	3.2	2.5	2.6	4.2	7.0	1.3	0.2	-3.6
Nonrailroad transportation	1.8	0.4	2.1	1.2	2.6	1.9	2.8	1.2
Communications	4.2	5.7	4.5	5.9	3.5	3.4	2.5	4.3
Public utilities	3.9	6.8	4.7	4.6	3.7	2.7	0.2	-3.8
Trade	2.4	2.1	1.6	1.8	3.6	1.0	2.9	—
Real estate	2.8	4.4	2.9	3.8	2.6	1.3	1.3	3.1

whole. Thus, despite the marked deceleration in business sector TFP 1966–69, above-average increases were recorded in farming, tobacco products, rubber products, and services. And although most manufacturing groups showed an improvement in TFP growth 1969–73, poorer performance was recorded for tobacco products, furniture, rubber products, fabricated metals, instruments, and miscellaneous products. The variation among industries in rates of productivity change provides a useful tool in analyzing causal factors.

In addition to variation in rates of productivity growth over the longer periods and subperiods, there are variations in productivity over the course of the business cycle in the nonfarm business economy, particularly within manufacturing. This mainly reflects the fact that there are cyclical variations in rates of change in output and in rates of utilization of capacity. As production rises from the trough of a cycle, rates of utilization of plant capacity increase from inefficient levels toward (and sometimes beyond) the most efficient rates. Further, overhead-type labor is utilized more fully as output expands. The opposite sequence takes place during contractions.

Thus, during the five postwar expansions (excluding the present one) calculations using the medians show that TFP in the private domestic business economy rose at an average annual rate of 2.8 percent, associated with output expansion of 5.3 percent. During the six contractions, TFP fell by 0.4 percent, associated with a drop of real product of 3.8 percent. In the farm economy, the median increase in TFP was at a 2.2 percent average annual rate in both expansions and contractions— although real product rose slightly less rapidly during contractions than during expansions. Thus, cyclicality in productivity changes is concentrated in the nonfarm sectors.

In the nonfarm, nonmanufacturing sector as a whole, median TFP rose during expansion at an average annual rate of 2.6 percent, while real product rose at a 4.9 percent rate. During contractions, the average increase was only 0.2 percent, associated with an annual rate of decline of 0.5 percent in real product. In three of the six contraction phases productivity dropped absolutely.

Manufacturing was much more volatile than the other sectors. In expansions, median TFP rose at a 3.6 percent average annual rate, and real product by almost 7 percent. In contractions, the median average annual rate of decline in TFP was 3.2 percent and in real product was almost 11 percent. In only one of the six contractions did TFP rise—from the fourth quarter of 1948 to the fourth quarter of 1949—despite a 6 percent decline in real product. The greatest fluctuations in TFP were registered by paper and paper products, rubber and rubber products, primary metals, and transportation equipment. Two industries showed increases in both output and TFP during contractions—food and petroleum refining—while two others showed increases in TFP despite declining output—tobacco products and nonelectrical machinery.

During the course of expansion, the rates of increase in TFP and the labor-productivity ratio begin to decelerate six quarters, on average, prior to the cycle peak—a quarter or so before deceleration in output and the output/capital ratio begins. In conjunction with continued increases in factor prices, this is associated with an acceleration in rates of increase in unit total costs and a decline in the ratio of price to unit cost. The associated retardation in unit profit increases, and the subsequent absolute decline in profit rates prior to the cycle peak, are an important aspect of the explanation of the cyclical process.

Conversely, the rates of increase in TFP and in output per labor-hour (but not in output and the output/capital ratio) accelerate at least one quarter before the cycle trough. This results in an increase in the ratio of price to unit total costs and unit labor costs an average of one quarter in advance of the trough. The widening of profit margins and associated increase in investment commitments contribute, of course, to the subsequent upturn of general business activity.[2]

PRODUCTIVITY, COSTS, AND PRICES

The main channel through which productivity change affects the economy is its relationship to unit costs and prices. At the macroeconomic level, product prices rise by less than factor prices (including profit) to the degree that productivity increases. This is the means whereby productivity gains are distributed to the owners of the factors. Since the same relationship holds at the industry level, relative changes in productivity tend to be positively correlated with relative changes in output, and thus affect economic structure.

The Macroeconomic Relationship
Before and After 1966

The macroeconomic impact is shown in Table 1–5 for the U.S. nonfinancial corporate sector (for which computations are simpler than for the entire business sector including proprietorships). Consider first the subperiod 1948–66, which spans almost two decades of only mild price inflation during which the implicit price deflator for the sectoral gross product rose at an average annual rate of 1.7 percent. Average factor prices rose at an average rate of 4.8 percent a year. If there had been no productivity growth, the price level would have risen at an average annual rate of 4.1 percent, a bit less than factor prices since

Table 1-5. Components of Price Changes in U.S. Nonfinancial Corporate Sector

	1948	1948–66			1966–76		
	Relative Weights (%)	Average Annual Rates of Change (%)	Contributions to Price Change (%)	Total	Average Annual Rates of Change (%)	Contributions to Price Change (%)	Total
Implicit price deflator	100.0	1.7	1.7	100.0	5.3	5.3	100.0
Unit indirect business taxes	8.8	2.4	0.2	12.4	5.3	0.5	10.2
Unit factor costs	91.2	1.6	1.5	87.6	5.3	4.8	89.8
Average factor price		4.8	3.9		6.7	6.0	
Total factor productivity		3.1	-2.4		1.3	-1.2	
Unit labor costs	63.9	1.7	1.1	63.1	5.7	3.6	67.8
Average hourly compensation		4.8	3.1		7.6	4.8	
Output per hour		3.1	-2.0		1.8	-1.2	
Unit capital costs	27.3	1.5	0.4	24.5	4.4	1.2	22.0
Average price of capital		2.9	0.8		4.4	1.2	
Output-capital ratio		1.4	-0.4		0	0	

Source: Kendrick and Grossman (forthcoming: Table 4–3).

indirect business taxes less subsidies per unit of output rose by less than product prices (but by more than unit factor cost). Thus, the increase in TFP, which averaged better than 3.1 percent a year, offset 76 percent of the hypothetical price rise.

Looking at the cost components, the 3.1 percent a year increase in output (real gross product) per labor-hour offset nearly two-thirds of the increase in average hourly labor compensation of 4.8 percent a year, so that unit labor costs rose by 1.7 percent a year. The average price of capital (including profits) rose by about 2.9 percent a year over the eighteen-year period. But the average annual rate of increase in capital productivity was almost 1.4 percent, so that unit capital costs rose by 1.5 percent a year—a bit less than the average rise in unit labor costs. Actually, unit fixed-capital charges (depreciation and interest) rose by more than 5 percent a year, but this was brought down by a slight decline in unit profits.

Developments between 1966 and 1976 were quite different from those in the earlier subperiod. The increase in factor prices accelerated to a 6.7 percent average annual rate, and if productivity had not grown, product prices would have risen by 6.5 percent a year. But the rate of increase in TFP decelerated by half to 1.3 percent a year, on average, offsetting only about 20 percent of the hypothetical price rise. Thus, the actual increase in the price deflator accelerated from 1.7 percent 1948–66 to 5.3 percent 1966–76, at average annual rates. Unit costs for each of the major factor classes accelerated, reflecting acceleration in the average price of each and deceleration in growth of each of the partial productivity ratios. In fact, the output/capital ratio showed virtually no growth at all, due in large part to the fact that real gross product in 1976 was still well below potential. Further cyclical recovery since 1976 has increased capital productivity, but not enough to offset further acceleration in factor price increases.

Interindustry Differentials

One could analyze rates of change in product prices for each of the thirty-one industry groups for which comparable estimates are available in the same manner as we have done for the nonfinancial corporate sector. But this would be of little general interest, and readers interested in seeing the extent to which productivity growth in particular industries have offset rising factor prices can refer to Table 1–6. Instead, we analyze interrelationships for the thirty nonfarm industries as a whole to see what kind of generalizations can be made.

A priori one can reason that if relative industry changes in productivity were not significantly correlated with relative changes in factor prices,

Table 1-6. Changes in Unit Factor Costs, and Product Prices by Major Industry Group

Part A: Average Annual Percentage Rates of Change: 1948-76

	Implicit Product Price Deflator	Unit Factor Cost	Average Factor Price	Total Factor Productivity
Farming	1.7	1.6	4.7	3.0
Manufacturing	2.8	2.9	5.0	2.1
Food	2.2	2.6	5.5	2.9
Tobacco	1.8	4.7	7.3	2.6
Textile	0.1	0.1	3.1	3.1
Apparel	1.5	1.5	4.0	2.5
Lumber	2.9	3.0	6.0	2.9
Furniture	2.9	2.8	4.7	1.8
Paper	2.9	2.8	4.9	2.0
Printing and publishing	3.5	3.5	5.1	1.5
Chemical	1.5	1.4	4.6	3.2
Petroleum	1.6	0.5	2.5	2.1
Rubber	2.9	3.2	5.0	1.8
Leather	2.9	2.8	4.0	1.1
Stone, clay, and glass	3.7	3.7	5.0	1.3
Primary metals	5.2	5.1	5.2	0.1
Fabricated metals	3.6	3.8	5.3	1.3
Nonelectrical machinery	3.8	3.8	4.9	1.7
Electrical machinery	1.2	1.3	5.1	3.7
Transportation equipment	2.5	2.7	5.5	2.7
Instruments	2.8	3.3	6.7	2.2
Miscellaneous	2.0	2.0	4.7	2.7
Nonfarm and Nonmanufacturing	3.3	3.2	5.2	2.0
Mining	3.7	3.5	5.2	1.7
Construction	4.2	4.2	5.3	1.0
Transportation, total	3.0	3.0	5.5	2.4
Railroads	2.2	2.4	4.9	2.5
Nonrail	3.9	3.8	5.4	1.6
Communications	2.0	2.3	6.7	4.2
Public utilities	2.5	2.5	5.6	3.0
Trade	2.9	2.6	4.7	2.1
Finance and insurance	4.7	4.5	4.7	0.1
Real estate	3.2	3.0	5.9	2.8
Services	4.4	4.4	6.1	1.6
Total	3.0	2.9	5.3	2.3

they would show a significant negative correlation with product prices. As the matrix of correlation coefficients in Table 1–7 shows, these presumptions do obtain in fact for the entire period 1948–76 and for each of the two subperiods. Although all the coefficients are significant at the .01 level, they are not extremely high since markets are not perfect, adjustments of price to reflect unit costs are imperfect, especially over shorter time periods, and implicit price deflators for gross product by industry reflect different levels and rates of change in unit indirect business taxes.

The next step in the reasoning process is that if relative industry changes in prices are negatively associated with relative changes in real sales and output, then there should be a positive correlation between relative industry changes in productivity and in output. The presumed direction of these relationships also holds in fact, as shown in Table 1–7. But the negative correlation between relative changes in price and in output, while negative in both subperiods, is significant (at the .01 level) only in the 1966–76 subperiod. The degree of correlation is affected, of course, by the extent of price elasticity of demand in the various industries, and by the extent to which price elasticities may be offset by income elasticities or changes in tastes working in the opposite direction (as in services, for example). Nevertheless, positive correlations between relative industry changes in productivity and in output obtain and are significant in both subperiods and over the twenty-eight-year period as a whole. The fact that this relationship is stronger than would be expected from the price-output correlations suggests that a reciprocal relationship is involved—that is, that relative changes in output affect productivity changes by industry through differing opportunities for economies of scale.

If relative changes in productivity and in output were *not* positively correlated, then one would expect a high negative correlation between relative changes in productivity and in factor input generally, and employment in particular. Although the latter relationship is negative it was not significant over the entire period nor in the 1966–76 subperiod, although it was barely significant at the .05 level in the earlier subperiod. Even so, employment did not decline absolutely in the high productivity growth industries, although it did rise strongly in some of the low productivity growth industries (particularly services) where high income elasticities of demand more than offset the effect of relative price increases.

Table 1-6. Changes in Unit Factor Costs, and Product Prices, by Major Industry Group
Part B: Average Annual Percentage Rates of Change: 1948–1966 and 1966–1976

	Implicit Product Price Deflator		Unit Factor Cost		Average Factor Price		Total Factor Productivity	
	1948–1966	1966–1976	1948–1966	1966–1976	1948–1966	1966–1976	1948–1966	1966–1976
Farming	-0.7	2.9	-0.9	6.2	2.6	8.6	3.5	2.2
Manufacturing	1.8	4.5	1.9	4.7	4.4	6.1	2.5	1.4
Food	1.3	4.0	1.4	4.8	4.4	7.5	3.0	2.6
Tobacco	1.4	2.6	3.6	6.7	6.2	9.5	2.5	2.6
Textiles	-1.8	3.6	-1.8	3.5	2.2	4.9	4.0	1.3
Apparel	0.8	2.8	0.8	2.7	2.9	6.0	2.1	3.2
Lumber	2.3	4.1	0.7	7.4	4.7	8.4	4.0	0.9
Furniture	2.3	4.1	2.3	3.8	4.5	5.1	2.1	1.3
Paper	1.8	5.0	1.7	4.9	3.9	6.8	2.2	1.8
Printing and publishing	2.2	6.0	2.2	5.9	4.6	6.0	2.4	-0-
Chemicals	0.5	3.3	0.4	3.3	4.0	5.8	3.5	2.5
Petroleum	0.7	3.4	-2.1	5.4	0.7	6.0	2.9	0.6
Rubber	1.9	4.6	2.0	5.3	4.2	6.5	2.2	1.1
Leather	2.2	4.2	2.2	4.1	3.3	5.2	1.1	1.1
Stone, clay, and glass	2.4	6.1	2.4	6.1	4.1	6.8	1.7	0.6
Primary metals	4.1	7.4	4.0	7.0	5.0	5.5	1.0	-1.4
Fabricated metals	2.2	6.1	2.1	6.8	3.8	7.3	1.7	0.5
Nonelectrical machinery	3.2	5.0	3.2	5.0	4.5	5.7	1.3	0.7
Electrical machinery	0.2	3.2	0.5	2.9	4.7	5.8	4.2	2.8
Transportation equipment	2.2	3.1	2.3	3.5	5.5	5.4	3.2	1.8
Instruments	2.6	3.2	3.0	4.1	6.1	5.0	3.1	0.8
Miscellaneous	1.0	3.9	1.0	3.8	3.9	6.4	2.8	2.5
Nonfarm and nonmanufacturing	2.0	5.7	1.9	5.6	4.4	6.7	2.5	1.1
	0.?	10.1	0	10.2	3.?	8.9	3.3	-1.2

	Price Deflator		Cost		Price		Productivity	
	1948–1966	1966–1976	1948–1966	1966–1976	1948–1966	1966–1976	1948–1966	1966–1976
Transportation, total	1.8	5.3	1.8	5.2	4.7	6.8	2.9	1.6
Railroad	-0-	6.2	0.4	6.1	4.6	5.4	4.2	-0.6
Nonrail	3.2	5.1	3.1	4.9	4.8	7.1	1.6	2.1
Communications	1.7	2.5	2.2	2.5	7.1	6.0	4.7	3.3
Public utilities	0.9	5.5	1.0	5.2	6.0	4.9	4.9	-0.3
Trade	1.3	5.9	0.9	5.7	3.4	7.2	2.5	1.4
Finance and insurance	4.5	5.2	4.4	4.8	4.8	4.4	0.4	-0.4
Real estate	2.6	4.3	2.3	4.3	5.7	6.2	3.4	1.8
Services	3.6	5.7	3.8	5.6	5.3	7.5	1.5	1.8
Total	1.7	5.3	1.6	5.3	4.6	6.7	2.9	1.4

Table 1-7. Matrix of Correlation Coefficients (Rates of Change in Total Factor Productivity and in Product Prices versus Rates of Change in Associated Variables)

	Average Factor Price	Unit Factor Cost Including Profits	Unit Factor Cost Excluding Profits	Average Product Price	Output (Real Product)	Total Factor Input	Persons Engaged
Total factor productivity							
1948–76	.179	-.674[a]	-.710[a]	-.809[a]	.475[a]	-.075	-.156
1948–66	.141	-.609[a]	-.752[a]	-.688[a]	.335[a]	-.243	-.310
1966–76	.167	-.690[a]	-.737[a]	-.773[a]	.622[a]	-.047	-.069
Average product price							
1948–76	.289	.871[a]	.863[a]		-.206	.262	.365[b]
1948–66	.479[a]	.880[a]	.889[a]		-.076	.460[b]	.551[a]
1966–76	.213	.789[a]	.670[a]		-.481[a]	.036	.115

[a]Significant at the .05 level.
[b]Significant at the .01 level.

SOURCES OF PRODUCTIVITY GROWTH AND OF THE RECENT SLOWDOWN

Productivity growth is the net result of a complex of forces reviewed in this section. The review focuses on proximate determinants of productivity change, but it must be remembered that these immediate causal forces are conditioned by the underlying values and institutions of a society. Nevertheless, changes in values and institutions are reflected in the proximate determinants, and the effect of those determinants on the growth of real product and productivity are discussed.

The discussion centers around Table 1–8, the stub of which lists the chief sources of economic growth. Part A shows the average annual percentage changes in real business product, factor inputs, and productivity ratios for three periods: 1948–66, 1966–73, and 1973–78. Part B shows the percentage point contributions to productivity growth of seven groups of causal factors.

The table is a somewhat modified and expanded version of the "growth accounting" framework pioneered by Edward F. Denison (1974). His estimates have been used for the majority of the entries for the period 1948–66, and from some of the subsequent periods. These estimates, however, whether Denison's or Kendrick's, are of varying degrees of precision. Some are quite firmly based, while others are somewhat "notional." But we believe they are quite useful for indicating the relative importance of the various factors, and their changing contributions over the three periods covered. Certainly the table is a convenient framework for organizing the discussion of causal forces.

Output, Inputs, and Productivity

Real gross product in the U.S. business economy grew at an average annual rate of almost 4 percent between 1948 and 1966. From 1966 to 1973 the most recent cycle peak, the growth rate slowed to 3.5 percent, then down to 2.4 percent from 1973 to 1978. Almost half of the retardation of the last period, however, reflects the fact that in 1978 the economy had not yet fully recovered from the 1973–75 recession.

Over the first two periods, increases in hours of labor input accelerated sharply from 0.4 percent a year to 1.4 percent, reflecting more rapid labor force growth. In the last period, the rate of increase receded slightly to a 1.3 percent annual average, reflecting the rise in unemployment between 1973 and 1978—from 4.9 percent of the civilian labor force to 6 percent. As a consequence the growth of real product per hour decelerated continuously across all three periods—from 3.5 percent a year 1948–66 to 2.1 percent 1966–73 to 1.1 percent in the final period. Fragmentary estimates suggest that the gain may be even less in 1979 than in 1973–78.

Since capital input has risen faster than labor input, total factor productivity has risen less rapidly than output per hour, but shows much the same pattern of deceleration—from an annual rate of 2.7 percent a year 1948–66 down to only 0.8 percent 1973–78. Even adjusting for cyclical effects (see below) it appears that the trend rate of increase in productivity since 1973 has been only about 1.1 percent a year, or less than half the earlier trend.

The difference between the growth rates of real product per unit of labor and of total factor productivity is accounted for by the rate of substitution of capital for labor. This is computed as the rate of increase in total input per unit of labor input (or, by the increase in capital per labor hour, weighted by the share of capital compensation in gross national income, which is almost one-third). As shown in Table 1–8, this rate of substitution decelerated a bit from 0.8 percent a year in the first period to 0.5 percent 1966–73, and to 0.3 percent in the final period.

Advances in Knowledge

The most important source of productivity growth is the advance in technological knowledge when applied to the ways and means of production through cost-reducing innovations. Denison estimates that this source contributed 1.4 percentage points—or about half of productivity growth—in the period 1948–66. The subsequent decline in its contributions can better be understood by looking at its main components.

The bulk of technological progress in recent decades has stemmed from formal research and development (R&D) programs, outlays for which increased steadily to 3 percent of GNP in the mid-1960s. Subsequently, R&D spending flattened out in real terms, and declined to 2.2 percent of GNP in 1978. The growth of the real stock of technological knowledge and know-how, obtained by cumulating outlays over the estimated lifetimes of the resulting new products and processes, showed a marked decline after 1966 (Kendrick 1976). This is the basis for the numbers shown in the table. Informal inventive and innovative activity, including the myriad small technological improvements devised by plant managers and workers, was the chief source of technological progress in the nineteenth century, and is still significant. In view of the deceleration in economic growth and the decline in major new inventions stemming from formal R&D, we estimate that the contribution of informal innovative activity declined from 0.3 in the first period to 0.2 in the third.

Changes in the rate of diffusion of cost-reducing technology throughout the producing units of the economy can also be a significant factor influencing productivity. Since the capital goods produced each year embody the latest technological advances, the average age of capital

Table 1–8. Sources of Growth in Real Gross Product

	1948–1966	1966–1973	1973–1978ᵖ
PART A: Average Annual Percentage Rates of Change			
Real gross product	3.9%	3.5%	2.4%
Total factor input	1.2	1.9	1.6
Labor	0.4	1.4	1.3
Capital	2.7	3.3	2.3
Real product per unit of labor	3.5	2.1	1.1
Capital labor substitution	0.8	0.5	0.3
Total factor productivity	2.7	1.6	0.8
PART B: Sources of Total Productivity Growth: Percentage Point Contribution			
Advances in knowledge	1.4	1.1	0.8
R&D stock	0.85	0.75	0.6
Informal	0.3	0.25	0.2
Rate of diffusion	0.25	0,1	—
Changes in labor quality	0.6	0.4	0.7
Education and training	0.6	0.7	0.8
Health and safety	0.1	0.1	0.1
Age/sex composition	–0.1	–0.4	–0.2
Changes in quality of land	—	–0.1	–0.2
Resource reallocations	0.8	0.7	0.3
Labor	0.4	0.2	0.1
Capital	0.4	0.5	0.2
Volume changes	0.4	0.2	–0.1
Economies of scale	0.4	0.2	–0.1
Intensity of demand	—	–0.1	–0.3
Net government impact	—	–0.1	–0.2
Services to business	0.1	0,1	0.1
Regulations	–0.1	–0.2	–0.4
Actual/potential efficiency, and n.e.c.	–0.5	–0.6	–0.4

p—preliminary; n.e.c.—not elsewhere classified.
Source: Based in part on estimates by Denison (1974, 1978, 1979).

goods is an important indicator of the rate of diffusion. Between 1948 and 1966 the average age declined about three years, contributing 0.25 to the growth rate. In the next period the decline slowed to one year, and between 1973 and 1978 there was virtually no change in the average age of capital goods, indicating no contribution from this source.

Changes in Labor Quality

The next group of factors has to do with the average quality of the work force. The most important of these variables has been the increase in average education and training per worker. Based on earnings differentials associated with different levels of educational attainment, Denison estimated that education contributed 0.5 percentage point to growth 1948–66, and even more since then. This is confirmed by the author's estimates of human capital, which also indicate another 0.1 percentage point contributed by increased training per worker in all three periods. This factor interacts with technological progress, whch upgrades the structure of demand for labor.

Also showing no deceleration has been the increase in average health and safety of workers, which reduces time lost because of illness and accident, and increases vitality and potential working life. The author's human capital estimates calculate this factor to have raised productivity by a yearly average of nearly 0.1 percent from 1948 through 1978. Denison contends that the decline in average hours worked per year has contributed to the energy content of hours worked, but the influence of this factor has become quite minor in recent years.

Changes in the age-sex composition of the labor force became a significant negative factor in the mid-1960s. The proportion of youth began increasing sharply, reflecting the baby boom after World War II, and the increase in the female labor force participation ratio accelerated. Because of the below-average value-added and compensation per worker of these groups, associated with less experience, and "learning by doing," increased proportions of youth and women reduced productivity growth by 0.1 percentage point 1948–66 and by 0.4 percent 1966–73, receding to 0.2 percent in the final period. Demographic projections indicate that the future contribution of this factor will become positive.

Changes in the Quality of Land

Changes in the average quality of land and other natural resources affect productivity in the extractive industries and thus in the business economy (although the share of these industries in gross income and product is less than 5 percent). Until the mid-1960s, the effect of "diminishing returns" appears to have been minor, and more than offset by technological advance—productivity in extractive industries grew substantially faster than in the rest of the economy. Since then, productivity growth has decelerated in agriculture, and productivity itself has declined in mining. The decline is due in part to safety and other regulations, but it also reflects the declining quality of natural resources. When the deceleration attributable to the latter cause is weighted by the sector's share of gross business product, it subtracts 0.1 percentage point from productivity growth rate 1966–73, and 0.2 percentage point in the following four-year period. The negative effect may well become larger in future years, particularly if the nation relies more heavily on domestic sources of energy.

Resource Reallocations

Productivity is affected by reallocations of labor and capital in response to different rates of remuneration in various industries which reflect continually changing supply and demand conditions. Inefficient allocation usually results from impediments to mobility, such as monopolistic practices by firms or unions, imperfect knowledge, or the sheer costs of movement.

With respect to labor mobility, Denison estimates that shifts from the farm to the nonfarm sector added 0.3 percentage point 1948–66, and shifts from nonfarm self-employment to employee status added another 0.1 percentage point. Since 1966 the effects of these shifts have become progressively less as the farm sector and self-employment have become much smaller proportions of the economy.

There have also been relative shifts of capital (including land) from uses with below average rates of return to higher value uses. Professors Gollop and Jorgenson (1977), using real capital estimates for over fifty industry groups, found that relative shifts added 0.4 percentage point to growth 1948–66, and somewhat more in subsequent period. But the contribution from this source declined in the final period.

Volume Changes

Economies of scale occur as growth opens up opportunities for greater specialization of workers, machines, and plants, and permits the spreading of overhead type functions over more units of output. Denison attributes about 10 percent of the growth rate to scale economies. On this basis their contribution dropped from 0.4 percent 1948–66 to 0.2 percent 1973–78, reflecting the deceleration in the rate of growth of real gross product.

Another volume factor is changes in the intensity of demand. Productivity changes along with the ratio of actual to potential real product changes, but to a lesser extent. Since capital input is assumed to move proportionately to real stocks unadjusted for changes in rates of utilization, capital productivity is obviously affected by utilization rates. Although employment and hours do fluctuate with output, there is an overhead component of labor input which also causes labor productivity to reflect to some extent cyclical movements in demand.

Since the economy was operating near capacity in both 1948 and 1966 (the unemployment rate was 3.8 percent in both years), this factor had a negligible effect on productivity growth in the first period. But according to the latest estimates of the Council of Economic Advisers, the ratio of actual to potential real GNP in 1973 was 1.5 percent below the 1966 ratio, and 2.7 percent lower in 1978. We estimate that this subtracted 0.1 percentage point from the growth rate 1966–73, and 0.3 in the final period. The influence of this factor depends on the cyclical position of the economy at the beginning and end of the period over which growth rates are calculated. But cyclicality and growth rates are negatively correlated, both for the economy as a whole and by industry. Less frequent and less severe economic contractions are associated with stronger growth of both output and productivity.

Net Government Impact

The positive contribution to business sector productivity from government-suppled infrastructure, such as roads, and labor services averaged about 0.1 percentage point a year over the entire period 1948–78. This rough estimate is based on the relative growth of factor services provided by governments at all levels.

But government rules and regulations also have a negative impact, causing unit real costs to rise. We estimate that the requirements on business from mandatory programs in effect before 1966 subtracted 0.1 percent from growth. Denison (1978) recently estimated that the effect of environmental and occupational safety and health regulations has added to that 0.1 percentage point 1966–73, and −0.3 thereafter. If improvements in the natural and working environments could be measured and included in real GNP, it is possible that the negative net government impact on productivity since 1966 would appear smaller. But given present methods of estimating real product and productivity, governments have contributed to the retardation of growth since 1966.

Actual/Potential Efficiency

As is the case with all growth accounting exercises, there is a residual. It averages −0.5 percentage point for the three periods covered by this study. To the extent that this does not merely offset an overstatement of the net impact of the other sources of growth, we interpret it as reflecting primarily a decline in the ratio of actual to potential labor efficiency, holding technology and other variables constant. One measurable element in the decline has been the reduction in hours actually worked relative to hours paid for, since the latter concept underlies most of the hours data used for the labor input measure. This decline has proceeded at near a 0.1 percent average annual rate, reflecting increased time paid for but not worked. In addition, University of Michigan surveys indicate that unproductive time at work (for coffee breaks, personal business, etc.) has also increased by at least 0.1 percent a year since the mid-1960s.

Beyond this, there is considerable speculation that the efficiency of hours actually worked as defined by standards or "norms" used in work measurement studies may have declined. Certainly, there are many instances of restrictive work rules and practices throughout industry, although it is difficult to ascertain whether their impact has increased. Some observers maintain that efficiency has been adversely affected during the past dozen years by social trends such as growing drug use and crime, loosening of the work ethic, and increased questioning of materialism and of most institutions, including business. Denison has adduced evidence to show that the increase in crimes against property has reduced the growth rate by about 0.05 percent a year since 1960. This type of factor affects the residual. Although the residual is negative, it has no clear trend.

Causes of the Slowdown

Recapitulation of this discussion of Table 1–8 will show the relative importance of the various causal forces in the slowdown of growth in total factor productivity between the first period, 1948–66, and the last period, 1973–78. Of the 1.9 percent decline in the productivity growth rate 0.5 percentage point, or about one-fourth, is due to the slower growth in the last period, 1973–78, largely reflecting the incomplete recovery from the 1973–75 recession. Three-fourths of the remaining 1.4 percentage point decline is accounted for by the 0.6 decline in the rate of technological progress and the 0.5 reduction in the positive effect of resource reallocations. The reminder is more than accounted for by the 0.3 negative net governmental impact, and the 0.2 percentage point estimated decline in the average quality of land and other natural resources.

The only positive changes were the 0.1 point increase in the average quality of labor, and the 0.1 point reduction in the negative residual, possibly reflecting a smaller decline in the ratio of actual to potential labor efficiency 1973–78 than in the earlier periods. The 0.5 percent larger decline in the ratio of real product to labor input than in total factor productivity is due to the slower growth of real capital per unit of labor in the 1973–78 period than in the 1948–66 period.

Although it is useful to know which causal factors accounted for the retardation of growth in recent years, the search for policy options to stimulate productivity need not be confined to them. All of the causes of productivity advance should be considered in developing policy recommendations. The subject of policy is treated in Chapter 8 below.

COMMENT

Jerome A. Mark
John R. Norsworthy

In most respects, we are in complete accord with Kendrick's methods and his findings. Our comments are directed toward points where we differ with his method or with the results of his analysis and measurement. Overall however, we are very pleased with the discussion—especially with its scope. Kendrick analyses total factor productivity growth not only at the aggregate level but also for individual industries. He examines price movements in these industries with considerable attention to cyclical detail. His choice of issues to examine specifies the kind of agenda that we believe it is most useful for him, and indeed for us at the Bureau of Labor Statistics (BLS), to be pursuing at this time. The link between productivity and unit factor cost, while well known, is seldom subjected to the kind of analysis that yields information as useful as what Kendrick offers here.

There are conceptual differences in output measurement in Kendrick's aggregate sector which he calls the U.S. Business Economy, and the Private Business Sector for which we at the BLS prepare productivity and cost measures. The most significant difference lies in Kendrick's inclusion of the imputed rental value of owner-occupied dwellings in output. This necessitates the inclusion of owner-occupied residences in the capital stock. We do not believe that inclusion of the rental value of owner-occupied dwellings is appropriate, because the labor input associated with this output is not measured. That is, we know that the owners of private residences expend considerable effort in their maintenance, and also that they purchase the time and materials of others for the purposes of home maintenance. The latter is of course classified as delivery to final demand, whereas if the rental value of owner-occupied dwellings is to be considered part of output, these expenditures should be considered as contributing to that output—that is, as intermediate input —and the hours of labor input of the owners and family members should also be included. Further, the output measure itself is based on an imputation. In general, in defining the private business sector at the Bureau of Labor Statistics, we have used two criteria. First, the availability of input and output measures for each subsector in the analysis, and second the requirement that output be the result of a market transaction. The rental value of owner-occupied dwellings seems clearly to fail on both criteria. This difference in output, and therefore in the labor and capital inputs required to properly analyze the sector, can lead to somewhat different conclusions about the role of capital in the recent productivity slowdown. We shall return to this point when we discuss Kendrick's analysis of the productivity slowdown.

While analysis of gross product originating as the output measure for a large aggregate sector is meaningful, it is less meaningful to analyze the same measure as output for two-digit manufacturing industries. Intermediate products, including energy, constitute 50 to 60 percent of total costs for most two-digit industries.

Consequently an analysis of price change or of total factor productivity change that excludes intermediate products is different in quality from an analysis for a large aggregate sector. While the recent econometric evidence examining the statistical legitimacy of a value-added measure of output is mixed, the preponderance seems to suggest such a measure which is a capital-labor aggregate cannot be constructed so as to represent output for manufacturing as a whole (Berndt and Wood 1975). If this is true, then one would suppose it to be even more dubious to construct such a measure for individual manufacturing industries because the rates of substitution between capital and labor are biased by the omission of energy and intermediate product inputs.

Kendrick's analysis of the cycle is most informative. In his discussion of the postwar cycles, Kendrick appears to be referring to quarterly data that are not included in the paper. Kendrick's analysis of price change in the U.S. nonfinancial corporate sector is very instructive. We are using this method of analysis in current work for the Council on Wage and Price Stability on price movement in the major sectors—it will strengthen our own presentation to be able to cite Kendrick's work. Ideally however, we would like to see the data subdivided to break at 1973. The U.S. economy appears to have been profoundly affected by the rapid change of energy prices since the oil embargo of 1974. There are thus substantial reasons for believing that the period since 1973 is different from earlier period. (Again, we will return to this point in our commentary on Kendrick's discussion of the slowdown in productivity growth.) Also, it would add to the presentation to break down changes in unit factor costs in the same way as in Table 1–15 showing the effects of changes in average factor price and in average factor productivity for capital and for labor. Furthermore we believe that a finer breakdown in time periods would add to the understanding of productivity and price change in recent and prior cycles. In particular, in our own work we have found that compensation per labor-hour has followed different paths in the last two cycles from earlier post war cycles, growing faster during the contractions than in the subsequent recoveries (Norsworthy and Fulco 1978). The reverse was true for business cycles prior to 1969.

It is also useful to examine in summary form the dispersion of rates of productivity growth by industry before and after the productivity slowdown. These data are included for changes in labor productivity growth in selected industries in Table 1-9. While no readily describable pattern emerges, the pervasiveness of the decline is striking.

Compared to other ways of measuring total factor productivity growth, which are based on different concepts, Kendrick's approach to the problem is very useful. His concept of total factor productivity growth is based on a measure that abstracts from changes in quality of capital and labor inputs and all other sources of growth, and thus is a maximum value for that concept. Part of the earlier debate between Denison and Jorgenson and his associates[1] turned on whose residual (after accounting for various sources of growth) was smaller, and whose could be properly labelled total factor productivity growth. If one accepts Kendrick's definition, analysis and attribution of the sources of total factor productivity growth are activities logically subsequent to measuring total factor productivity growth itself. Then, the issue as to what constitutes growth in factor inputs and what constitutes growth in productivity is reduced in importance. Alternative analytic frameworks can then be compared based on the maximum size of the residual, and the decomposition of that residual among various sources of growth.

Kendrick's assessment of sources of growth in real output in the economy is a hybrid of his own work and of Denison's earlier work extended to the period 1973-78. In Table 1-8 real product per unit of labor input can be regarded as the sum of contributions from several kinds of influences, including total factor productivity growth. In some of our work at the Bureau of Labor Statistics, we use a share-weighted framework to analyze some of these influences. We obtain rather different results from Kendrick—we find that between 1965 and 1973 there was no reduction in the contribution of the growth of the capital stock to the growth in output per unit of labor input while Kendrick finds a substantial contribution—0.3 percent per year—for the period 1966-73. There are two probable sources of this difference in findings. As noted earlier, Kendrick includes the rental value of owner-occupied dwellings in output and the corresponding residential capital stock as part of capital input. This factor appears to account for the most of the difference between Kendrick's findings and our own. Leaving the differences in the output and associated labor input measures aside, and even including this piece of GNP in the sector, it still appears that, from the perspective of policy analysis, the implications of the two approaches are different. His approach shows a slowdown in capital formation beginning in the mid-1960s whereas our approach shows a slowdown in capital formation contributing to labor productivity growth beginning only after 1973. Insofar as this slowdown is attributable to the inclusion

Table 1–9. Productivity Growth by Industry

Industry	1973–77 Falloff from 1947–73	Average Annual Rate 1947–73	1973–77
Candy and other confectionary products	8.5%	3.6%	−4.9%
Iron mining, usable ore	8.0	3.5	−4.5
Iron mining, crude ore	7.7	4.8	−2.9
Intercity trucking, general freight	7.6	2.4 (54-73)	−5.2
Coal mining	7.4	3.8	−3.6
Bituminous coal and lignite mining	7.3	3.9	−3.4
Crushed and broken stone	6.4	4.3 (58-73)	−2.1
Wood household furniture	5.9	3.0 (58-73)	−2.9
Petroleum refining	5.6	5.7	0.1
Copper rolling and drawing	5.4	3.4 (53-73)	−2.0
Motors and generators	5.4	3.8 (54-73)	−1.6
Gas and electric utilities	5.1	6.4	1.3
Railroad transportation, revenue traffic	5.1	4.6	−0.5
Nonmetallic minerals except fuels	5.0	4.2 (54-73)	−0.8
Hydraulic cement	4.9	4.5	−0.4
Clay refractories	4.8	3.8 (58-73)	−1.0
Railroad transportation, car miles	4.4	4.0	−0.4
Aluminum rolling and drawing	4.3	6.1 (58-73)	1.8
Air transportation	3.9	7.9	4.0
Concrete products	3.7	3.8	0.1
Structural clay products	3.6	3.8 (58-73)	0.2
Paper, paperboard and pulp mills	3.5	4.1	0.6
Ready-mixed concrete	3.5	1.9 (53-73)	−1.6
Primary aluminum	3.4	3.7	0.3
Lighting fixtures	3.4	3.5 (61-73)	0.1
Steel	3.4	2.2	−1.2
Radio and TV receiving sets	3.2	4.9 (58-73)	1.7
Clay construction products	3.2	3.8 (58-73)	0.6
Flour and other grain mill products	3.2	3.0	−0.2
Hotels, motels and tourist courts	3.2	2.4 (58-73)	−0.8
Retail food stores	2.7	2.4 (58-73)	−0.3
Household furniture	2.5	2.6 (58-73)	0.1
Major household appliances	2.2	5.8 (58-73)	3.6
Sawmills and planing mills, general	2.1	2.9 (58-73)	0.8
Veneer and plywood	2.0	5.1 (58-73)	3.1
Primary copper, lead and zinc	1.9	2.7	0.8

of rental value of owner-occupied dwellings in the capital stock, the implications for stimulating investment are vastly different from those then if the slowdown is understood to be a result of the decline in capital formation associated with the rise in energy prices and substantial rise in interest rates that have characterized the period since 1973. Another minor difference that may contribute to our different findings with regard to the effect on labor productivity growth of capital formation may derive from the methods of aggregation. We have tested for the conditions required for direct aggregation of the components of capital stock—equipment, structures, land, and inventories—and found that the conditions did not hold (Norsworthy and Harper 1979). We have also tested for the conditions for Divisia or translog aggregation of the capital stock and found that those conditions did hold. This aggregation method depends essentially on aggregating the growth rates of the various components of the capital stock weighted by their shares in total capital costs. The differences amount to as much as 10 percent of the growth rate of the capital stock for some subperiods. Our findings are shown in Tables 1–10 and 1–11.

Finally, with respect to the last category of sources of growth, it is puzzling that the residual is described as the combination of two effects, the ratio of actual to potential efficiency and sources not elsewhere classified. Further, it is difficult to believe that the residual effect would be relatively large and negative. Quite possibly the residual is in fact just a catchall for overexplained resources of growth in total factor productivity. The overexplanation of total factor productivity growth may arise because a framework that examines so many separate categories of growth cannot properly account for interactions among them. A case in point is that of resource reallocations. Kendrick's category attempts to measure the impacts of changes in the industry distributions of labor and capital inputs. Our analysis, based on a share-weighted approach to the sources of labor productivity growth, finds that the contributions of labor and capital combined from 1948 to 1965 average 0.4 percent per year and 0.33 percent per year from 1965 through 1973. In addition, we get a much smaller result for the period 1973 to 1978—less than 0.1 percent per year. In our more limited approach, while we cannot consistently handle as many sources of growth as the Kendrick-Denison analysis does, we can be certain that there is no overlap in the attribution of sources of growth.

With respect to the analysis of sources of growth, we have two broad categories of comments. The first is almost semantic. The category of net government impact seems to understate substantially the role of government as a source of total factor productivity growth. In addition to services to business and the impact of regulations, the government has clearly also contributed to advances in knowledge through the growth of

Table 1-10. Average Annual Growth Rates of Capital Stock, Nonfarm Business Sector, for Direct and Translog Aggregation of Equipment, Structures, Land, and Inventories

	Direct Aggregation	Translog Aggregation	Total Composition Effect $\dot{q}_K$	Asset Effect $\dot{q}_A$	Intersectoral Shift Effect $\dot{q}_M$	Interaction Asset and Shift $\dot{q}_I$
1948-1955	3.00	3.33	0.33	0.22	0.08	0.03
1955-1965	3.24	3.19	-0.05	-0.01	-0.08	0.04
1965-1973	4.30	4.56	0.26	0.24	-0-	0.02
1973-1977	2.04	2.18	0.14	0.18	-0-	-0.04

Table 1-11. Effect of Net Capital Stock and Other Factors on Labor Productivity Growth in Nonfarm Business Sector

	Labor Productivity Growth $\frac{\dot{O}}{L_o}$	Capital Labor Ratio $w_K \frac{\dot{K}_o}{L_o}$	Effect of Changes In: Composition of Capital Stock $w_K \dot{q}_K$	Effect of Changes In: Intersectoral Allocation of Labor $w_L \dot{q}_L$	Other Factors $\dot{A}$	Total Effect of Capital Stock $w_K \frac{\dot{K}}{L_o}$
1948-55	3.00	0.66	0.12	0.02	2.20	0.78
1955-65	2.80	0.76	-0.01	-0.03	2.08	0.75
1965-73	1.96	0.80	0.09	-0.01	1.08	0.89
1973-77	1.09	0.41	0.05	-0.09	0.72	0.46

the stock of research and development, to education and training (as pointed out by Kendrick in some of his earlier work measuring human capital), and in the area of health. In the last two cases, it would require some extraordinary analysis or assumptions regarding the elasticity of demand for health and for education and training in order to separate out the impact of government from other causes. However, the labeling of the category described as net government impact seems to suggest that the net effect of government is negative. While this may be true, considerably more analysis than is embodied in this framework is required to demonstrate it.

Another general category has to do with changes in output. Kendrick's framework recognizes in this general category economies of scale, intensity of demand and the ratio of actual to potential efficiency. The first and last of these categories imply nonhomogeneity of the underlying production function. However, homogeneity of the production function is relied upon elsewhere in the analysis of the effects of changes in labor quality, and also in the partitioning of growth in labor productivity to changes in the capital labor ratio and in total factor productivity.

NOTES TO CHAPTER 1
1. The table is adapted from one prepared by the author for Kendrick (forthcoming).
2. The timing of the relationships is spelled out in greater detail in Kendrick and Grossman (forthcoming: Chapter 5).

NOTES TO COMMENT
1. This debate is colleted in *The Measurement of Productivity,* a special supplement to the *Survey of Current Business* (May 1972).

Chapter 2

Productivity Trends
in Canada

*Sylvia Ostry and P.S. Rao**

There has, over the past few years in Canada, developed a considerable degree of anxiety over the level and growth of Canadian productivity compared to other developed countries, and recently even compared to the less developed countries. This concern is in many ways similar to a longer standing concern in the United States since the mid-1960s that has intensified since the OPEC-induced oil crisis and recession of 1974–75.

Productivity is, of course, a vital *indicator* of economic performance. In more pragmatic terms, it is a prime *determinant* of economic well-being, especially as it affects job creation, the balance of payments, the rate of inflation, and, perhaps most important, as it determines future economic development. In this chapter we present some preliminary observations on the development of productivity in Canada over the past twenty years not in order to establish hard and fast facts about the subject, but to provide additional information upon which to base our judgments. This is not an apology for the results of our investigations, but rather is recognition of the complex and perplexing nature of the factors affecting productivity growth and economic progress. The Economic Council will be undertaking intensive research on the macro- and microeconomic determinants of productivity and growth; over the next several years we hope to have much more to report in this area. It must be emphasized that the results that follow are preliminary and in no way reflect the views of the Economic Council of Canada.

*The authors are grateful to Peter Sagar for his assistance in the preparation of this chapter. The findings of this study are the personal responsibility of the authors and, as such, have not been endorsed by members of the Economic Council of Canada.

One shortcoming of this chapter, at least for popular purposes, is that data limitations prevent us from discussing—except in the broadest of generalities or by inference—the productivity developments from 1977 on. The estimates presented here are, for most part, based on *gross output* data that, unlike *net* output data, include the contributions to output made by intermediate inputs—material and energy. Our preference for the gross figures is based on work by Star (1974) and Denny and May (1978a, 1979) that shows net output figures give upwardly biased estimates of total labor productivity growth when used in studies of this kind. This result is confirmed by recent investigations by Rao (forthcoming). Unfortunately, gross output figures are not as timely as net output data. Only for manufacturing industries were data available for the year 1976; for other industries, data were available only to 1975.

One final caveat, perhaps unnecessary, is that aggregative macro-based approaches may hide as much information as they yield, and may prove more misleading than accurate, especially when data series are of limited reliability, and theoretical foundations such as the capacity utilization and capital stock series are involved. However pessimistic this may sound, it is a necessary caution that we might do well to add to every highly aggregative study of this kind; but it does not constitute a prohibition. With care, a great deal of information can be obtained from the aggregative mines.

Obviously however, not all issues can be studied using such an approach, especially in the case of productivity growth where an enormously broad range of issues has received attention over the past few years. We have been variously informed of the impact on productivity growth of such diverse factors as rising energy prices, regulations, weakened industrial relations, the decline of the work ethic, and shortages of skilled labor and management. Broad factors, such as low rates of capital accumulation, demographic and structural shifts, slow demand growth, and inadequate levels and promulgation of research and development, have also been raised. In this chapter we cannot and will not attempt to address all of these issues directly, yet in some ways, all are touched upon at least implicitly.

Before becoming too deeply enmeshed in more detailed discussion, we should present our definition of productivity. Productivity is defined in most of this study as the level of gross real output per man-hour worked.[1] It must be understood that the choice of this measure of productivity, or more precisely labor productivity, does not in any way signify a belief that all productivity stems from labor, or that efforts to increase productivity are tantamount to attempts to "get more output for the same wages." We recognize, and presume that the reader recognizes, that the productivity phenomenon is the product of a very wide range of inputs to the production process from capital, energy, and labor to technology, management skills, the organization of production, and other even less concrete factors. No one factor of production can be held entirely responsible for reduced productivity growth; nor can any one factor be responsible for high rates of growth.

If one were inclined to tell good news-bad news stories, then Canadian productivity growth might provide a fertile source of material. One could very easily imagine the good news: Canadian productivity growth has consistently outstripped the growth of the most advanced nation in the world, the United States. Followed by the bad news: the *level* of productivity is still higher in the United States than in Canada, the most advanced countries have higher rates of productivity growth than does Canada. These countries are catching up both to Canada, and to the United States.

The truth of this unfunny story is well illustrated by the following example (Table 2-1). In 1960, output per man-hour in manufacturing in Canada amounted to just 65 percent of the level in the United States, while Japanese productivity amounted to only 30 percent of the U.S. level. By 1977, Canadian productivity had risen to 75 percent of the U.S.level, but Japanese productivity had risen to a level almost equal to Canada's.

In the next section the broad pattern of productivity growth from 1957 to 1976 is described prior to a more detailed examination of the factors affecting productivity developments and some consideration of several of the very important questions regarding our recent experience. Appendix A contains details of the data sources and definitions used in the rest of the chapter.

Aggregate Performance

One of the most striking and disconcerting features of productivity performance in the recent past has been the remarkable diversity in the movements between various sectors, and indeed within sectors between years. Therefore it is less than perfectly clear that there is a great deal to be gained by expounding at any great length on the aggregate productivity growth in the Canadian economy. Yet intellectual curiosity demands a certain amount of attention to be paid to such figures. Simply put, everyone wants to know the bottom line.

In fact, between the years 1957 and 1966, and the years 1967 and 1973, the average pace of productivity growth for all Canadian industries remained relatively unchanged, increasing at average rates of 3.1 percent during both periods (Table 2-2). This fairly strong growth was, it seems,

**Table 2–1. Output Per Man-Hour in Manufacturing
(Index: U.S. = 100)**

	Canada/U.S.	*Japan/U.S.*
1958	n.a.	23[a]
1960	65[a]	30[a]
1967	68[a]	45[a]
1973	75[a]	69[a]
1974	80	73
1975	77	68
1976	74	72
1977	76	75

[a]Average of U.S. and domestic price weights.
Source: Walters (1979).

**Table 2–2. Average Annual Percentage Change in Inputs and
Outputs**

	1957–66	*1967–73*	*1974*	*1975*
Gross output (1971$)	4.75	5.09	3.95	.53
Man-hours	1.65	1.98	3.83	.97
Capital per man-hour	3.48	2.81	2.04	4.89
Intermediate inputs per man-hour	3.21	3.13	–.22	–1.05
Output per man-hour	3.05	3.07	–.12	–.44

Source: Based on data from Statistics Canada and estimates by the authors.

based on increased usage of capital and materials per man-hour, and technological progress. As well, during the 1957–66 period, shifts in the share of employment from lower productivity level industries to higher productivity industries resulted in increased aggregate productivity growth by .68 percent per year. During the latter period, from 1967 to 1973, this effect became negligible, as shown in Table 2–3.

The year 1974 brought, as we know all too well by now, a major economic slowdown. Total productivity growth in 1974 and 1975 actually fell as did material and energy usage per man-hour.[2] Even employment shifts reduced aggregate productivity growth.

These developments are seen best in the light of the developments in the constituent sectors of the Canadian economy—to which we now turn.

Manufacturing Sector

In terms of competitive performance (and our collective sense of national esteem) the manufacturing sector is paramount in the minds of many Canadians. This same sort of emphasis is given to manufacturing performance in the United States as well where a number of observers have noted the apparent slowdown of productivity growth dating from the mid-1960s. Yet despite the close economic ties between Canada and the United States, Canadian productivity growth did not show the same degree of lethargy over the 1967–73 period. In fact, spurred on by increased levels of investment, Canadian productivity levels accelerated in the latter part of the 1960s relative to their performance in the period from the late 1950s.

From 1957 to 1966, output per man-hour in manufacturing industries grew at average annual rates of 2.9 percent based on increases in capital, materials, and energy per man-hour of 2.2 percent, 3.6 percent, and 4.3 percent respectively (Table 2–4). The growth continued and, as noted above, strengthened between 1966 and 1973, with average annual productivity increases of 4.0 percent. Once again, increases in the utilization of other inputs, coupled with the ongoing process of technical progress, were responsible for this period of relatively strong advances in the level or productivity. Capital utilized per man-hour advanced on average, by 3.1 percent over this period, while materials inputs showed even stronger annual gains on the order of 4.2 percent. Only energy use slowed from the previous period, although it certainly showed little promise of regressing. According to our estimates, the amount of energy used for each man-hour worked increased over this period by 3.3 percent per year, just slightly faster than did the amount of capital per man-hour.

In short then, at the same time the U.S. manufacturing segment was undergoing a productivity growth slowdown, the Canadian manufacturing productivity growth pace actually quickened. The crunch, such as it was, did not appear in Canada until 1974, following the shocks of the OPEC price hikes and the related economic slowdown. In this year, productivity growth slowed to just 0.6 percent, and its 1975 gain of only 1.6 percent continued the slow pace.

In part, the productivity slowdown in 1974–75 represented a cyclical phenomenon associated with the rate of labor hoarding—the holding by companies of labor that is surplus to needs during short-term cyclical downturns in order to save the expenses of firing and rehiring when the recovery comes and, in some cases, to avoid the loss of relatively scarce skilled labor.[3] According to the estimates of a recent Economic Council discussion paper, in 1974 and 1975, the rate of paid labor hoarding in manufacturing industries rose to levels three to five times above the 1961 to 1970 average (Siedule and Newton 1979).

By 1976, the effects of the slowdown were beginning to wear off in manufacturing as output rose 5.2 percent over 1975 levels. Productivity increased by 5.8 percent, as the number of man-hours worked actually declined slightly. As a result, the annual productivity growth rate for the three years following the oil crisis averaged about 2.7 percent, just slightly below the 1957–66 average.

Primary Sector

Primary industries constitute very important elements in the Canadian economic milieu, yet are often the forgotten components in productivity studies. This history of omissions might be because of the motley composition of the sector, which consists of such diverse industries as mining, agriculture, fishing, and forestry.

In the period from 1957 to 1966, this sector led manufacturing, construction, and services with productivity gains averaging 7.9 percent per year (Table 2–5). These gains are well explained by the high levels of capital investment and output expansion in these sectors during these years. Capital per man-hour rose at average rates of 8.8 percent, the use of materials and energy per man-hour rose by 8.4 percent, and the level of output rose at a pace of 3.7 percent per year; employment actually declined at a rate averaging 3.8 percent per year.

Coming into the period from 1967 to 1973, primary sector expansion slackened somewhat but remained strong. Productivity growth continued at an average rate of 6.4 percent as capital per man-hour growth remained strong, and material and energy input growth slowed.

In 1974, primary sector output declined by 2.4 percent, but man-hours *increased* by 1.4 percent. The implications for productivity performance are obvious; productivity fell 3.7 percent. By 1975, employment also began to fall, but the slight 0.2 percent man-hours decline was not sufficient to offset the continued output drops and productivity fell a further 2.7 percent.

Service Sector

The first difficulties encountered in studying any sector are those related to measurement. This is doubly true of the service sector. In certain service sector industries, notably public administration, business, and personal services, output is measured to a significant extent simply by the quantity of inputs used; as inputs rise, output as measured rises by an identical amount. Hence, productivity growth by definition is nil.

The extent to which this measurement effect may result in downward-

Table 2–3. Aggregate Labor Productivity Growth and Interindustry Shifts

Component	1957–66	1967–73	1974–75
Total shift effect	0.6524	0.0089	–0.4928
Employment	0.6761	0.0037	–0.6809
Output	–0.0237	0.0052	0.1881
Actual productivity growth	3.0600	3.0700	–0.1621

Source: Based on data from Statistics Canada and calculations by the authors. For details of calculations, see Rao (forthcoming).

Table 2–4. Average Annual Percentage Change in Inputs and Outputs: Manufacturing Industries

	1957–66	1967–73	1974	1975	1976
Gross output (1971$)	5.28	5.39	3.26	–3.07	5.23
Man-hours	2.36	1.36	2.61	–4.56	–.38
Capital per man-hour	2.15	3.12	2.97	9.55	3.10
Intermediate inputs (less energy) per man-hour	3.57	4.23	0.70	2.76	5.56
Energy per man-hour	4.28	3.27	–4.30	3.27	13.74
Output per man-hour	2.86	4.00	0.63	1.57	5.79

Source: Based on the data from Statistics Canada and estimates by the authors.

Table 2–5. Average Annual Percentage Change in Inputs and Outputs: Primary Industries

	1957–66	1967–73	1974	1975
Gross output (1971$)	3.73	3.65	–2.38	–2.84
Man-hours	–3.81	–2.55	1.38	–.16
Capital per man-hour	7.92	6.39	–3.71	6.24
Intermediate inputs per man-hour	8.42	6.80	–1.25	–5.04
Output per man-hour	7.92	6.39	–3.71	–2.69

Source: Based on data from Statistics Canada and estimates by the authors.

biased estimates of total service sector productivity growth is illustrated by the fact that on a net-value basis service sector productivity growth amounted to an average annual rate of 1.8 percent between 1950 and 1977 (Table 2–6). Yet when those service industries whose output is improperly measured are excluded from this measure, the average rate of growth amounts to 2.9 percent (Economic Council of Canada 1978).

In this paper, we have not excluded those industries where the measurement of productivity is biased. It is therefore necessary to keep in mind that the estimates presented here are biased downwards significantly. To the extent that the importance of this bias has changed over time, or cyclically, the results of our econometric estimates will also be affected.

From 1957 to 1966, the service industries made the lowest productivity gains of the three sectors considered here. Average annual productivity growth amounted to just 1.6 percent, despite increases in the capital per man-hour of 2.8 percent, and increases in the use of materials and energy per man-hour of 1.2 percent. As indicated above, this slow progress is due in large extent to measurement problems. The individual service industries for which output is adequately measured, such as utilities, trade, and transportation, communication, and storage, made much better gains in productivity over this, and subsequent, periods.

For the service sector as a whole, productivity growth improved in the years from 1967 to 1973 to an average annual rate of 2.2 percent, because of the increased rate of utilization of materials and energy inputs and despite a slowing in the rate of increase of capital per man-hour. In 1974, the service sector productivity showed greater resistance to the effects of the demand slowdown by increasing by 1.5 percent, a greater increase than for the other sectors despite the downward measurement bias. In 1975, productivity growth remained positive but slowed to just 0.3 percent, as output growth slowed to 3.6 percent from 5.6 percent in 1974.

Construction Sector

Productivity growth in the construction industry has lagged behind improvements in manufacturing and primary industries, and has barely outpaced gains in the service sector. From 1957 to 1966, productivity increases in the construction industry were limited to average annual gains of just 1.7 percent, based on slight increases in the use of materials and energy inputs per man-hour, and despite actual declines of capital per man-hour averaging 0.5 percent per year (Table 2–7).

As with other sectors, productivity gains improved in the 1966–73 period to average annual rates of 2.5 percent, still relatively weak, but

Table 2–6. Average Annual Percentage Change in Inputs and Outputs: Service Industries

	1957–66	*1967–73*	*1974*	*1975*
Gross output (1971$)	4.65	5.59	5.57	3.61
Man-hours	3.02	3.30	4.06	3.29
Capital per man-hour	2.81	1.74	2.08	3.12
Intermediate inputs				
per man-hour	1.22	2.43	2.12	3.15
Output per man-hour	1.58	2.22	1.46	.31

Source: Based on data from Statistics Canada and estimates by the authors.

Table 2–7. Average Annual Percentage Change in Inputs and Outputs: Construction Industries

	1957–66	*1967–73*	*1974*	*1975*
Gross output (1971$)	4.38	2.87	4.48	3.78
Man-hours	2.89	.44	9.45	.43
Capital per man-hour	–.52	3.56	–3.16	4.13
Intermediate inputs				
per man-hour	1.68	2.54	–4.54	3.38
Output per man-hour	1.66	2.53	–4.54	3.35

Source: Based on data from Statistics Canada and estimates by the authors.

improved over the previous years. During this period, the capital-labor ratio improved strongly in contrast to previous declines, and the increased usage of materials and energy inputs increased at a faster pace. This stronger performance was cut short in 1974, when productivity declined by 4.5 percent despite strong output growth. A partial recovery occurred in 1975 with an increase in productivity of 3.3 percent, insufficient to offset the 1974 decline.

Such, then, is the story of the recent Canadian productivity performance. If one were forced to provide a capsule description of it based on nothing more than has been presented so far in this paper, it might well take the following form. Compared to the movements of productivity in the United States, the recent Canadian performance has been remarkably stable and assured. From 1957 to 1973, this growth, despite some relatively minor setbacks, continued at a strong pace with little or no sign of weakening arising from domestic sources. Then in 1974 and 1975, after the oil price increases began, and in the midst of pervasive demand weaknesses, productivity stagnated.

Yet we still have not explained anything. We do not know for example what were the sources of the slowdown and their relative contributions to it, any more than we know what were the sources of the relatively strong growth during the 1960s. Questions such as these have usually been investigated either directly, using explicitly defined production functions,[4] or residually, using the distribution of inputs, where a production function is implicit in the estimates.[5]

In this paper, we have used the direct approach, with a fairly extensive econometric investigation based on the method using KLEM (capital, labor, energy, materials) production functions. A full technical description of the procedure is given in Appendix B along with some information on the multitude of tests that we were able to make. However, for the casual reader, the following brief explanation should suffice.

In the broadest form of the model tested here, we posited a fairly general production function that was manipulated to yield a functional form expressing output per man-hour as a function of capital per man-hour, energy used per man-hour, materials input per man-hour, and technical factors that may reflect the effects of, among other things, the rate of capacity utilization, the prime age male unemployment rate, demographic effects, and Hicks-neutral and factor-augmenting technical change. It was not assumed that returns-to-scale effects were constant but rather this constituted an additional test within the equations.

Thirty-five individual equations were fitted over the period from 1957-1974 under a number of varied hypotheses and, on the basis of several factors, the most appropriate for each industry and several of the aggregates was chosen. This process and the chosen equations are presented in Appendix C. Because data are unavailable, only for manufacturing industries could energy and materials contributions be separated.

We are not presenting these results as anything more than further pieces of preliminary evidence regarding an extremely complex case— evidence obtained from the application of one particular technique. There remains a great deal of work to be done before we can hope to understand well the influences of the myriad factors that determine productivity levels and growth.

There is little to be gained here from detailed examinations of the results and meanings of each equation—even the entrails of chickens may be dissected usefully only to a certain point. Instead we would like to present some of the more general observations that may be drawn from the results and that bear most closely on the questions of productivity growth over the 1957 to 1974 period.[6]

1. For all industries, with the exception of agriculture, fishing and trapping, forestry, and nonautomobile transportation equipment, technical progress appears to be of the Hicks-neutral type.[7] That is, technical progress appears to have increased the efficiency of all inputs at the same rate.

2. For manufacturing industries as a whole, technical progress appears to have contributed approximately 1 percentage point per year to productivity growth from 1957 to 1974.[8]

3. Industry-specific capacity utilization effects have a significant impact on productivity performance in manufacturing. As capacity utilization rates increase so does productivity; while during a demand slowdown, when capacity utilization rates fall, productivity levels also diminish.[9]

4. In general, a slightly diminishing or constant returns-to-scale assumption is supported for most manufacturing industries.[10]

5. The impact of demographic changes in the labor force is probably negative, but is quite small in manufacturing.[11]

Of these findings, one that may stand out to many readers is the conclusion that diminishing or constant returns-to-scale were exhibited by many of the manufacturing industries examined. It has long been one of the central tenets of those most deeply concerned with Canadian productivity study that a principal reason for Canada's lagging behind the United States is that Canadian industries do not produce on a worldwide, efficient scale. Therefore among the most commonly proffered cures for our productivity malaise have been those based on attempts to increase the scale of Canadian production. Yet if many industries really do operate on a constant or diminishing returns-to-scale basis, then one must question the appropriateness of this approach. At the very least it would be prudent to explore this issue much more deeply and to keep in mind the need for a broader range of policy thrusts.

Two points in this regard must, however, be made. First, the particular inferences that may be drawn from any econometric time-series study are subject to any number of sources of error, large and small. Therefore, very specific tests are usually designed to test the validity of specific postulated hypotheses in a manner that reduces the probability of errors, or more precisely, inaccuracies creeping into the tests. In the case at hand, we did not set out to study explicitly the presence or absence of scale economies in Canadian manufacturing and therefore our tests were not designed in an optimal way to eliminate possible sources of error in this regard. Time-series-based statistical tests are generally blunt tools, often used to work on the least reliable data under relatively crude conditions; while they serve as guides, they cannot be taken for gospel.

Second, while scale effects have been of considerable concern, there has been equal, if not greater, emphasis placed on the possible advantages to Canada of obtaining greater levels of in-plant specialization (Gorecki 1977). This proposal could not be tested in our model, although, for example, some of the benefits that may have flowed from the increased specialization of Canadian industry following the Kennedy Round of tariff changes may well be included in the technical change factor in the equations (Lermer 1973).

Therefore, while our results do not support the hypothesis that there are vast untapped gains to be made from exploiting economies of scale, they should not be taken as strong refutation of this view. Moreover, there is no evidence here to confirm or reject the presence of economies of specialization in the Canadian economy. In our view, such facets of the issue require microeconomic-based testing and are unlikely to yield to the sort of macro approach used in this chapter.

SOURCES OF PRODUCTIVITY GROWTH

Based on the empirical results of this econometric investigation, we were able to look at the relative contributions of various factors of productivity growth. The interested reader should consult Rao (forthcoming) for detailed, disaggregated estimates.

Between 1957 and 1966, the greatest contribution to manufacturing productivity increases derived from the increased use of material inputs per man-hour, which accounted for roughly two-thirds of the total increase. Somewhat surprisingly, increases in the capital-labor ratio accounted for less than 7 percent of the growth, while technical progress contributed average annual gains of 1.3 percentage points, or 37 percent of total productivity advances.

In other sectors, there seemed a tendency for factors other than increased material usage to play major roles. For example, in the utilities sector, capital formation was responsible for some 39 percent of the increased productivity during the 1957 to 1966 period, a contribution matched by technical progress.

It is of some interest to follow the developments in the manufacturing sector through the latter part of our estimation period in order to observe the developments that have molded recent productivity progress. In the interest of brevity, and recognizing the presence of diminishing marginal returns in detailed descriptions, a similar exercise will not be repeated for all of the individual sectors.

The contribution of materials to productivity growth remained dominant during the 1967 to 1973 period, rising from roughly a 65 percent share during the 1957 to 1966 period to 69 percent between 1967 and 1976, while the contributions made by other fators remained in line with the previous experience. In particular, demographic effects continued to detract slightly from the progress added by other factors, as did the apparent effects of diminishing marginal returns.

The relatively short period from 1974 to 1976 reflects the impact of the economic slowdown. The actual manufacturing productivity gain would have been much larger, by almost one-third, had not cyclical factors played such a large, and negative, role. In fact, productivity performance would have been in line with growth from 1957 to 1966, although lower than in the 1967 to 1973 period, had not cyclical factors intervened.

In brief, looking at the performance of manufacturing in this way, we have seen that the reason for the slower growth during the years 1974–76 appears to be due to the effects of the lower output levels experienced during this period. It remains an open question, however, as to what extent the prolonged slowdown experienced since then has reduced the level of potential productivity growth in the near future.

The importance of the increased usage of material inputs per man-hour as a source of productivity growth is, of course, a result unique to gross output-based studies; and it is one whose underlying causes we do not well understand. It could be, for example, that this phenomenon of increased materials usage reflects nothing more than a decline in materials prices relative to other factors' prices. Or it may reflect an underlying shift in the structure of the economy, to an increased degree of production specialization, for example, or to a shift toward the production of more highly finished goods requiring more intermediate inputs. We simply do not know; we might suggest that this would prove a fertile ground for future investigation.

Energy

Much of the recent productivity debate and research in the United States centers around the proposition that the energy crisis or, more correctly, the increase in energy prices associated with the OPEC cartel in late 1973, has led to some form of structual break in productivity performance. This break is usually assumed to be either a once-and-for-all lowering of productivity levels, or a once-and-for-all lowering accompanied by a permanently lower long-run productivity growth rate. The former scenario hinges around, so it seems, the concept that the energy price rises had the immediate effect of rendering obsolete a substantial portion of formerly productive capital, thus lowering the effective capital-labor ratio and productivity. The second, a case argued effectively by Jorgenson, is predicated around the assumption that capital and energy enter production as complementary items.[12] Thus the energy price increase effectively served to diminish the utilization of energy and capital in production and to raise the utilization of labor (whose relative wage was now lower relative to the energy-capital costs). Over the long run, if energy prices remained high, then the rate of substitution of capital for labor would remain depressed, and therefore productivity growth would be permanently subdued.

Unfortunately it would be slightly premature to reach any definite conclusions based on the work we have been able to carry out to date. While we can report the findings of our work that relate only to the period up to 1976, it is important to realize that the energy price increases were particularly traumatic experiences for Western economies for which the relative price of energy had been falling for many years. Therefore, to expect that the full effects of the increases would be felt only two years after the event would be inappropriate, especially since the government acted to cushion the effects of the shock by allowing Canadian oil prices to rise more slowly than world prices so that domestic industries were not subject to the full effects of the increases immediately. Indeed, according to our estimates, even by 1976 the price of energy relative to the GNP deflator was lower than its average relative position during the 1957 to 1966 period.

Therefore the results of our investigations for manufacturing industries provide, not surprisingly, therefore, little evidence in support of either the once-and-for-all lowering of productivity proposition, nor for the permanently lower long-run growth proposition (Table 2–8). If a large-scale retirement of capital had taken place, as posited in the first scenario—and such would not be reflected in the official capital stock measures used here[13]—then our equations would have tended to over-predict seriously the level of productivity gains made, and the level of productivity itself in the 1974–76 period. This, in fact, has not happened to any significant extent. The second assumption, that the longer run rate of productivity growth has been negatively affected has also not been supported by either the equations we have estimated, or the movements of energy per man-hour in manufacturing. The movements of this series are shown in Table 2–8, from which it is easily seen that the level of energy per man-hour has in fact *increased* since the energy crunch, at a rate similar to rates established for earlier periods.

Thus the evidence for manufacturing for the 1974–76 period does not seem to support the structural shift hypotheses. Whether this should be construed as evidence that Canadian industry is not adjusting to the world of higher energy prices, or whether it is simply an indication of the long lags in operation in the economy, remains unclear. For the present all we can note is that energy prices seem likely to remain at high relative levels in the future, and that to survive in a highly competitive world,

Table 2-8. Energy Use in Canadian Manufacturing

	1957-66	1967-73	1974	1975	1976
Growth of energy consumption (%)	6.69	4.61	-1.80	-1.44	13.14
Energy/man-hour ($)	.20	.27	.28	.29	.33
Energy/unit output ($)	.02	.02	.02	.02	.02
Price of energy/ GNE deflator	1.22	.97	1.12	1.14	1.18

Source: Based on data from Statistics Canada and estimates by the authors.

industry must make some adjustment to these higher levels. Such adjustment need not necessarily result in lower productivity. We face a tremendous challenge certainly, but inherent in this challenge is an opportunity to make technological improvements and gains on a scale and in manner that may result in productivity gains through production avenues, products, and technologies that would not otherwise have been considered. Higher prices and increased international competition provide the challenge and the incentive; stagnation and reduced standards of living are the unpleasant alternatives.

Regulations

Another of the frequently diagnosed causes of the productivity growth malaise has been economic regulation, especially the new regulations directed towards health and safety standards, pollution controls, zoning restrictions, product standards, and the like. It has been argued for example, that regulations reduce productivity growth by diverting capital and research expenditures away from more productive uses, by inducing long delays into the innovative process and by slowing the adoption of new production techniques (Meadows 1978). An alternative view, that regulations, if used in an appropriate manner, may serve to stimulate the innovative process, and hence increase potential productivity growth, has also received some attention of late (Allen et al. 1978).

Unfortunately, our model does not incorporate the effects of regulatory activity directly. However, because the pattern of regulatory growth has not been smoothed over our estimation period—for example, as many regulations were passed in the period from 1970 to 1977 as were passed in the previous three decades at the federal level alone (Economic Council of Canada 1978)—some of the effects might have been expected to have been in evidence in our residuals. This did not turn out to be the case, however; no pattern readily attributable to the effects of regulations could be found.

This sort of negative finding, or inference, obviously proves nothing. There are any number of alternative explanations that might be compatible with the type of nonresult of this sort. There are undoubtedly cases where regulatory interventions have reduced the potential rate of productivity increase and others where they may have augmented the productivity level. It is equally certain that the existing regulatory process can be improved. Overlapping, redundant, and ineffective regulations can be eliminated, or at least their incidence can be reduced, and future and existing regulations can be reviewed to ensure they are used effectively and efficiently in achieving the goals of our society. In particular, the effects that regulations may have on productivity and economic growth must be recognized and evaluated in the formulation of new regulations, and in the revision of existing legislation. At present, the Economic Council, under a reference from First Ministers, is undertaking a full-scale investigation into the topic of economic regulation from which it is hoped an improved understanding of the regulatory process will evolve.

Demographic Effects

The demographic composition of the working force has been called into question a number of times in past productivity studies.[14] In particular, as the effects of the baby boom are now passing through the labor force, it might be expected that the resultant decline in the average age and experience level of the labor force would have a deleterious impact on productivity. Compounding this effect has been the recent influx of female workers into the labor force with relatively little (on a "for-pay" basis) work-related experience (Table 2–9). As a crude test of the effects of these changes in the composition of the labor force, a variable that expressed the ratio of women and youths in the labor force to the total labor force was incorporated into the equations. For manufacturing, the effect of this variable turned out to be negative, although quite small. Over the 1966 to 1973 period for example, the contribution of the demographic variable was to lower the growth of total labor productivity by only 0.36 percent per year.

Research and Development

One of the areas of greatest concern over the past few years has been the question of the adequacy of Canadian investment in research and

Table 2–9. Demographic Changes in Canada

	1957–66	1967–73	1974	1975
Growth in youth and female labor force	4.80%	4.82%	8.54%	4.88%
Growth in the "prime age male" labor force	1.33	1.80	2.97	2.31
Youth and female labor force as percentage of total labor force	33.11	39.80	43.80	44.36
Ratio of unemployed youth and females to unemployed prime age males	.99	1.36	1.60	1.55
Employed youth and females as a percentage of total employment	33.29	39.57	43.35	43.81

Source: Based on data from Statistics Canada and estimates by the authors.

development.[15] This, unfortunately, is one where this chapter can say relatively little.

In the equations used in this chapter, technical progress is calculated on the basis of linear time trends, which cannot detect directly any changes over the estimation period in the rate of technical progress. Therefore our results do not permit us to make any robust statements regarding the hypothesis that the rate of technical progress has declined over this period. We might however note that if any such decline has occurred, it has not been of sufficient magnitude to cause a significant error to appear in our results over the estimation period from 1957 to 1974, nor in simulations performed with the results for the years 1975 and 1976.

The entire technology research and development question and its role in the progress of the economy is an enormously complicated one not given to simplistic solutions or studies. To say that more research and development would be beneficial is to issue a motherhood statement. What is needed is a much improved understanding of the relative costs and benefits of such goal. There remains a great deal of work to be done in this and other aspects of industrial development policies. We need a better understanding, for example, of the process of diffusion of new technologies, the role to be played by governments, the effects of multinational corporations on technological diffusion, and of many other aspects of this and other issues before we make informed proposals for Canada's industrial future.

Regional Problems

One particular aspect of the industrial development policy question that very clearly needs an improved understanding is in the sphere of regional development. Just as we found substantial differences among individual sectors in terms of productivity, there are very substantial differences among regions. An Economic Council background study to the Council document "Living Together" contains analysis of these differences in some detail (Auer 1979). The study was based on value-added measurement and so is not directly comparable to this chapter, but the results are in and of themselves of considerable interest.

In brief, the study found that on a region-to-region basis productivity levels differed by up to 50 percent of the national average with Alberta productivity some 14 percent above, and Prince Edward Island productivity 40 percent below. Moreover, these differences are not mere reflections of differences in industrial structure, which overall accounted for only 20 percent of the differences, but reflect more deeply rooted differences in the efficiency of production in those areas. For example, those regions that had below average rates of aggregate productivity also tended to be below average within specific industry groups. This tendency is well illustrated by Table 2-10.

The primary causes of these variations in productivity appear to be related to differences in the workforce and to differences in the capital stock. As well, it was noted that the lower productivity regions tended to benefit last from improvements in technology and other advances.

Remedying these problems is by no means a simple task, but the rewards in terms of increased domestic productivity, and the easing of regional income disparities should justify a significant effort in this regard, especially one directed toward upgrading the labor force and toward improving the current management and technological processes, and increasing the availability of new technologies to firms in low productivity regions.

CONCLUSION

The story of recent productivity trends in Canada has been an extremely complicated one. In the initial stage of this chapter we sought to show that, although productivity growth in Canada has outstripped that of the United States, it was not sufficient to offset the substantial gains made in other generally less developed, countries, nor was it sufficient to reach the overall level of productivity of the United States. However, it was clear that the Canadian economy did not go through the sort of productivity slowdown evidenced in the United States following

Table 2–10. Variations in Output per Worker (Standardized for Industrial Structure): 1970–73

Province	Total Economy	Goods-Producing Industries	Manufacturing Industries
Newfoundland	85%	83%	76%
Prince Edward Island	76	81	65
Nova Scotia	78	71	73
New Brunswick	81	74	80
Quebec	92	84	93
Ontario	103	104	106
Manitoba	92	89	89
Saskatchewan	111	118	106
Alberta	118	137	104
British Columbia	109	112	109
Canada	100	100	100

Source: Auer (1970: 42).

the mid-1960s (Table 2–11). In general, the ultimate conclusion to be drawn from the earlier part of this effort might be that between 1957 and 1973 Canadian productivity growth remained remarkably stable and strong, although there remain significant regional problems.

During the 1970s Canadian industry was subjected to an increasing number of shocks and hindrances including increasing regulation, soaring energy prices, and a pronounced economic slowdown of a duration and extent not experienced in the postwar period. While for the relatively short period from 1974 to 1976 we were unable to detect the impact of regulations or the energy crisis on productivity, it was abundantly clear that the continued low levels of demand were having a pronounced and deleterious impact.[16] It is not fair to conclude from this that regulations and rising relative energy prices have not had an effect on productivity and output, but only that we were not able to detect it using macroeconometric tools in the period up to 1976.

Productivity growth depends on a great number of factors including the growth of aggregate demand and the levels of various inputs available for use in the production process, the scale and specialization of production runs, technological advance, management techniques, research and development, and the skill and attitude of the labor force. It has become quite clear that strong future productivity growth will depend on our ability to make advances over the broad front of all of these factors. But, where do we begin? How much emphasis should be given to each factor, and at what costs, in the effort to improve productivity? These are questions to which a major part of the Economic Council's ongoing research will be directed.

Table 2–11. Average Annual Growth in Labor Productivity

Industry	1957–66	1967–73	1974	1975
Agriculture, fishing, trapping	7.4621%	4.2615%	−.600%	4.224%
Forestry	8.6293	5.5404	−2.483	5.399
Construction	1.6605	2.5322	−4.543	3.343
Mining	7.2309	7.0413	−3.998	−10.450
Transportation and communications	4.2508	3.7797	2.461	3.137
Trade	2.5675	3.0495	1.848	.207
Finance, insurance, real estate	−.1084	2.0721	−2.087	4.001
Utilities	6.2973	5.5491	11.230	−12.084
Services	.8476	1.8904	1.585	−1.683
Manufacturing	2.8627	3.9965	.628	1.568
Durables	3.7913	4.2213	.595	3.463
Nondurables	3.2338	3.8027	.663	−.317

APPENDIX A
DATA SOURCES

Most of the data series are drawn from the Candide Model 2.0 data bank. However, we will explain briefly the primary source for each variable used in the research reported in this chapter.

Employment series for the eleven major industries[1] are obtained from the Labour Force Survey Division, Statistics Canada. Since the LF Survey does not give the employment breakdown either for manufacturing or for mining, we had to construct the employment series for twenty-two manufacturing and four mining industries. For this purpose, we made use of the employment data from the Establishment Survey, obtained from the Labour Division, Statistics Canada.

The employment data from these two sources are not compatible primarily because of differences in coverage. Generally, the Establishment Survey covers companies having twenty or more employees. This drawback limits the use of these data. The coverage varies from industry to industry. For example, in 1972 the coverage for service industry is only 20 percent. For the same year, the coverage for the manufacturing industries is about 95 percent. Generally, the coverage for both the mining and manufacturing industries is fairly good—between 91–95 percent.

Using the data from these two surveys, we constructed employment series for all mining and manufacturing industries. Let N_{ML} be the total employment for the manufacturing industry, obtained from the Labour Force Survey (LFS).

N_{MiE} is the employment of the ith manufacturing industry given by the Establishment Survey (ES), and N_{ME} is the total employment of the total manufacturing industry from the ES:

$$\sum_{i=1}^{22} N_{MiE}$$

then, the employment data for the ith manufacturing industry is constructed as:

$$N_{MiL} = N_{MiE} * (N_{ML}/N_{ME})$$
$$i = 1, 2, \ldots 22. \tag{2.1}$$

Equation (2.1) implicitly assumes that the coverage for each of the components is the same as the coverage of total manufacturing industry. This assumption is somewhat restrictive. However, in the absence of any information on individual industry coverage, this assumption may not be unreasonable. Moreover, without much effort the components add up to the LFS total. A similar procedure is used for the construction of employment data for the components of the mining industry.

For the eleven major industries, the data on average weekly hours worked are obtained from Mr. A.B. McCormick of the Productivity Section, Statistics Canada. To construct the average weekly hours series for each of the manufacturing and the mining industries, the ES data on average weekly hours of production workers and production and non-production worker employment is used. For each component industry the following four steps are involved in the construction of the average weekly hours series.

Step 1.

Construction of the ES average weekly hours series for each industry. For this purpose, we used the ES data on the production and nonproduction workers and the average weekly hours of production workers. Let H_{PMiE} be the average weekly hours worked by the production workers of the *i*th manufacturing industry. N_{PMiE} is the number of production workers in the *i*th manufacturing industry, and H_{MiE} is the average weekly hours worked in the *i*th manufacturing industry. Then H_{MiE} is calculated as

$$H_{MiE} = H_{PMiE} * (N_{PMiE}/N_{MiE}) + 40$$
$$* [1 - (N_{PMiE}/N_{MiE})] \qquad (2.2)$$
$$i = 1, 2, \ldots 22$$

Equation (2.2) assumes that the nonproduction workers work forty hours a week and it is invariant over time.

Step 2

Making use of the employment, average weekly hours data computed in (2.2), we construct a pseudo man-hour series for each component:

$$\hat{M}_{Mi} = H_{MiE} * N_{MiL} * 52$$
$$i = 1, 2, \ldots 22 \qquad (2.3)$$

where M_{Mi} is the pseudo man-hours for the *i*th manufacturing industry.

Step 3

Using employment data from the LFS and average hours data given by the productivity division, first we have constructed the man-hours series for the eleven major industries.

$$M_M = N_{ML} * H_{MP} * 52 \qquad (2.4)$$

where N_{ML} is total manufacturing employment, obtained from the LFS, H_{MP} is the average weekly hours of the manufacturing industry, and M

$_M$ is the total man-hours of the manufacturing industry. The corresponding pseudo man-hours is given by:

$$\hat{M}_M = \sum_{i=1}^{22} \hat{M}_{Mi}. \tag{2.5}$$

Next, we construct the man-hours series for each individual manufacturing industry as:

$$M_{Mi} = \hat{M}_{Mi} * (M_M / \hat{M}_M)$$
$$i = 1, 2, \ldots 22. \tag{2.6}$$

Step 4

Using the man-hours series from (2.6) and the employment series from (2.1), the average weekly hours are computed:

$$H_{Mi} = M_{Mi} / (N_{Mi} * 52)$$
$$i = 1, 2, \ldots 22 \tag{2.7}$$

Similarly, the average weekly hours data are constructed for all four mining industries.

For all the industries, both the current and constant dollar value-added data are obtained from the Industry Product Division, Statistics Canada.

For the eleven major industries, wage bill data are drawn from CANSIM data bank. Using the ES data on average weekly earnings, we constructed the wage bill series for each of the manufacturing and the mining industries.

$$WB_{Mi} = W_{MiE} * N_{Mi} * 52 \tag{2.8}$$

where W_{MiE} is the average weekly earnings of the ith manufacturing industry from the ES, and WB_{Mi} is the wage bill of the ith manufacturing industry. Similarly the wage bill data for the individual mining industries is computed.

Making use of benchmark capital stock data, time series on investment and an industry-specific depreciation into capital stock series are constructed. All the raw data are obtained from the Construction Division, Statistics Canada.

For all the thirty-five industries, data on gross output and intermediate inputs, both in current and constant dollars are obtained from the Industry Product Division, Statistics Canada.

For all the manufacturing industries, data on current dollar energy consumption are directly taken from *General Review of the Manufacturing Industries of Canada,* Statistics Canada Publication, Catalogue No. 31–203.

To obtain constant dollar consumption of energy, we need time series on energy prices by industry. Since these data are not readily available, we have constructed energy price indexes making use of data on gross output prices of these industries: coal mining, crude petroleum and natural gas, petroleum and coal products, and utilities. First, we have obtained the deliveries of these industries for each of our manufacturing industries from the 1971 input-output tables. The sum of these values is approximately equal to the energy and fuel consumption given in census of manufacturing industries. This information is used to construct the weights and these in turn are used to construct a weighted energy price index by industry:

$$P_{Eit} = a_{cli}\, P_{clt} + a_{cpi}\, P_{cpt} + a_{pci}\, P_{pct} + a_{ui}\, P_{ut}$$
$$i = 1, \ldots 22 \tag{2.9}$$

where P_{Eit} is the price index of energy for the i*th* industry in the time t, $\alpha_{cli}, \alpha_{cip}, \alpha_{pci},$ and α_{ui} are the shares of coal, crude petroleum and natural gas, petroleum and coal products, and utilities in the energy input of the i*th* industry, respectively, and P_{clt}, P_{cpt}, P_{pct}, and P_{ut}, are the gross output price indexes coal, crude petroleum and natural gas, petroleum and coal products, and utilities, respectively.

Quarterly time-series data on the capacity utilization is obtained from Statistics Canada Publication Catalogue No. 31–003. These data in turn are converted to an annual basis. These data are available only from 1961. Using regression techniques, we have obtained estimates of capacity utilization for the period 1957–1960. For the nonmanufacturing industries, capacity utilization data are obtained from the Research Department of the Bank of Canada.

Data on normal average weekly hours by industry are constructed as a four-year moving average of actual hours worked.

APPENDIX B
PRODUCTIVITY ESTIMATES BY INDUSTRY

Estimates of total factor productivity growth can be obtained either by directly estimating the technical progress parameter of a well-defined production function[1] or derived residually using a distribution theory, where the production function is implicit.[2]

If we assume a four-factor, twice differentiable, homogenous production function f, with disembodied technical progress A:

$$Q = A \, f \, (K, \, L, \, E, \, M) \tag{2.10}$$

where K, L, E, M are capital, labor, energy, and material inputs, respectively, and Q is the gross output in constant dollars.

Differentiating (2.10) with respect to time and dividing it through by Q and rearranging the terms, gives us:

$$\frac{dA}{A} = \frac{dQ}{Q} - F_K \frac{K}{Q} \frac{dK}{K} - F_L \frac{L}{Q} \frac{dL}{L}$$
$$- F_E \frac{E}{Q} \frac{dE}{E} - F_M \frac{M}{Q} \frac{dM}{M} \tag{2.11}$$

where dA/A is the measure of factor productivity and F_K, F_L, F_E, and F_M are the partial derivatives of output with respect to capital, labor, energy, and material inputs respectively.

It is clear from (2.11) that both the magnitude and the stability of the technical progress parameter (dA/A) depends on: (1) the appropriate measurement of output and inputs, (2) the functional form of f(.), and (3) the importance of omitted variables from the production process (such as entrepreneural ability, capacity utilization, government regulation, etc.).

The productivity estimates given in Rao (1978) were based on the value-added rather than the gross output data. The use of value-added data in productivity analysis can be justified only if there is no substitution between intermediate inputs and other inputs—capital and labor. In spite of this restrictive assumption, the use of value-added will always overestimate the total factor productivity (except those industries in which the material content is zero), and this bias will be serious in industries where the material content is large.[3]

In this section, using the KLEM production approach, we will obtain estimates of factor productivity for each industry. The estimated parameters of the productivity equations will enable us to analyze the sources of productivity growth in each industry in all three periods. Hopefully, this would help us to identify the causes of the productivity slowdown experienced in the 1970s.

We begin with the Cobb-Douglas production function with Hicks-neutral technical change and constant returns to scale:

$$Q_{it} = A_{oi}\, e^{\lambda_i t}\, K_{it}^{a_i}\, E_{it}^{\beta_i}\, M_{it}^{\gamma_i}\, L_{it}^{1-(a_i+\beta_i+\gamma_i)} \tag{2.13}$$

where Q_{it} is the gross output (constant 1971$) in the ith industry in time t, K_{it}, E_{it}, M_{it}, L_{it}, are, respectively, capital, energy, raw materials, and labor, inputs of the ith industry in time t, t is the time trend and λ_i is the technical progress parameter of the ith industry. Dividing both sides of (2.13) by L_{it} gives the labor productivity equation for the ith industry.

$$(Q_{it}/L_{it}) = A_{oi}\, e^{\lambda_i t}\, \frac{K_{it}^{a_{it}}}{L_{it}}\, \frac{E_{it}^{\beta_i}}{L_{it}}\, \frac{M_{it}^{\gamma_i}}{L_{it}} \tag{2.14}$$

$$q_{it} = A_{oi} e^{\lambda_i t}\, K_{it}^{a_i}\, e_{it}^{\beta_i}\, m_{it}^{\gamma_i} \tag{2.14a}$$

where q_i is the output per man-hour and k_{it}, e_{it}, and m_{it} are capital, energy, and materials per unit of labor respectively.[4]

Relaxation of the constant returns to scale assumption is straightforward.[4]

$$q_{it} = A_{oi}\, e^{\lambda_i t}\, k_{it}^{a_i}\, e_{it}^{\beta_i}\, m_{it}^{\gamma_i}\, L_{it}^{\theta_i - 1}$$

where $$\tag{2.15}$$

$$\theta_i = a_i + \beta_i + \gamma_i + \delta_i$$

and δ_i is the exponent of labor input in (2.13). If the exponent of L_{it} in (2.15) is positive and statistically significant, increasing returns to scale are implied; decreasing returns to scale are implied if the coefficient is significantly negative and a coefficient not significantly different from zero implies constant returns to scale.

In order to get unbiased estimates of the parameters of the production function, we have to make corrections for the cyclical movements of productivity. Clear evidence exists that short-run increasing returns arise from the short-run movements in output. While in aggregate studies,[5] cyclical adjustments are usually made by using the aggregate unemployment rate (standardized for age-sex composition of labor force) as a proxy for the utilization of inputs, this variable above will not be able to satisfactorily purge the cyclical elements from trend productivity at the industry level. We could overcome this problem by introducing a measure of industry-specific capacity utilization in addition to the aggregate unemployment rate in the productivity equation (2.15):

$$q_{it} = A_{oi} \, e_{it}^{\lambda_i t} \, k_{it}^{\alpha_i} \, m_{it}^{\gamma_i} \, L_{it}^{\pi_i} \, e^{(\phi_i \, URATE_t + \eta_i \, CU_{it})}$$

where: (2.16)

$$\pi_i = \theta_i - 1$$

URATE $= $ aggregate unemploment rate standardized for age-sex composition of labor force, and

CU_{it} $= $ capacity utilization measures for the i*th* industry in time t.

Labor input should reflect changes in skill, age, sex, and education over time. Most of the aggregate studies on productivity made some effort to quantity the impact of these demographic changes in labor productivity.[6]

Since time-series data on industry-specific employment by age, sex, education, and so forth are not available, it is not possible to standardize the labor input of each industry for these demographic changes. However, we can introduce the ratio of female and teenage male labor force to the total labor force as a rough proxy for the labor quality variable in the industry-specific productivity equation (2.16). This variable might help us to identify the industries that are most affected by the dramatic changes in the composition of labor forces in recent years. The productivity equation with correction for labor quality is written as:

$$q_{it} = A_{oi} \, e^{\lambda_i t} \, k_{it}^{\alpha_i} \, e_{it}^{\beta_i} \, m_{it}^{\gamma_i} \, L_{it}^{\pi_i} \, e^{(\phi_i \, URATE_t + \eta_i \, CU_{it} + \epsilon_i \, LQ_t)} \quad (2.17)$$

where LQ_t is the ratio of female and teenage male labor force to total labor force.

The logarithmic form of (2.17) is written as:

$$
\begin{aligned}
ln\ q_{it} = & ln\ A_{oi} + \lambda_i t + \alpha_{it}\ ln\ k_{it} \\
& + \beta_i\ ln\ e_{it} + \gamma_i\ ln\ m_{it} \\
& + \pi_i\ ln\ L_{it} + \phi_i\ URATE_t + \eta_i\ CU_{it} \\
& + \epsilon_i\ LQ_t + U_{it}
\end{aligned}
$$

where

$$U_{it} = \text{The disturbance term.}$$

Hicks-neutral technical progress assumption can be easily relaxed by slightly modifying the productivity equation (2.17):[7]

$$
\begin{aligned}
ln\ q_{it} = & ln\ A_{oi} + \lambda_i t + \alpha_i ln\ k_{it} + \beta_i\ ln\ e_{it} \\
& + \gamma_i\ ln\ m_{it} + \pi_i\ ln\ L_{it} + \phi_i\ URATE_t \\
& + \mu_i\ CU_{it} + \epsilon_i\ LQ_t + \theta_{ki}\ ln\ (K_{it})t \\
& + \theta_{mi}\ ln\ (M_{it})t + \theta_{ei} ln\ (E_{it})t + U_{it}.
\end{aligned}
$$

2.18

If the coefficient of the three interaction terms θ_{ki}, θ_{mi}, θ_{ei}, turn out to be statistically insignificant, equation (2.18) implies Hicks-neutral technical progress and the factor shares will be constant. However, in the case of factor augmenting technical progress, factor shares will vary over time.[8]

Klein and Preston (1967), Bodkin and Klein (1967), Preston (1967), and Hickman and Coen (1976) have argued against the direct estimation of the parameters of the production function. In the case of translog functions, production function and factor share equations have to be estimated as a system of equations subject to the relevant constraints. Moreover, because of the expected multicollinearity among factor inputs and time trend, we will not be able to get precise estimates of the parameters of the production sunction. We could overcome these problems by using a constrained estimation on equation (2.18). From the observed factor shares data, we get estimates of α_i, β_i, $_i$, and $_i$ as:

$$
\hat{\delta}_i = \frac{1}{T} \sum_{t=1}^{T} (WB\$_{it} / Q\$_{it})
$$

(2.19)

$$for\ i = 1, \ldots 35$$

$$\hat{\beta}_i = 1 \quad \sum_{t=1}^{T} \quad (E\$_{it} / Q\$_{it}) \qquad (2.20)$$

$$\text{for } i = 1, \ldots 35$$

$$\hat{\gamma}_i = 1 \quad \sum_{t=1}^{T} \quad (M\$_{it} / Q\$_{it}) \qquad (2.21)$$

$$\text{for } i = 1, \ldots 35$$

and

$$\hat{a}_i = 1 - \hat{\delta}_i - \hat{\beta}_i - \hat{\gamma}_i \qquad (2.22)$$

$$\text{for } i = 1, \ldots 35$$

where $WB\$_{it}$, $E\$_{it}$, $M\$_{it}$, and $Q\$_{it}$ are respectively wage bill, energy, materials, and gross output (all in current dollars) for the ith industry in the time t.

Then the constrained productivity equation is written as:

$$ln \; q_{it} - \hat{a}_i \; ln \; k_{it} - \hat{\beta}_i \; ln \; e_{it} - \hat{\gamma}_i \; ln \; m_{it}$$

$$= ln \; A_{oi} + \lambda_i t + \pi_i \; ln \; L_{it} + \phi_i \; URATE_t$$

$$+ \eta_i \; CU_{it} + \epsilon_i \; LQ_t + \theta_{ki} \; ln \; K_{it} t \qquad (2.23)$$

$$+ \theta_{mi} \; ln \; M_{it} t + \theta_{ei} \; ln \; E_{it} + U_{it}$$

To check for the robustness of technical progress parameter with the inclusion or exclusion of certain variables, we have estimated several variants of equation (2.23). For comparison purposes, we have also estimated productivity equations for each industry without imposing any constraints on α_i, β_i, and γ_i.

APPENDIX C
EMPIRICAL RESULTS

Here we will discuss the empirical estimates of the parameters of the productivity equation (2.23), for each industry. To study the sensitivity of estimates with the inclusion or exclusion of some variables,[1] we have estimated several variants of (2.23). These results are recorded by industry in Tables 2.12 and 2.13. After a thorough review of these equations, for each industry we have chosen a representative productivity equation. In selecting the representative equation, the following criteria are used: (1) goodness of fit of the equation, (2) standard error of estimate, (3) Durbin-Watson statistic, and (4) signs, sizes, and robustness of coefficients. In selecting these equations we have paid special attention to the description of technical change. These selected productivity equations for the manufacturing and nonmanufacturing industries are given in Tables 2-12 and 2-13, respectively. Each row contains the estimated coefficient of the variable with the t-ratio in the parenthesis.[2] A blank space in any row indicates that this particular variable is not included in the equation. The last three rows give (1) R^2, the coefficient of determination adjusted for degrees of freedom, (2) S.E.E., standard error of estimate, and (3) D.W., the Durbin-Watson statistic.

The results are encouraging in several respects. First, with the exception of agriculture, fishing, and trapping, mining (aggregate), and metal mining, more than 90 percent of variation in labor productivity is explained. Second, this assures that all the estimates are free from problems of autocorrelation. Third, with few exceptions, both the signs and sizes of all the coefficients are in accordance with prior expectations. Fourth, because of the multicollinearity problem among factor inputs and time trend, for none of the industries did the unconstrained estimation give reasonable estimates of the factor shares and the factor productivity growth. Fifth, as expected, in every industry the estimates of gross factor productivity are smaller than the value-added productivity given in Rao (1978). Sixth, only for agriculture, forestry, the four mining industries and nonautomobile transportation equipment industries did the factor augmenting technical progress model give superior results. For all the other industries, Hicks-neutral technical progress is not rejected on the basis of the goodness of fit and the reasonableness of the signs and sizes of all of the coefficients. Lastly, the estimated residuals of these equations were fairly random in the 1970s. If there is any productivity break, we would have either consistently over or underestimated the actual labor productivity in this period. This result is consistent with the findings of Rao (1978) and Denny and May (1978b), Clark (1978), and Norsworthy and Harper (1979).

Table 2-12. Selected Productivity Equations (Gross Output) Manufacturing Industries: 1957–74.
Dependent Variable ln Q/L

Variable	Nonferrous Metal Mining	Metal Fabricating	Nonelectrical Machinery	Nonauto Transportation Equipment	Motor Vehicle Parts and Accessories
ln (K/L)	0.09184	0.12669	0.06299	0.05467	0.04902
ln (M/L)	0.65220	0.59560	0.61004	0.56888	0.82914
ln (E/L)	0.00460	0.01029	0.00732	0.00969	0.00364
Time trend	0.00623	0.00956	0.01582	0.13865	0.01449
	(6.16)	(3.48)	(3.30)	(1.73)	(10.88)
Capacity utilization	—	0.00112	0.00242	0.00420	—
		(7.88)	(2.86)	(2.44)	
Actual normal hours	-0.88887	—	1.00800	—	—
	(1.76)		(2.76)		
Labour quality	—	—	0.00439	—	—
			(0.55)		
DMURATE 25.54 distributed lag	-0.01729	-0.00138	—	0.05738	0.01033
	(8.87)	(3.50)		(2.92)	(1.63)
ln (L)	0.023273	—	0.00600	—	—
	(3.50)		(0.17)		
ln (K)*T	—	—	—	-0.00679	—
				(0.74)	
ln (M)*T	—	—	—	-0.02551	—
				(14.42)	
ln (E)*T	—	—	—	0.01655	—
				(8.02)	
$\bar{R}^2$	0.963	0.994	0.992	0.966	0.895
SEE	0.0056	0.0043	0.0057	0.0403	0.0253
D.W.	2.197	1.605	2.861	2.622	2.257

Table 2-12. Selected Productivity Equations (Gross Output) Manufacturing Industries: 1957-74. Dependent Variable in Q/L (Continued)

Variable	Total Manufacturing	Manufacturing Durables	Wood	Furniture and Fixtures	Iron and Steel
ln (K/L)	0.10823	0.09623	0.08411	0.13456	0.12655
ln (M/L)	0.64648	0.63469	0.65252	0.57460	0.54484
ln (E/L)	0.01821	0.01630	0.01698	0.00945	0.03299
Time trend	0.01318	0.01695	0.00525	0.00793	0.00868
	(5.63)	(5.51)	(4.34)	(18.91)	(6.68)
Capacity utilization	0.00106	0.00146	—	0.00288	—
	(2.23)	(2.62)		(4.71)	
Actual/normal hours	—	—	1.09126	—	3.81923
			(4.14)		(2.11)
Labor quality	-0.00448	-0.00614	—	—	—
	(1.28)	(1.35)			
DMURATE 25.54 (Distributed lag)	-0.00527	-0.01021	-0.011447	0.00291	-0.00955
	(2.87)	(3.39)	(6.37)	(0.78)	(2.01)
ln (L)	-0.08371	-0.13916	-0.12461	—	—
	(1.25)	(1.70)	(2.47)		
ln (K)*T	—	—	—	—	—
ln (M)*T	—	—	—	—	—
ln (E)*T	—	—	—	—	—
$\bar{R}^2$	0.994	0.993	0.947	0.976	0.902
SEE	0.0037	0.0049	0.0055	0.0080	0.0160
D.W.	2.478	2.204	1.853	1.597	1.820

Table 2-12. Selected Productivity Equations (Gross Output) Manufacturing Industries: 1957-74. Dependent Variable in Q/L (Continued)

Variable	Motor vehicles (Excluding Parts and Accessories)	Electrical Products	Nonmetallic Mineral Products	Manufacturing Nondurables	Food and Beverage
ln (K/L)	0.09548	0.09033	0.18020	0.12268	0.11379
ln (M/L)	0.58559	0.60935	0.50792	0.65766	0.73496
ln (E/L)	0.01203	0.00654	0.05636	0.01801	0.01166
Time trend	0.01170	0.03234	0.00825	0.01106	0.00953
	(14.15)	(6.35)	(12.19)	(6.16)	(5.47)
Capacity utilization	—	0.00483	0.00417	0.00080	0.00024
		(5.64)	(4.54)	(1.63)	(1.31)
Actual/normal hours	1.06614	1.91845	—	—	—
	(2.84)	(2.54)			
Labor quality	—	-0.02717	—	-0.00406	-0.00688
		(3.70)		(1.57)	(2.80)
DMURATE 25.54	-0.02382	—	0.01215	-0.00161	-0.00459
	(3.73)		(3.13)	(1.33)	(5.00)
Distributed lag ln (L)	—	-0.10418	—	-0.06565	-0.04902
		(1.29)		(1.53)	(1.32)
ln (K) *T	—	—	—	—	—
ln (M) *T	—	—	—	—	—
ln (E) *T	—	—	—	—	—
R̄²	0.976	0.985	0.932	0.996	0.987
SEE	0.0101	0.0075	0.0129	0.0026	0.0027
D.W.	2.680	2.139	2.429	2.394	1.916

Table 2-12. Selected Productivity Equations (Gross Output) Manufacturing Industries: 1957-74. Dependent Variable in Q/L (Continued)

Variable	Tobacco Products	Rubber and Plastic	Leather	Textiles	Knitting and Clothing
ln (K/L)	0.13214	0.12798	0.04324	0.08327	0.10566
ln (M/L)	0.71484	0.58851	0.62496	0.60960	0.60354
ln (E/L)	0.00344	0.01655	0.00729	0.01626	0.04438
Time trend	0.00984	0.01784	0.01078	0.01204	0.01964
	(3.97)	(15.62)	(3.73)	(1.62)	(4.67)
Capacity utilization	0.00153	0.00358	0.00124	—	-0.00098
	(4.16)	(4.77)	(3.49)		(0.74)
Actual/normal hours	—	—	—	1.84371	—
				(3.19)	
Labor quality	-0.00473	—	-0.00626	0.00889	-0.01474
	(1.43)		(1.58)	(0.88)	(2.55)
DMURATE 25.54 (Distributed lag)	0.00032	0.01969	-0.00270	—	-0.00438
	(0.26)	(3.18)	(1.51)		(1.51)
ln (L)	-0.13531	—	-0.1088	—	—
	(4.92)		(2.78)		
ln (K) *T	—	—	—	—	—
ln (M) *T	—	—	—	—	—
ln (E) *T	—	—	—	—	—
$\bar{R}^2$	0.993	0.957	0.988	0.995	0.982
SEE	0.0037	.0190	0.0041	0.0056	0.0066
D.W.	1.615	1.941	2.559	2.440	1.996

Dependent Variable in Q/L (Continued)

Variable	Paper and Allied Products	Printing and Publishing	Petroleum and Coal Products	Chemical and Chemical Prod.	Miscellaneous Manufacturing
ln (K/L)	0.13635	0.19062	0.07330	0.14500	0.18137
ln (M/L)	0.56008	0.45494	0.82974	0.62310	0.55965
ln (E/L)	0.05311	0.00662	0.00841	0.03235	0.00919
Time trend	0.00771	0.00970	0.00561	0.02324	0.00723
	(19.82)	(12.07)	(10.59)	(5.53)	(9.56)
Capacity utilization	0.00084	—	—	0.00050	—
	(1.28)			(1.27)	
Actual/normal hours	—	1.24749	0.83607	—	-0.65530
		(1.49)	(2.38)		(1.47)
Labor quality	—	—	—	-0.01435	—
				(2.46)	
DMURATE 25.54 (Distributed lag)	0.00183	0.00600	-0.00190	-0.00395	0.00183
	(0.92)	(1.99)	(1.43)	(1.72)	(0.62)
ln (L)	—	—	-0.19307	—	—
			(4.34)		
ln (K) *T	—	—	—	—	—
ln (M) *T	—	—	—	—	—
ln (E) *T	—	—	—	—	—
$\bar{R}^2$	0.971	0.945	0.972	0.991	0.910
SEE	0.0074	0.0102	0.0037	0.0068	0.0100
D.W.	1.654	2.047	1.610	2.412	1.573

Table 2-13. Selected Productivity Equations (Gross Output) Nonmanufacturing Industries: 1957–74
Dependent Variable: ln Q/L

Variable	Agriculture	Forestry	Mining Total	Coal Mining	Metal Mining	Crude Petroleum
ln (K/L)	0.49243	0.08894	0.33945	0.15051	0.26889	0.19587
ln (M/L)	0.43046	0.37568	0.42145	0.38460	0.55192	0.63656
ln (E/L)	—	—	—	—	—	—
Time trend	0.14272	0.11989	0.00533	0.01182	-0.02046	-0.05475
	(1.78)	(4.92)	(1.79)	(1.57)	(0.86)	(0.50)
Capacity utilization	0.00191	-0.00103	—	-0.00090	-0.00180	-0.00045
	(1.04)	(0.67)		(0.15)	(0.63)	(0.16)
Actual/normal hours	—	—	0.32704	—	—	—
			(0.82)			
Labor quality	—	—	—	—	—	—
DMURATE	-0.02815	-0.02478	0.00577	0.06044	0.02660	0.02323
	(2.17)	(2.94)	(0.78)	(4.07)	(4.68)	(3.26)
ln (L)	—	—	-0.23139	-0.00200	—	—
			(3.84)	(2.28)		
ln (K) *T	-0.02449	-0.01325	—	-0.00200	-0.00392	-0.00338
	(3.27)	(4.16)		(2.28)	(3.56)	(0.42)
ln (M) *T	0.01151	0.00387	—	0.00551	0.00673	0.01060
	(2.47)	(1.34)		(4.48)	(3.67)	(5.57)
ln (E) *T	—	—	—	—	—	—
$\bar{R}^2$	0.569	0.987	0.825	0.893	0.807	0.906
SEE	0.0308	0.0246	0.0188	0.0516	0.0209	0.0235
D.W.	1.872	2.217	2.49	2.288	2.56	1.86

Variable	Non-Metal Mining	Construction	Finance, Insurance and Real Estate	Communications and Transportation	Trade	Utilities
ln (K/L)	0.44137	0.54973	0.33987	0.22666	0.24932	0.51349
ln (M/L)	0.30785	0.14845	0.38110	0.32106	0.32050	0.18983
ln (E/L)	—	—	—	—	—	—
Time trend	-0.02984	0.01166	-0.02450	0.02624	0.01989	0.02424
	(0.61)	(1.64)	(1.92)	(14.67)	(10.40)	(4.18)
Capacity utilization	-0.00012	0.00313	-0.00090	—	0.00244	0.00328
	(0.33)	(4.63)	(0.92)		(2.55)	(1.92)
Actual/normal hours	—	-0.43539	2.94830	-0.03992	2.11826	—
		(1.27)	(4.64)	(0.09)	(5.87)	
Labor quality	—	0.00176	0.00992	—	—	0.01235
		(0.18)	(0.62)			(1.50)
DMURATE	0.04486	—	—	-0.00973	-0.00669	0.01134
	(2.38)			(2.53)	(2.59)	(3.75)
ln (L)	—	-0.23036	-0.31463	—	-0.32487	-0.35675
		(2.85)	(1.01)		(2.78)	(6.83)
ln (K) *T	-0.00469	—	—	—	—	—
	(2.38)					
ln (M) *T	0.00962	—	—	—	—	—
	(2.24)					
ln (E) *T	—	—	—	—	—	—
R̄²	0.807	0.968	0.918	0.989	0.995	0.996
SEE	0.0310	0.0073	0.0153	0.0153	0.0076	0.0092
D.W.	2.284	2.297	2.783	1.549	1.962	1.842

COMMENT
Noah M. Meltz

The chapter by Ostry and Rao on "Productivity Trends in Canada" represents a very useful background piece setting out the main factors underlying productivity trends in Canada from 1957 to 1976. The following comments deal with some of the implications of the findings particularly in relation to the labor market. Four subjects are discussed:
1. Long-term trends in productivity growth by industry,
2. Changes in the distribution of output and employment by industry sector,
3. The reasons why productivity growth didn't decline between the mid-1950s and early 1970s,
4. Productivity growth in 1974 and subsequently.

Long-term trends in productivity growth by industry

The growth trends by industry that Ostry and Rao observed for the two subperiods 1957–66 and 1967–73 represent continuations of patterns that existed almost thirty years earlier as shown in Table 2–14. The high-ranking utilities and primary industries consistently had the greatest rate of productivity growth while the reverse was true of the low-ranking services, finance, and trade industries.

Changes in the distribution of output and employment by industry sector

Two other long-term historical patterns are shown in Table 2–15. These patterns are output (measured by gross domestic product at factor cost) and employment by industry sector. There was a slight shift of output away from the primary sector toward services and construction and a large shift of employment from primary to services. The authors found that the shift in employment to higher productivity industries, which raised aggregate productivity by .68 percent during the period 1957–66, only had a negligible impact (less than .01 percent) in the period 1967–73.

The reasons why productivity didn't decline between the mid-1950s and early 1970s

One of the surprising findings in the Ostry and Rao chapter is that until the early 1970s in contrast with the experience in the United States, there was no decline in the rate of aggregate labour productivity growth

Table 2–14. Ranking of Average Annual Growth in Labor Productivity in Canada

	1931–61	1957–66	1967–73
Primary			
Agriculture	3.	2.	4.
Fishing, trapping	7.	2.	4.
Forestry	7.	1.	3.
Mining	2.	3.	1.
Manufacturing	4.	6.	5.
Construction	6.	8.	8.
Service			
Transportation and communications	5.	5.	6.
Trade	8.	7.	7.
Finance, insurance, real estate	10.	10.	9.
Utilities	1.	4.	2.
Services	9.	9.	10.

Source: 1931–61 Meltz (1965: 88); 1957–66, 1967–73, Ostry and Rao, p. 58.

in Canada. The reason for this lack of decline[1] is that productivity growth accelerated in manufacturing, construction and services (see Table 2–16).

In the case of manufacturing the main contributor to productivity growth was the increased use of material inputs, while for construction the major factor appears to have been the increase in capital per manhour and to a lesser extent the increase in intermediate inputs. For services, the growth of productivity during 1967–73 appears to be due to the increase in intermediate inputs[2]. (see Table 2–16).

Productivity growth in 1974 and subsequently

From 1974 to 1977 there were two years, 1974 and 1975, in which the growth in the aggregate output per man-hour was far below the long-term average, and two years that were about or close to the average (see Table 2–16). Since 1974 contained some peculiar developments it has been singled out for special examination even though there are difficulties in focusing on one particular year.

The chapter suggests that the productivity decline may have been due to labor hoarding in the face of a major economic slowdown. Unfortunately the evidence is very confusing. Although gross output did not increase as fast as the previous year or as in the 1967–73 period, there were signs

Table 2–15. Percent* Distribution of Output and Employment by Industry Sector in Canada, Selected Years

	1931	1961	1967	1973	1977
Output					
Total	100.0	100.0	100.0	100.0	100.0
Primary	12.8	9.5	9.0	9.5	8.2
Manufacturing	22.2	26.0	24.9	22.9	20.5
Construction	4.8	5.9	6.7	7.1	7.2
Services	60.2	58.6	59.3	60.5	64.1
Employment					
Total	100.0	100.0	100.0	100.0	100.0
Primary	35.4	14.5	10.6	7.9	7.3
Manufacturing	18.7	24.0	23.8	22.5	19.6
Construction	5.8	6.7	6.4	6.3	6.6
Services	40.2	54.8	59.2	63.3	66.6

Sources: Output is Gross Domestic Product at Factor Cost; Statistics Canada, *National Income and Expenditure Accounts 1926–1974* (Catalogue 13-531).
Employment: 1931, 1961 from Meltz (1965). 1967, 1973 from Statistics Canada, *The Labour Force,* March 1974 (70-001) and *Historical Labour Force Statistics* 1979 (71-201).

suggesting strong labor demand. The Help Wanted Index experienced its biggest year-over-year increase ever (*Economic Review 1978*) the vacancy rate rose sharply (*Statistics Canada, Quarterly Review of Job Vacancies* 1978), and man-hours increased at more than double the long-term rate. Although the unemployment rate fell only slightly, it was accompanied by the second largest increase in the labor force—the largest occurred the year before.

Normally one would associate labor hoarding with a decrease in employment, yet the study by Siedule and Newton (1979) indicates that there was, on the contrary, an increase in labor hoarding after 1973, at a time when employment was increasing (and the unemployment rate decreasing).

There are a number of possible explanations of this development that may have implications for the whole period of the 1970s. One explanation relates to the impact of the sharp increase in oil prices. If it were possible to quickly substitute among factors of production we would expect labor in particular to be substituted for energy inputs. There is strong support for this possibility. Table 2–16 shows that while man-hours rose sharply in manufacturing, energy inputs fell sharply. Similarly, in the case of the primary sector and construction, man-hours rose and intermediate inputs fell significantly.

This would seem to support the view that energy price changes caused

Table 2–16. Average Annual Percentage Change in Inputs and Outputs by Industry Sector in Canada

	1957–66	1967–73	1974	1975	1976	1977
Output per man-hour	3.05	3.07	–0.12	–0.44	5.0*	2.8*
Primary	7.92	6.39	–3.71	–2.69		
Manufacturing	2.86	4.00	0.63	1.57	5.79	
Construction	1.66	2.53	–4.54	3.35		
Service	1.58	2.22	1.46	0.31		
Gross Output (1971$)	4.75	5.09	3.95	0.53	5.9*	3.4*
Primary	3.73	3.65	–2.38	–2.84		
Manufacturing	5.28	5.39	3.26	–3.07	5.23	
Construction	4.38	2.87	4.48	3.78		
Service	4.65	5.59	5.57	3.61		
Man-hours	1.65	1.98	3.83	0.97		
Primary	–3.81	–2.55	1.38	–0.16		
Manufacturing	2.36	1.36	2.61	–4.56	–0.38	
Construction	2.89	0.44	9.45	0.43		
Service	3.02	3.30	4.06	3.29		
Capital per man-hour	3.48	2.81	2.04	4.89		
Primary	7.92	6.39	–3.71	6.24		
Manufacturing	2.15	3.12	2.97	9.55	3.10	
Construction	–0.52	3.56	–3.16	4.13		
Service	2.81	1.74	2.08	3.12		
Intermediate inputs						
per man-hour	3.21	3.13	–0.22	–1.05		
Primary	8.42	6.80	–1.25	–5.04		
Manufacturing						
Excluding Energy	3.57	4.23	0.70	2.76	5.56	
Energy	4.28	3.27	–4.30	3.27	13.74	
Construction	1.68	2.54	–4.54	3.38		
Service	1.22	2.43	2.12	3.15		

Source: All data are from various tables in the Ostry and Rao chapter except for the change in output per man-hour in 1976 and 1977 which are from *Aggregate Productivity Measures*.
ªCommercial industries only.

the decrease in labor productivity. Ostry and Rao do not find support for this view from the 1974–76 data. Rao (1978) also did not find any structural break during this period. The decline in productivity was mostly caused, according to Rao, by reductions in the rate of growth of the capital-labor radio and the decline in capacity utilization.

A second possible explanation is that the sharp increase in strike activity during this period led employers to attempt to hire additional labor in anticipation of strikes in order to increase their inventories. This hypothesis remains to be tested. A third possibility is that the change in the demographic structure of the labor force toward youth and women was the primary factor in the sudden productivity decline. Ostry and Rao show that this factor contributed only a small decrease of 0.36 percent.

A fourth factor could be changes in government programs, particularly Unemployment Insurance (UI). Professor Frank Reid and I found that the 1972 revisions in the UI Act contributed 1.9 percentage points to the upward shift in the vacancy-unemployment relationship (Reid and Meltz, 1979). This is turn could have lead to an increase in labor turnover, thereby lowering productivity. Unfortunately, turnover statistics are not available to assess this possibility.

Further research is necessary to determine whether the absolute declines in productivity growth which occurred in Canada in 1974 and 1975 were to be expected or whether they signal changes in the long-run situation.

Final Comment

Perhaps the most significant finding is the existence of diminishing or constant returns to scale. This contradicts the general view and raises major questions for future Canadian policy. If there are no economies of scale to be captured, then Canada need be less concerned with attempting to expand its markets and perhaps more concerned with increasing domestic competition. This is also an important consideration in efforts to explain Canada's lower productivity levels in relation to the United States.

NOTES TO CHAPTER 2

1. That is, the value of output adjusted for changes in prices divided by the total number of man-hours worked.

2. Even though 3 of the 4 individual industrial components (manufacturing, primary, construction, and services) had *positive* productivity growth in 1975, aggregate labor productivity *declined* due to interindustry shifts in output and man-hours. During the period 1974–1975, aggregate interindustry shifts reduced labor productivity growth by 0.5 percent per annum. (See Rao forthcoming).

3. See, Okun (1962), Solow (1957), Kuh (1965), Nordhaus (1972), Hickman and Coen (1976), Freedman (1977), and Clark (1978).

4. Solow (1957), Brown (1966), Ferguson (1965), Jorgenson (1965), Mitchell (1968), Nordhaus (1972), Gollop and Jorgenson (1977), Denny and May (1978a, 1978b, and 1979), Clark (1978), Brown and Medoff (1978).

5. Kendrick (1961), Denison (1962). Griliches (1968), Jorgenson and Griliches (1967), Kendrick (1970), Star (1974), and Nishimizu and Hulten (1978).

6. For full details see Rao (forthcoming).

7. Since most manufacturing industries exhibit little or no variation in factor shares during the sample period, this result is not surprising.

8. This estimate is very similar in size to the total factor productivity growth estimate by Denny and May (1978b), for Canadian manufacturing industries.

9. In each equation two measures of industry-specific utilization variables may be included: (1) capacity utilization obtained from Statistics Canada and (2) the ratio of actual to normal weekly hours worked as a proxy for the utilization of labor and capital inputs in that industry. The construction of normal hours series is explained in Appendix A.

10. Here we remind the reader that the short-turn effects due to increased utilization of factor inputs are captured by the capacity utilization variables.

11. Similar results are obtained in most aggregate studies on U.S. productivity. See, Nordhaus (1972), Clark (1978), and Norsworthy and Harper (1979).

12. For example see Berndt and Wood (1975) and Hudson and Jorgenson (1978).

13. See Appendix A for details.

14. See, Denison (1962), Perry (1971), Nordhaus (1972), Clark (1978), McCarthy (1978), and Nishimizu and Hulten (1978).

15. See, for example, Britton and Gilmour (1978).

16. This result is consistent with the findings of Clark (1978), Mark (1978), and Norsworthy and Harper (1979), for USA, and Rao (1978) for Canada.

NOTES TO APPENDIX A

1. The eleven industries are: agriculture, fishing and trapping; construction; communications and transportation; finance, insurance and real estate; forestry; manufacturing; trade; mining; services; utilities; and public administration.

NOTES TO APPENDIX B

1. Solow (1957), Brown (1966), Ferguson (1965), Jorgenson (1965), Mitchell (1968), Nordhaus (1972), Gollop and Jorgenson (1977), Denny and May (1978a, 1978b, and 1979), Clark (1978), Brown and Medoff (1978).

2. Kendrick (1961), Denison (1962), Griliches (1968), Jorgenson and Griliches (1967), Kendrick (1970), Star (1974), and Nishimizu and Hulten (1978).

3. The relationship between the two estimates of productivity can be represented as:

$$\frac{\dot{A}}{A} = \beta \frac{\dot{A}^*}{A^*} \tag{2.12}$$

where $\dot{A}/A$ and $\dot{A}^*/A^*$ are estimates of factor productivity based on gross and net outputs respectively and β is the share of capital and labor in gross output. Equation (2.12) says that the true factor productivity growth will be some fraction of value-added factor productivity. Since for most of the manufacturing industries, the value of β is approximately 0.5, use of value-added data will result in substantial overestimates of factor productivity growth in these industries. For details, see Star (1974), pp. 127–28.

4. See Griliches and Ringstad (1971), and Brown and Medoff (1978).

5. Okun (1962), Solow (1957), Nordhaus (1972), Hickman and Cohen (1976), and Rao (1978).

6. See Denison (1962), Perry (1971), Nordhaus (1972), Clark (1978), McCarthy (1978), and Nishimizu and Hulten (1978).

7. See Berndt and Wood (1975), Denny and May (1978a, 1978b).

8. It can be easily shown that the implied production function in (2.18) is a specific form of the popular translog production frontier. See Berndt and Jorgenson (1975), Hudson and Jorgenson (1972) and Denny and May (1978b). Equation (2.18) assumes that all coefficients of the factor inputs in the share equations are zero.

NOTES TO APPENDIX C

1. The sample period used in this paper is the same as in Rao (1978). Recently, we have obtained consistent data on gross output and material inputs (both current and constant dollars) for the years 1975 and 1976 for all the twenty-two manufacturing industries. For the nonmanufacturing industries, we could update this data only for 1975. Because of its late arrival, we could not make use of these data for estimation purposes. However, we make use of the estimated parameters of the productivity equation and productivity performance of the Canadian industries for the period 1971–1976 is analyzed.

2. Since all the selected equations are constrained type (2.23), t-ratios are not available for the coefficients on all the three factor intensity variables.

NOTES TO COMMENT

1. Rao (1978) examined the impact of the changes in output and employment shares and changes in productivity relatives over time for three periods: 1957–74, 1966–74, and 1971–74. He found that the predicted aggregate growth was very close to the actual and that the effects of changes in employment and output shares and changes in productivity relatives was very small (page 51).

2. Rao (1978) found that for some of the service sector industries (finance and services) capital contributed at least 50 percent of the measured productivity growth (page 35) while for others (transport, trade, and utilities) the contribution during the 1966–74 period was much smaller (Table 7).

Part II

Causes and Effects

The Importance of Productivity Change in the Economic Growth of Nine Industrialized Countries

*Charles R. Hulten & Mieko Nishimizu**

The prime mover in the process of economic growth is the readiness to absorb technical changes combined with the willingness to invest capital.

Nicholas Kaldor (1957)

INTRODUCTION

The purpose of this chapter is to provide an assessment of the importance of productivity change as the source of economic growth. The conventional methodology and measure of productivity change, often referred to as "residual," is the most common measure of total factor efficiency, and has been the subject of extensive research.[1] One of its main uses is the assessment of the relative contribution of productivity change to the process of economic growth. It has been pointed out, however, that this assessment is valid only under a set of highly restrictive assumptions.[2] In general, the conventional measure of total factor productivity change ignores the change in the accumulation of capital generated by productivity change, and therefore understates the impact of increases in factor efficiency on economic growth.

This chapter discusses a methodological framework for measuring the impact of productivity change on economic growth in which capital is treated as an endogenously determined factor of production. The methodology is based on the intertemporal economic theory of production. The point of departure for this theory is a variant of the Malinvaud-type intertemporal technology (Malinvaud 1953, 1961). We assume that the observed relative prices reflect intertemporal decisions, and that the

*We thank Odette Dekezel and Janis McCallum for their able research assistance in this project.

estimated rate of return to capital equals the rate of time preference. To analyze the effective rate of productivity change, we consider the change in the Malinvaud intertemporal production frontier because of factor efficiency, and allocate the change in total consumption between the rate of change of total primary input and productivity change, the "dynamic residual." Capital accumulation is endogenous in the intertemporal framework, and the dynamic residual retrieves the impact of changes in factor efficiency to economic growth through induced capital accumulation.

The intertemporal framework is then applied to aggregate data for the following nine countries over the post-World War II period: Canada, France, West Germany, Italy, Japan, Korea, the Netherlands, United Kingdom and the United States. Our basic conclusion is that productivity change was the primary source of economic growth in all countries.

The next section presents a brief discussion of our methodology. The third section discusses the data and presents our empirical results. Further interpretation of our results and conclusion are given in the last Section.

THE METHODOLOGY

Conventional analysis of patterns of aggregate economic growth allocates the rate of growth of output between the share-weighted growth rates of capital input and labor input, and a residual measure of total factor productivity change. The measure is intended to represent changes in the efficiency with which capital and labor are employed, and can be interpreted as a Hicks-neutral shift of an aggregate production function. The corresponding share-weighted growth rates of factor inputs can be interpreted as movements along the production function. In Figure 3-1 the shift in the function is depicted by the move from b to a and the factor accumulation effect by the move from d to b

This conventional methodology provides a valid measure of changes in total factor efficiency under the assumptions that (1) the production possibility set can be approximated by a constant return-to-scale Hicks-neutral technology, and (2) that factors of production are paid the value of their marginal product at every point in time. The methodology, however, does not provide a correct measure of the relative importance of productivity change as a cause of economic growth. The reason is that capital is a *produced* means of production that depends on total factor productivity change. This effect can be illustrated in Figure 3-1. If the economy is in stationary equilibrium at point d, a shift in factor efficiency from A_0 to A_1 will presumably cause the economy to establish

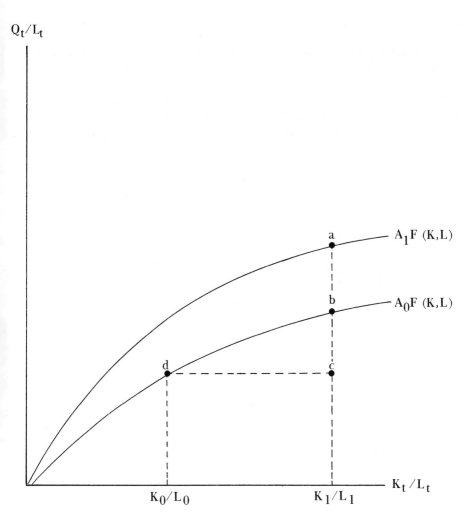

Figure 3–1. Output per Worker as a Function of the Capital-Labor Ratio.

a new equilibrium at some point on the more efficient technology, such as point a. The resulting change in output is the line segment ac; the total factor productivity change is, as before, equivalent to the segment ab. Thus, part of the true productivity effect, ac, is attributed to capital formation—that is, the segment bc—and thus understates the full effect of the efficiency change A_0 to A_1.

The source of the problem is the extra capital induced by the change in factor efficiency. This suggests a production accounting system in which capital formation is endogenous, corresponding to a theoretical framework where an intertemporal production possibility frontier replaces the aggregate production function of conventional productivity analysis, and where the conventional identity between value of input and value of output is replaced by the corresponding wealth concepts. For a finite horizon, consumption and terminal capital stock are determined by the initial stock, labor supply, and level of factor efficiency at each point in time. Variations in labor supply and factor efficiency lead, *mutatis mutandis,* to changes in consumption and terminal capital; the impact of efficiency change can therefore be estimated with capital formation responding endogenously.

Let Q, K, and L denote aggregate output, capital, and labor respectively, and let p, c, and w denote the corresponding prices. If output is a stable function of capital and labor, and if this function can be characterized by constant returns-to-scale and Hicks-neutral technical progress, then

$$Q_t = A_t \, F(K_t, \, L_t). \tag{3.1}$$

The factors are paid the value of the marginal product under producer equilibrium:

$$\frac{\partial Q_t}{\partial K_t} = \frac{c_t}{p_t}, \; \frac{\partial Q_t}{\partial L_t} = \frac{w_t}{p_t}. \tag{3.2}$$

Together, (3.1) and (3.2) imply

$$\frac{\dot{A}_t}{A_t} = \frac{\dot{Q}_t}{Q_t} - \frac{c_t K_t}{p_t Q_t} \frac{\dot{K}_t}{K_t} - \frac{w_t L_t}{p_t Q_t} \frac{\dot{L}_t}{L_t}, \tag{3.3}$$

where dots over variables indicate logarithmic differentiation with respect to time.

The left-hand side of equation (3.3) is residual output not accounted for by the growth of factor input. It is thus evident that the residual is equivalent to the rate of change of the A_t given (3.1) and (3.2). Equation (3.3) implies that $\dot{A}_t/A_t$ can be estimated directly from price and quantity data. The contribution of productivity change to growth in this conventional framework is measured by the ratio of $\dot{A}_t/A_t$ to $\dot{Q}_t/Q_t$

The endogenous capital model of productivity change is based on the intertemporal production possibility frontier,

$$\phi (C_1, \ldots C_N, K_N, K_O, L_1, \ldots L_N, A_1, \ldots A_N) = 0, \qquad (3.4)$$

where C_t denotes consumption at time t. Under the assumption that discounted prices reflect marginal rates of transformation, that is,

$$\frac{\partial\phi/\partial C_{t+s}}{\partial\phi/\partial C_t} = \frac{p^*_{t+s}}{p^*_t} \cdot \frac{1}{(1+r_{t+1}) \ldots (1+r_{t+s})}, \qquad (3.5)$$

where r_{t+s} is the rate of discount at time $t+s$ and asterisks denote prices discounted to the initial period $t = 0$. Equation (3.5) reflects the price normalization $p_{t+s} = 1$ for all s[3]. Differentiation of (3.4) yields

$$T(0, N) = \sum_{t=1}^{N} \frac{(\partial\phi/\partial A_t) \, A_t}{W_N} \frac{\dot{A}_t}{A_t}$$

$$= \sum_{t=1}^{N} \frac{p^*_t C_t}{W_N} \frac{\dot{C}_t}{C_t} + \frac{p^*_N K_N}{W_N} \frac{\dot{K}_N}{K_N} \qquad (3.6)$$

$$- \sum_{t=1}^{N} \frac{w^*_t L_t}{W_N} \frac{\dot{L}_t}{L_t} - \frac{p^*_O K_O}{W_N} \frac{\dot{K}_O}{K_O}.$$

The actual period-by-period growth rates have been substituted in (3.6) for the logarithmic differentials. We define W_N as the net wealth accumulated during the period O to N:

$$W_N = \sum_{t=1}^{N} p^*_t C_t + p^*_N K_N - p^*_O K_O$$

$$= \sum_{t=1}^{N} w^*_t L_t. \qquad (3.7)$$

Equation (3.7) is derived from (3.4) and (3.5) by assuming that production occurs under constant returns-to-scale in each period. The first equality in (3.7) defines wealth as the present value of net production over the period O to N. The second equality indicates that the net intertemporal product is exhausted under constant returns by the present value of the payments to the primary factors of production. Equation (3.7) is thus the intertemporal analogue to the conventional production account identity between value of output and value of total factor outlay implicit in equations (3.1) and (3.2).

We refer to T(O,N) as the "dynamic residual". It captures the change in intertemporal real product not associated with the changes in the factors of production. It can be thought of as the contribution to net wealth made by the change in total factor efficiency from one production period to the next, *where in each production period the level of efficiency is fully achieved*. The dynamic residual is thus a "local" measure of the importance of productivity change, and should be distinguished from a "global" concept, which measures the total effect of productivity change relative to the technology of initial production period.[4]

In order to further understand the concept of the dynamic residual, it is useful to examine the relationship between T(O,N) and the conventional residuals. First, note that the first equality in (3.6) can be written as

$$T(O, N) = \sum_{t=1}^{N} \frac{p_t^* Q_t}{W_N} \frac{\dot{A}_t}{A_t}. \tag{3.8}$$

This equality indicates that the dynamic residual is the weighted sum of the conventional residuals, where the weights sum to the ratio of gross intertemporal product to net intertemporal product: $\Sigma_t p_t^* Q_t / W_N$ The weighting scheme sums to a quantity greater than 1, and can be interpreted to reflect the magnification effect caused by the expansion in investment goods induced by the increased efficiency of factor input in all production periods. This is, of course, precisely the effect that T(O,N) is intended to capture.

Second, we note that although the conventional residuals measure period-by-period changes in factor efficiency, analyses of the conventional residual seldom focus on the individual $\dot{A}_t/A_t$ Instead, the residuals are frequently smoothed by calculating N-period geometric means:[5]

$$1 + A(O, N) = (1 + \frac{\dot{A}_1}{A_1}) (1 + \frac{\dot{A}_2}{A_2}) \ldots (1 + \frac{\dot{A}_N}{A_N}) \doteq \left(\frac{A_N}{A_O}\right)^{\frac{1}{N}} \quad (3.9)$$

The smoothed conventional residual A(O,N) is obviously an N-period concept and thus has the same time dimension as the dynamic residual. The smoothed conventional residual and the dynamic residual may therefore be regarded as alternative functions of the individual $\dot{A}_t/A_t$ — the former portraying the average compound rate of efficiency change, and the latter portraying the *impact* of that efficiency change. The conventional and dynamic residuals are thus complementary concepts, both of which depend on a common set of prices and quantities.

THE DATA AND EMPIRICAL RESULTS

We employ the price and quantity data on output and factor input from the aggregate production accounts developed by Christensen, Cummings, and Jorgenson (1977) for the private domestic sector of nine industrialized countries in their study of comparative factor efficiency. Their production accounts are constructed annually for the post-World War II period up to 1973 with a different initial period for each country. The data satisfy the fundamental identity for production accounts between the value of total product and total factor outlay in each period. Within the framework developed by Christensen and Jorgenson (1969, 1970, 1973), the product and factor outlay accounts are linked through capital formation and property compensation. In order to make this link explicit, they construct the price and quantity indexes of total output based on the price and quantity indexes of consumption goods and investment goods. Our endogenous capital model assumes a constant marginal rate of substitution between consumption and investment goods. Although we have extended the model to two-good specification, we did not have available separate price indexes employed in their data development. We therefore adopted their price index of total output to represent the price of the "homogeneous" good, and reconstructed the Christensen, Cummings, and Jorgenson production accounts. Although the homogeneity assumption is not attractive, we observed that the original accounts are not significantly sensitive to the respecification of prices.

It will be recalled from the previous section that the calculation of the dynamic residual requires that all prices be discounted to a common base-period. The choice of discount rate is not arbitrary and must be consistent with the equilibrium assumed in the calculations. Equations (3.2) and (3.5) specify two conditions of economic equilibrium. The third condition that must be satisfied under perfect foresight is the relationship between the price of investment goods and the present value of the net income flow associated with each capital asset:

$$1 = R_0 p_0 = R_1 c_1 + R_2 (1-\delta) c_2 + R_3 (1-\delta)^2 c_3 + \ldots + R_N (1-\delta)^{N-1} c_N + R_N (1-\delta)^N p_N$$

$$p_1^* = R_1 p_1 = R_1 c_2 + R_3 (1-\delta)\ c_3 + \ldots + R_N (1-\delta)^{N-2} c_N + R_N (1-\delta)^{N-1} p_N$$

$$\vdots$$

$$\text{(3.10)}$$

$$\vdots$$

$$p_N^* = R_N \bar{p}_N = \quad \vdots$$

where δ is the rate of replacement, R_t is the cumulative discount factor, that is,

$$R_t = \frac{1}{(1+r_1)(1+r_2)\ldots(1+r_t)} \qquad \text{(3.11)}$$

and where r_t denotes the rate of return to capital.[6] The prices p_t in (3.10) are shown for the sake of clarity; since the normalization implies that $P_0 = p_1 = \ldots = p_N = 1$, they can be omitted. Given this normalization and the rate of replacement, equation (3.10) can be solved recursively to yield estimates of the rentals:

$$c_t = r_t + \delta \qquad \text{(3.12)}$$

The individual r_t can then be imputed as

$$r_t = \frac{V_t - w_t L_t - \delta K_t}{K_t}. \qquad \text{(3.13)}$$

Given the r_t the discount factor R_t can be calculated and applied to the product and factor input prices.

Since taxes are not included in the asset-pricing equation (3.12) to preserve the simplicity of the one sector model, the estimated rates of return are before-tax measures.[7] This contrasts with the after-tax approach of Jorgenson and Griliches (1967) and Christensen and Jorgenson (1969, 1970, 1973).

We construct the estimates of the dynamic residual based on the translog discrete approximation to the continuous time index represented in the second equality in equation (3.6). The translog approximation replaces the continuous growth rates with the discrete time differences in the natural logarithms of the variables, and replaces the corresponding shares with the arithmetic average of the shares from one period to the next.[8] Table 3-1 presents the average annual rates of change in net real wealth, that is, the change in intertemporal product, the average annual rates of change in value added by labor, and the average annual rates of change in the dynamic residual for the entire postwar period as well as two sub-periods for each country. Table 3-2 presents the contribution of the dynamic residual to the change in intertemporal product, as well as the contribution of labor to the change in intertemporal product. Table 3-3 reports the conventional average annual rate of change of real product, total factor input, and total factor productivity for each of the nine countries as estimated by Christensen, Cummings, and Jorgenson. The average annual rate of growth of capital and labor input are also presented. Table 3-4 presents the conventional measures of contribution to growth by total factor input and productivity change.

These estimates permit an evaluation of the sources of growth and an assessment of the importance of productivity change in the aggregate economic growth of the nine industrialized countries. Table 3-3 shows that the ratio of change in total factor productivity measured within the conventional framework is significant relative to the changes in total factor input in all countries. Indeed, Table 3-4 shows that approximately one-third to one-half of growth in aggregate output can be attributed to the conventional measure of productivity change in these countries. Of the change in total factor input, growth in capital input is a far more important contributing factor to output growth relative to labor in most of the countries. Again, approximately one-third to one-half of growth in output can be attributed to the growth in capital input for those countries.

The overall implication of these estimates is clear: capital accumulation and improvement in total factor efficiency were the two important sources of aggregate economic growth. This conventional view of the sources of growth, however, is not an accurate representation of the prime motive force of economic growth. It ignores the accumulation of capital induced by productivity change, and therefore understates the

Table 3-1. Average Annual Growth Rates of Intertemporal Output, Input, and the Dynamic Residual

	Canada	France	West Germany	Italy	Japan	Korea	Netherlands	United Kingdom	United States
	1947-73	*1950-73*	*1950-73*	*1952-73*	*1952-73*		*1951-73*	*1955-73*	*1947-73*
Real wealth	.057	.060	.064	.062	.113	—	.065	.034	.046
Value added by labor	.014	.004	.004	.011	.033	—	.008	.001	.015
Dynamic residual	.043	.056	.061	.051	.080	—	.057	.033	.031
	1947-60	*1950-60*	*1950-60*	*1952-60*	*1952-60*		*1951-60*	*1955-60*	*1947-60*
Real wealth	.060	.061	.092	.081	.118	—	.071	.031	.044
Value added by labor	.011	.003	.016	.022	.048	—	.015	.002	.011
Dynamic residual	.049	.058	.076	.059	.070	—	.056	.029	.034
					1960-1973				
Real wealth	.053	.060	.038	.047	.110	.117	.060	.036	.050
Value added by labor	.019	.005	-.008	.002	.025	.049	.003	.001	.022
Dynamic residual	.034	.055	.046	.045	.085	.068	.058	.035	.028

Table 3-2. Intertemporal View of the Importance of Productivity

	Canada	France	West Germany	Italy	Japan	Korea	Nether-lands	United Kingdom	United States
	1947-73	*1950-73*	*1950-73*	*1952-73*	*1952-73*		*1951-73*	*1955-73*	*1947-73*
Contribution of labor	.245	.064	.055	.171	.291	—	.126	.037	.324
Contribution of productivity	.755	.936	.945	.829	.709	—	.874	.963	.676
	1947-60	*1950-60*	*1950-60*	*1952-60*	*1952-60*		*1951-60*	*1955-60*	*1947-60*
Contribution of labor	.187	.053	.172	.267	.405	—	.208	.054	.238
Contribution of productivity	.813	.947	.828	.733	.595	—	.792	.946	.762
					1960-1973				
Contribution of labor	.352	.076	-.215	.044	.226	.420	.052	.029	.443
Contribution of productivity	.648	.924	1.215	.956	.774	.580	.948	.971	.557

Note: Contributions of labor and productivity are the ratio of value added by labor and dynamic residual respectively to the growth of real wealth in Table 3-1.

Table 3-3. Average Annual Growth Rates of Real Product, Real Factor Inputs, and Total Factor Productivity

	Canada	France	West Germany	Italy	Japan	Korea	Netherlands	United Kingdom	United States
	1947-73	1950-73	1950-73	1952-73	1952-73		1951-73	1955-73	1947-73
Real property	.051	.055	.064	.052	.098	—	.053	.037	.038
Real factor input	.034	.025	.029	.024	.057	—	.029	.017	.027
Total factor productivity	.017	.030	.036	.029	.041	—	.025	.019	.013
Real capital input	.058	.056	.070	.045	.088	—	.055	.045	.043
Real labor input	.015	.004	.003	.010	.035	—	.008	.000	.016
	1947-60	1950-60	1950-60	1952-60	1952-60		1951-60	1955-60	1947-60
Real product	.051	.048	.082	.060	.081	—	.048	.033	.036
Real factor input	.035	.020	.036	.026	.047	—	.027	.018	.025
Total factor productivity	.029	.029	.047	.033	.033	—	.023	.015	.014
Real capital input	.068	.047	.069	.033	.044	—	.040	.044	.046
Real labor input	.011	.003	.016	.022	.048	—	.014	.002	.012
				1960-1973					
Real product	.051	.059	.050	.047	.109	.097	.056	.038	.041
Real factor input	.033	.029	.024	.022	.064	.058	.030	.018	.029
Total factor productivity	.018	.030	.028	.025	.045	.040	.025	.021	.012
Real capital input	.049	.063	.070	.054	.115	.072	.066	.046	.040
Real labor input	.020	.004	-.007	.002	.027	.050	.003	.000	.022

Source: Christensen, Cummings, and Jorgenson (1977).

Table 3-4. Conventional View of the Sources of Growth

	Canada	France	West Germany	Italy	Japan	Korea	Netherlands	United Kingdom	United States
	1947-73	1950-73	1950-73	1952-73	1952-73		1951-73	1955-73	1947-73
Contribution of real capital input	.492	.408	.424	.347	.339	—	.453	.482	.451
Contribution of real labor input	.166	.041	.095	.100	.277	—	.085	.009	.258
Contribution of total factor productivity	.348	.550	.562	.553	.417	—	.462	.509	.293
	1947-60	1950-60	1950-60	1952-60	1952-60		1951-60	1955-60	1947-60
Contribution of real capital input	.549	.365	.310	.220	.197	—	.381	.513	.497
Contribution of real labor input	.127	.039	.120	.215	.380	—	.155	.042	.204
Contribution of total factor productivity	.325	.595	.568	.565	.421	—	.465	.445	.303
					1960-1973				
Contribution of real capital input	.430	.444	.520	.435	.437	.264	.509	.468	.401
Contribution of real labor input	.209	.043	-.074	.020	.147	.324	.031	-.006	.317
Contribution of total factor productivity	.361	.513	.556	.545	.414	.412	.460	.538	.282

Source: Christensen, Cummings, and Jorgenson (1977).

impact of increases in factor efficiency on economic growth. Table 3–1 shows that when the technology-induced expansion in capital is allowed for through the dynamic residual, the growth rates associated with efficiency change rise considerably for every country. In many of these countries, the dynamic rate of change of efficiency is approximately double the conventional total factor productivity change. Table 3–2 shows that when measured as a fraction of the change in real wealth the importance of productivity change in growth increases dramatically, accounting for from more than one-half up to the entirety of the aggregate economic growth in these countries. Thus, the alternative approach suggested in this paper implies that changes in the efficiency with which factors are used at a given point in time is the single most important force in the economic growth process in the subsequent periods of production.

CONCLUSION

That productivity change should emerge from our analysis as the prime source of economic growth should not be surprising. The dynamic residual reassigns part of the historically observed growth rate of capital to the productivity change. When the additional capital available as a direct result of the increase in factor efficiency is built into a composite measure like the dynamic residual, the importance of productivity change becomes intuitively reasonable. The interesting question then is the extent of the contribution made by productivity change. The purpose of this chapter is to provide one such estimate.

This is not to say that capital formation is irrelevant. A zero rate of capital formation, or, alternatively, a zero net marginal propensity-to-save, would have had a dire effect on the growth rate of output. In the first place, capital formation would have occurred even in the absence of productivity change,[9] and second, the induced accumulation effect underlying the dynamic residual depends on a positive net marginal propensity-to-save. Furthermore, any complete description of the growth process would include the partial dependence of productivity change on the rate of capital accumulation (through the embodiment of technology in new capital goods). The complete cycle would then involve (1) increases in technical efficiency leading to additional capital formation, and in turn to more output, and so forth, and (2) the resulting increase in capital stock permitting further increases in technical efficiency, and so on. A complete description would also allow for the effect of productivity change on the supply of labor. However, since the embodiment hypothesis has not received general empirical support,[10] and since the direction of the labor supply effect is ambiguous, the results of this paper do provide one indication of the contribution of productivity change to economic growth.

We note further that many conventional analyses of the importance of productivity change have assigned a leading role to productivity change. This does not imply, however, that the dynamic residual is then an irrelevant concept. On the contrary, equation (3.8) shows that the dynamic residual is a weighted sum of the conventional residuals. If the conventional approach indicates that productivity change was the most important source of growth, the dynamic residual approach will show that productivity change made an even larger contribution to growth.

Finally, it is important to point out that the dynamic residual can be reinterpreted within the framework of neoclassical growth theory. In a one-sector model of optimal growth, Hulten (1975) considered technical change in terms of the rate of shift of the production frontier evaluated along the long-run optimal growth path. In order to assess the importance of technical change in the growth process, he allows for the impact of reproducibility of capital by introducing intertemporal consumption decisions. The resulting "long-run Fisherian rate" of technical change, say Z_t, is shown to be related to the conventional rate of productivity change as follows:

$$Z_t = [1 + \frac{\pi}{1-\pi} \sigma] A_t, \qquad (3.14)$$

where π is capital income share, and δ is the elasticity of substitution between capital and labor. We computed the long-run Fisherian rate, using the same data base as before and assuming $\delta = 1$ and $\delta = 1.5$ for each of the nine countries. Table 3–5 presents these results in terms of the average annual rates for the relevant time periods. Comparison of these results with the dynamic residual presented in Table 3–1 reveals a striking similarity between these two estimates. Each estimator captures the interaction between the reproducibility of capital and the factor efficiency with different sets of assumptions. In particular, the long-run Fisherian rate assumes a Ramsey utility function, a constant rate of time preference, and a parametric value for the elasticity of substitution between capital and labor. The dynamic residual assumes that the observed relative prices reflect intertemporal decisions, and thus the equivalence between the estimated rate of return on capital and the rate of time preference. The similarity between these two estimates thus provides a comforting additional support in our assessment of the importance of productivity change.

Table 3-5. The Long Run Fisherian Rates of Technical Change (Z)

	Canada	France	West Germany	Italy	Japan	Korea	Netherlands	United Kingdom	United States
	1947-73	1950-73	1950-73	1952-73	1952-73	—	1951-73	1955-73	1947-73
Z: $\delta=1.0$	.032	.050	.059	.048	.068	—	.044	.031	.022
Z: $\delta=1.5$	.039	.060	.070	.058	.082	—	.054	.037	.026
	1947-60	1950-60	1950-60	1952-60	1952-60	—	1951-60	1955-60	1947-60
Z: $\delta=1.0$	.030	.048	.074	.058	.053	—	.043	.024	.023
Z: $\delta=1.5$	.036	.057	.088	.069	.062	—	.054	.028	.027
					1960-73				
Z: $\delta=1.0$	.034	.052	.047	.042	.078	.065	.044	.034	.021
Z: $\delta=1.5$	.042	.063	.056	.051	.094	.077	.054	.040	.025

Note: δ is the elasticity of substitution between capital and labor. See equation (3.14) in the text.

COMMENT

Orley Ashenfelter

Technical change is the phrase used to describe our ignorance about the causes of economic growth. It represents a measure of those factors that affect output growth but that cannot be accounted for by known measures of the growth in the number of men and machines used in the economy. Since it is a measure of our ignorance, estimates of the amount of technical change are really an indicator of the research we need to do to explain productivity growth. This paper does not attempt to reduce that ignorance, but instead is a method of repackaging it. Hulten and Nishimizu, building on Hulten's earlier work, observe that exogenous productivity change will increase savings and hence capital accumulation. Thus, the total effect of any given exogenous technical change on productivity is the direct effect plus the induced effect due to the increased capital accumulation that results from the technical change.

At first blush this seems to imply that the productivity growth *caused* by any exogenous technical change will be underestimated because part of the "credit" for its effect on output will have been attributed to the effect of capital's growth on output. I have deliberately stated the problem in this way to bring out the similarity of Hulten and Nishimizu's work to the estimation of the structural as opposed to the reduced form effects of a policy change in conventional econometric models. If increases in the capital stock increases output, and if technical change increases the capital stock, then it follows that ignoring the effect of technical change on the capital stock leads to a downward bias in the estimates of the reduced form effects of technical change on output. Measuring the extent of this "bias" or, alternatively, the difference between the structural and reduced form effects of technical change on output growth is the purpose of Hulten and Nishimizu's work. At best, therefore, their work will only tell us that a better unraveling of the causes or components of technical change is a more important item for our research agenda than we once thought, but it will not carry us any further along on that agenda. Judging from the results of their computations this is indeed the case. Surely this general finding is beyond serious dispute, but its importance is another matter.

The bulk of Hulten and Nishimizu's work explains how the induced effect of technical change on capital accumulation is to be measured. As they observe, under some assumptions it is possible to use conventional measures of the amount of direct technical change to estimate the amount of induced capital accumulation, and the sum of these induced and direct effects is the end result of their work. A disturbing feature of the description of their methods is the difficulty of discerning just what assumptions they have used for this purpose and how relaxation of these assumptions would affect the results. Constant returns to scale is one assumption maintained here and throughout much of the growth-accounting literature. There are two further implicit assumptions that are less common, however, and whose importance is difficult to evaluate.

The first is an implicit assumption that the structure of the savings (or capital accumulation) process is independent of the amount or form of technical change. It would be easy to paint a scenario in which (correctly) anticipated technical change, for example, is treated as current wealth. Presumably this would reduce the extent to which current output growth should then be attributed to current induced capital accumulation. The general point is that the presence of technical change is likely to change what are taken to be the underlying structural parameters of the economy so that the implied reduced form effect of technical change may not be invariant to its magnitude or composition. Since Hulten and Nishimizu do not test whether capital accumulation is a result of technical change, but instead assume that it is these issues cannot be resolved in the framework they use and the sensitivity of their results to them remains unknown.

A second implicit assumption is that technical change, as measured, is the exogenous variable influencing capital accumulation and not the reverse. In view of the ignorance that surrounds the nature and causes of technical change it is always possible that both are related to other unspecified variables. Of course, the measurement process that Hulten and Nishimizu undertake need not be affected by this argument so long as their relationships are stable, but then the implications of public policies toward various aspects of the determinants of technical change might be vastly different. Uncovering these more fundamental relationships may be difficult or even impossible, but doing so remains the real challenge for growth accountants.

COMMENT
Frank Reid

To begin let me say that I am in general agreement with both the substance and conclusions of Chapter 3. The main conclusion of the chapter is that, as explanations of the rate of growth of per capita real income over time, productivity growth is substantially more important relative to capital accumulation than is indicated in a conventional Solow-type analysis. Hulten and Nishimizu (hereafter H-N) support this conclusion by applying to nine industrialized countries the new conceptual framework for measuring the contribution of productivity change to economic growth developed by Hulten in two papers in the *American Economic Review* (Hulten, 1975, 1979).

In these comments I hope to do two things. First, I want to emphasize the importance of developing a more accessible exposition of the theoretical argument and to encourage H-N to undertake such an exposition. Second, and perhaps as a contribution towards the first goal, I want to offer a very crude alternative model that, although it relies on much stronger assumptions, provides a much simplier derivation and yields very similar conclusions to the H-N model.

The H-N exposition of the model is suited to professional economists who are specializing in the area. I think it would be desirable to develop a less technical exposition of the model for several reasons. First, in order for the paper to receive the widespread academic recognition I think it deserves, it is necessary for it to be accessible to a relatively large audience. Second, the contribution this chapter makes is in developing a new conceptual framework for measuring the importance of productivity growth. There are no hypotheses tested in the paper—rather it develops what the authors call a new "production accounting system." One cannot turn to the data to verify the analysis or indicate whether the ideas presented are correct or incorrect. A new measure is developed and it is simply applied to the data. In order to judge whether the method is an improvement on conventional methods the reader must be very clear about the advantage of the new conceptual framework.

The third and most important reason why I think it is essential to attempt a simpler exposition of the model is that this is a policy-oriented volume. Governments clearly have a great interest in the determinants of productivity growth—witness the list of sponsors of the conference on which this volume is based. These include, among others, the Economic Council of Canada, the Ontario Ministry of Labour, and the Ontario Economic Council. My impression is that policymakers are reluctant to base decisions on results of economic analysis unless they have at least some basic idea of the concepts involved.

I think that the brief introductory discussion in Chapter 3 gives an excellent intuitive explanation of the problem addressed. But there is no analogous explanation of how the problem is approached, in either the conventional or modified methods. The discussion of the model, which starts with the intertemporal production possibility frontier in equation (3.4), and its total differentiation in (3.6) to give the dynamic residual is an elegant derivation but not one that gives much of an intuitive feeling for the working of the model.

If, in such a situation, one simply relies on the great prestige of our profession and asks the policymaker to accept the results on faith, two unfortunate things may happen. The most likely one is that the policymaker will be a skeptic and will not believe the results. Or, what is probably worse, the results may be believed but attributed an unwarranted degree of precision, leading to their misuse. The policymaker will then *become* a skeptic.

To develop the kind of exposition I am suggesting is often difficult and, in this instance, may not be possible. In addition to expositional skills, it requires an excellent understanding of the workings of the model. For this reason I will not attempt to undertake such an exposition myself but will simply encourage the authors to do so.

What I will do is develop a very simple model that, together with the Solow model, provides the two extreme limits of the more general model employed by H-N. I will then show that empirically the H-N model turns out to give very similar results to the simple model used here.

If there are constant returns-to-scale, then output per capita q depends only on the capital-labor ratio k, as shown in Figure 3–2 below, which is a slight variant of Figure 3-1. The basic problem is that at two points in time one observes points such as d and a, which are on different production functions and correspond to different levels of capital per unit of labor.

Solow in his classic *Review of Economics and Statistics* paper implicitly assumes that changes in k over time are exogenous, that is, not affected by productivity change. The problem is then to determine point b so that the total proportionate increase in q can be separated into the part caused by capital accumulation and the part caused by technical change; that is

$$\frac{q_2 - q_1}{q_1} = \frac{q_4 - q_1}{q_1} + \frac{q_2 - q_4}{q_1} \tag{3.15}$$

where the rate of technical change is defined as the second component:

$$\frac{\Delta A}{A} \quad \frac{q_2 - q_4}{q_1} \tag{3.16}$$

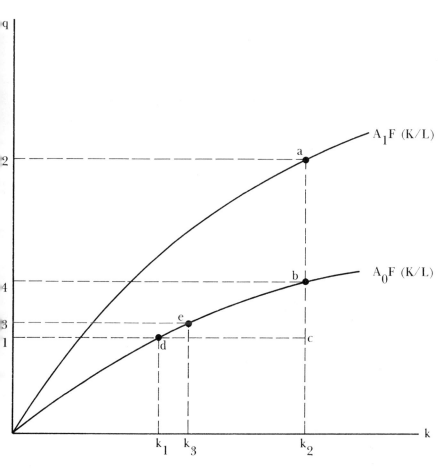

Figure 3–2. Change in Output per Worker as a Function of the Change in Capital per Worker and Technical Change.

If the slope of the production function, 2q/2k were known, then an approximation to point *b*o could be calculated as

$$q_4 = q_1 + \frac{\partial q}{\partial k}(k_2 - k_1).$$
(3.17)

By assuming that capital is paid its marginal product *(r)*, that is,

$$\frac{\partial q}{\partial k} = r,$$
(3.18)

it is then possible to determine q_4 as

$$q_4 = q_1 + r\,(k_2 - k_1). \tag{3.19}$$

Substituting equations (3.19) and (3.15) into (3.16) yields

$$\frac{\Delta A}{A} = \frac{q_2 - q_1}{q_1} - \frac{r(k_2 - k_1)}{q_1} \tag{3.20}$$

which, with some minor algebraic manipulation, may be written

$$\frac{\Delta A}{A} = \frac{\Delta q}{q_1} - \beta\,\frac{\Delta k}{k_1} \tag{3.21}$$

where $\beta = rk_1/q_1$, that is, the share of capital in total output, and q and k refer to the observed changes in q and k.

Equation 3.21 can easily be expressed in aggregate rather than per capita terms by substitution in $\Delta q/q = \Delta Q/Q - \Delta L/L$ and $\Delta k/k = \Delta K/K - \Delta L/L$, yielding

$$\frac{\Delta A}{A} = \frac{\Delta Q}{Q} - \beta\,\frac{\Delta K}{K} - (1 - \beta)\,\frac{\Delta L}{L} \tag{3.22}$$

This is, of course, Solow's famous estimating equation for the rate of productivity growth.

The main point that H-N make is that part of the increase in k is induced by the rise in q because of productivity growth. In Figure 3–2 the rise in k that would have occurred if there had been no technical change $(k_3 - k_1)$ is indicated by the movement from d to e. The remainder is the induced increase in k.

The model that H-N use to take account of the effect of capital accumulation induced by productivity growth was developed by Hulten in his 1979 *American Economic Review* paper. It is actually a Mark III model—the Mark I and Mark II models were presented in Hulten's 1975 *American Economic Review* paper. Generally, all three types of model give similar results but, generally speaking, they progressively rely on more complicated analysis and less restrictive assumptions in their derivations. The Mark I ("long-run Fisherian") model assumes the economy is always in a long-run equilibrium state with the optimal k. The Mark II model ("short-run Fisherian") allows the economy to be out of equilibrium but approaching the optimal k. The Mark III model uses an intertemporal production possibility frontier and determines the rate

Table 3–6. Rate of Economic Growth Due to Productivity Change

Country	Mark Zero $\frac{\Delta Q}{Q} - \frac{\Delta L}{L}$	Mark I Long-run Fisherian	Mark III Dynamic Residual
Canada	.036	.032	.043
France	.051	.051	.056
West Germany	.061	.059	.061
Italy	.042	.048	.051
Japan	.063	.063	.080
Netherlands	.045	.044	.057
United Kingdom	.037	.031	.033
United States	.022	.022	.031

of productivity growth as a "dynamic residual" over time.

A very crude and simple model that I will call the "Mark Zero" model (and perhaps a zero mark is what it deserves!) is the following. If it is assumed that the economy was initially at its optimal level of k (in a Phelps golden age growth sense) then, in the absence of technical change, k would have been unchanged at its initial value. This would imply that all capital accumulation that occurred is due to productivity growth and the entire increase in q is due to technical change. This assumption, that all capital accumulation is induced by technical change, is the extreme opposite of the Solow assumption that none of the increase in k is induced. Together these two simpler models provide extreme limits for the more general case H-N analyzed.

In the crude Mark Zero model the amount of economic growth caused by productivity growth is computed very simply as $\Delta A/A = \Delta q/q = \Delta Q/Q - \Delta L/L$. In this case labor only affects $\Delta Q/Q$ through the scale effects of increasing the population. Table 3–6 gives the rate of economic growth caused by productivity growth for the Mark Zero model for the eight countries in the H-N sample that have data up to 1973. It also reproduces the "dynamic residual" estimates from Table 3-1 and the "long-run Fisherian" estimates from Table 3-5. All three models give very similar estimates. The Mark Zero model estimates are highly correlated with those from both the Mark I model (r = 0.97) and the Mark III model (r = 0.91). The long-run Fisherian and dynamic residual estimates, which H-N refer to as showing a "striking similarity" have a correlation of r = 0.94.

What these estimates show is, I think, that the main results of Chapter 3 can be derived using a highly simplified model that can be easily explained. It is also a rather obvious way of highlighting the main conclusion that virtually all capital accumulation is induced by technical change.

NOTES TO CHAPTER 3

1. Brown (1966) and Nadiri (1970) provide general surveys of the productivity literature. See also Hulten (1979) and Nishimizu and Hulten (1978) for additional references for the United States and Japan respectively. Kravis (1976) and Nadiri (1972) provide surveys on international productivity comparisons.

2. See Hulten (1975, 1979) and references cited therein.

3. The normalization implies that contemporaneous prices are measured relative to the price of the homogeneous output.

4. The global effect would be conceptually equivalent to the difference between the equilibrium level of output in each period and the equilibrium output that would have resulted if the economy had been constrained to growth at the initial level of factor efficiency (i.e., at A_0.

5. The result of this procedure would be to calculate arithmetic averages of the annual residuals, although this procedure ignores the compound nature of the growth process.

6. The rates of replacement for each country are the implicit average rates for all depreciable assets employed in Christensen, Cummings, and Jorgenson (1977).

7. Taxes could be incorporated by assuming that they are used to generate transfer payments. This is, however, a rather artificial assumption and a two-sector model would be required to adequately incorporate taxes into the framework. The error made by ignoring taxes results in higher rate of discount than would be the case with an after-tax rate of discount.

8. For a discussion of the translog function and its application to index numbers, see Christensen, Jorgenson, and Lau (1973), and Diewert (1976).

9. This assumes that total saving would exceed the replacement requirements generated by the existing stock of capital (which is, in fact, a reasonable assumption).

10. See, for example, Gregory and James (1973).

Chapter 4

The Downturn in Productivity Growth: A New Look At Its Nature And Causes

Randall K. Filer

The question of the rate of growth of productivity has captured a great deal of attention in recent years from both the academic community and the popular press. Indeed, reading some of the comments on this issue might incline one to a deep pessimism concerning the state of the American economy. For example, the New York Stock Exchange study "Reaching a Higher Standard of Living" begins with the following comments:

Productivity gains have dropped nearly in half during the past decade, contributing both to an escalation of inflation and a slower rate of economic growth.

The decline in productivity is a long-run problem which cannot be overcome by short-run solutions. Current inflation took time to wind up and it will take time to decelerate. Productivity can play a key role in that process, as this study shows. (New York Stock Exchange 1979).

It is certain that the rate of growth of labor productivity plays a key role in the economy. In an age when all sectors of society seem to feel that they are entitled to an ever-increasing standard of living, it is growth in output per man-hour of labor input that enables each worker to increase his or her standard of living without that increase coming at the expense of another worker. If workers are going to demand and obtain increases in nominal wages, it is increases in productivity that enable these dollar wage increases to be translated into real wage increases, rather than simply becoming another round in the endless cycles of inflation. Clearly, any decline in the rate of increase in labor productivity is cause for serious concern, since it entails a reduction in the rate of sustainable increase in standards of living the society can support.

This chapter has two tasks. The first is to summarize the world view and previous conclusions of economists looking at the question of productivity growth in the United States (and to a certain extent in the closely linked Canadian economy). The second is to attempt to extend these investigations in new directions. Due to time and space considerations, the first of these tasks will be given only minimal attention. Much of what can be said will emerge in the course of the second task. In addition, there are several other places where interested individuals can turn to find these previous results summarized.

Throughout the current work, the definition of productivity will be one of output per man-hour of labor input. There are other possible measures that take into account the changing mix of capital and labor inputs, but these measures closely parallel the trends of gross labor productivity as defined above and there are certain reasons for choosing the former. First, it is the time-series for which we have the most and the most reliable data. Second, the concept of gross labor productivity has an intuitive appeal since it represents each worker's actual command over goods and services (ignoring adjustments for changes in chosen hours of labor supplied). If it is the economic well-being of working members of society that concern us, then this seems to be an approrpiate measure.

A cursory examination of the annual rates of growth in gross labor productivity for the past thirty years (see Table 4–1) reveals a pattern of rates that varies considerably from year to year. While there may have been a secular deline in these rates of growth, such a conclusion is not overwhelmingly obvious from simply glancing at the data. The highest rate of growth (8 percent) occurred in 1950 and the lowest (–3.4 percent) in 1974. Yet one of the lowest (1.7 percent) occurred in 1949 and the third highest (4.5 percent) in 1976. In order to make sense out of the time-series presented in Table 4–1, the numbers must be reduced to some sort of summary statistic.

Table 4–1. Annual Rate of Gross Labor Productivity Growth

1948	3.9%	1958	2.7%	1968	3.3%
1949	1.7	1959	3.6	1969	0.3
1950	8.0	1960	1.6	1970	0.7
1951	2.9	1961	3.3	1971	3.2
1952	2.5	1962	4.6	1972	2.9
1953	3.7	1963	4.0	1973	1.9
1954	1.8	1964	4.1	1974	-3.4
1955	4.1	1965	3.7	1975	2.1
1956	1.4	1966	3.2	1976	4.5
1957	3.0	1967	2.3	1977	1.8

Unfortunately, the choice of how one goes about reducing the time-series to a single statistic for analytical purposes radically affects the conclusions that are drawn. The most frequently used method is to compare the years before the late 1960s with those since then. Such a comparison does indicate a significant fall-off in the rate of productivity growth. To take one frequently used division, between 1948 and 1966 gross labor productivity in the United States grew at an average annual rate of 3.36 percent in the private domestic business sector, while between 1967 and 1977 the average annual rate of increase fell to only 1.78 percent. Certainly this would seem to indicate a serious problem.

A division into two groups with the dividing point set in the late 1960s, however, is the method of analysis of the data that gives the single greatest indication of a serious problem. It is interesting by way of contrast to consider the average annual rates of growth over each of the three most recent decades. Between 1951 and 1960, gross labor productivity grew at an average annual rate of 2.73 percent; while between 1961 and 1970, the average rate of growth increased slightly to 2.95 percent. Since 1971 there has been a lower rate of growth, averaging only 1.86 percent. Before reaching doomsday conclusions regarding the future of the American economy, however, it is important to analyze this average further. It appears to be heavily influenced by one unusual year, the truly extraordinary year of 1974. This is the only year in recent history when there was an actual decrease in the level of reported gross labor productivity. It is also the year of the serious disruptions in the economy caused by the Arab oil embargo. If this year is excluded as an outlier with a known, highly probable cause for its unusual status, then the average annual rate of growth in output per man-hour in the 1970s turns out to be 2.73 percent, exactly the same rate of improvement as two decades earlier.

This sensitivity to the point or points at which the time-series is split for comparison purposes leads to a desire for less arbitrary methods to examine the supposed downturn in rates of productivity growth. For the years 1948 to 1977, a simple correlation between the rate of productivity growth and time yields a correlation coefficient (Pearson r) of -0.36, which is significant at the 5 percent level, but, here again qualifications must be raised. Figure 4-1 presents the rates of productivity growth for the past thirty years plotted against time. It is clear from the figure that there are two obvious outliers among the data points, the year 1974 discussed above and the year 1950 when output per man-hour grew at an annual rate of 8 percent, almost 3.5 percent more than any other year since World War II. The existence of these two somewhat unusual years suggests that a simple Pearson r coefficient may not be an appropriate measure of the degree of correlation between rates of productivity growth and time.

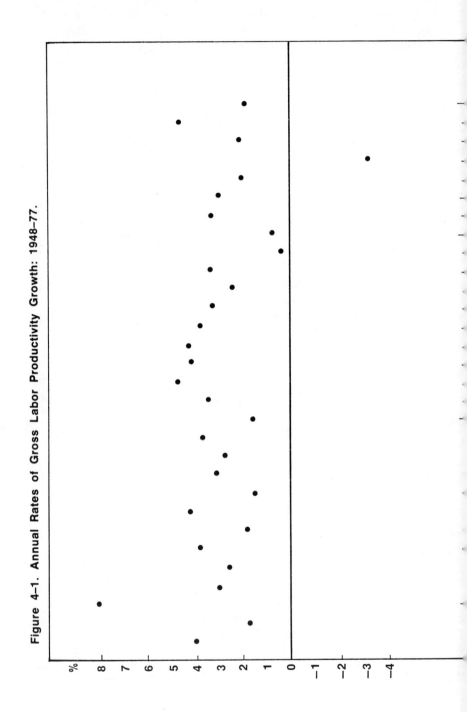

Figure 4–1. Annual Rates of Gross Labor Productivity Growth: 1948–77.

Several alternative statistical tests are possible, all of them designed to minimize the importance of the outliers. One could minimize the absolute value of the deviations from the trend line rather than the square of the deviations. Alternatively, the outliers could simply be dropped from the analysis. When these two years are removed from the data set, visual inspection can discern no obvious trend to the time-series. Indeed, the Pearson r coefficient for the relationship between the rate of productivity growth and time (excluding 1950 and 1974) is only -0.12, a value that is *not* statistically significant at any conventional level. This indicates that time alone can explain a scant 1 percent variation in rate of growth of output per man-hour over the past thirty years. However, the exclusion of these two years might be seen as another arbitrary decision designed to make the data conform to a specific set of beliefs. There is a clear explanation for the abnormal performance in 1974, but 1950 remains at this point a fact in search of a rationale. It is true that the Korean War started in that year, and one is tempted to attribute the rapid rise in productivity to a process of gearing up for the war at the same time that the country was coming out of the recession of 1949. Unfortunately, almost all of the unusual rate of productivity growth came in the first quarter of 1950, when there was an annual rate of growth of over 18 percent, while the Korean War did not start until June 25, 1950. Since it does not seem that the war was expected in advance, it is hard to consider this explanation reasonable.

An alternative that avoids the ad hoc exclusion of the two years in question, yet avoids as well the problem of giving undue weight to outlying data points, is the use of a nonparametric rather than a parametric correlation statistic. Computation of a Kendall tau coefficient for the entire thirty-year period yields a rank-order correlation coefficient of -0.18, which does not indicate a statistically significant level of relationship between time and rates of growth of gross labor productivity.

The implication of the above analysis is that the data do not reveal an unquestionable downturn in growth of output per labor hour. The world may not be as bleak as we have been telling ourselves.

Given this background, is it possible to detect reasons for the patterns of productivity growth in recent years? Previous work by economists looking at the question of productivity growth falls into two categories. The first of these is the familiar "growth accounting" study in which the researcher attempts to actually attribute the growth in output in the economy to each of several causal factors, especially economies of scale, growth in inputs, shifting mixes of inputs, and changing quality of inputs. There are several studies of this type that have been widely circulated.[1] The second type of study measures directly the effects of one or more of the factors that usually are left as part of the residual in the growth accounting studies. An example of this type of research would be studies that attempt to measure the link between productivity growth and research and development expenditure (R&D).

The growth accounting studies have in common a world view that might be called "engineering" in nature. They attempt to measure *physical* output as a function of *physical* inputs. If we start with a typical economic production function of the form:

$$Q = f\ (K,\ L,\ R),$$

where Q represents output and K, L, and R stand for capital, labor, and resource inputs, respectively, then it is easy to see that a change in output can only come from changing either the form of the production function or changing the effective amounts of one or more of the inputs. Obviously, a change in the quality of an input will result in a change in the effective amount of that input even if the physical amount does not change.

Indeed, starting with the economist's favorite plaything, the generalized Cobb-Douglas production function:

$$Q = AK^{\alpha}L^{\beta}R^{\gamma}$$

and manipulating gives the final conclusion that the percentage change in output per man-hour (productivity) is equal to the percentage changes in the inputs weighted by their exponents in the expression for Q.[2]

This formulation leads to the obvious conclusion that analyses of productivity growth should focus on changes in the inputs or the production function (changes in A or the exponents α, β, and   ). At a more fundamental level, however, changes in amounts of inputs are the direct result (given a constant technology) of changes in the prices of these inputs or of a change in the final amount of output. This relationship leads to the estimation of a regression equation relating growth in labor productivity in the private domestic business sector to changes in the prices of inputs, plus scale effects and some factors that might pick up changes in the quality of certain inputs or the shape of the production function.

Formally, the process under discussion involves the maximization of a constrained output function (not a cost function) and requires very few restrictive assumptions. With output written as $Q = f\ (L,\ K,\ R,\ A)$, then an assumption of constant returns to scale allows the function to be rewritten as:

$$\frac{Q}{L} = f\ (\frac{K}{L},\ \frac{R}{L},\ A)\ .$$

But with a constraint of profit maximization imposed, input demand equations take on the typical form:

$$\frac{K}{L} = K\ (P_L,\ P_K,\ P_R,\ P_O,\ A)$$

and:

$$\frac{R}{L} = R\ (P_L,\ P_K,\ P_R,\ P_O,\ A).$$

Substitution of these input demand equations into the production function above gives rise to the basic system for which linear approximations have been estimated.

The results of such a regression are reported in Table 4-2.

Several results reported from this regression are both interesting and important. The first thing to notice is that even though there are a limited number of degrees of freedom (the equation covers only the early 1960s to the middle 1970s), there is a remarkable ability to predict the rate of growth of gross labor productivity. The R^2 value of 0.99 is truly extraordinary for time-series analyses where the variables are changes rather than levels. In addition, one might expect that with limited degrees of freedom and at least some potential for multicollinearity, the standard errors of the estimated coefficients might tend to blow up and become unsatisfactorily large. This problem does not occur and all of the estimated coefficients are comfortably significant. In addition, they are relatively robust when different specifications or time periods are used, or when the time period of the estimation is extended. An example of such an extension is reported in the appendix to this chapter.

The estimated coefficients are, for the most part, of a magnitude and direction that make good intuitive sense and conform to standard economic theory. The notable exception to this generalization is the set of coefficients on past years' expenditure on research and development in the industrial sector, which is negative. One might expect these coefficients to be positive, indicating that a larger past expenditure on R&D leads to a larger current increase in productivity. Several points can be made concerning this apparent anomaly. First, the bulk of research and development in the Western economies is directed not toward improvements in technologies that might increase productivity, but rather toward improvements in products. This situation might weaken any positive relationship that existed, but should not generate a significant negative relationship. A model consistent with this observed fact can be postulated, however. While there may be a causal relationship between past expenditures on R&D and productivity increases, this relationship

Table 4–2. Regression Results with Change in Gross Labor Productivity as Dependent Variable

Explanatory Variable[a]	*Coefficient (t-value)*
Change in relative energy prices[b]	−1.67
	(4.23)
Change in relative investment prices	−64.72
	(8.47)
Change in GNP	−0.023
	(2.90)
Lagged industrial research and development	−2.06
	(10.38)
Two years lagged industrial research and development	−0.430
	(2.65)
Change in percentage of employed workforce who are female	−4.74 (13.52)
Time	5.58
	(10.55)
Time squared	−0.29
	(11.31)
Constant	15.42

$\overline{R}^2 = .996$ $F = 390.92$

[a]Other variables tried in various formulations that proved to be insignificant included: change in unemployment rate, change in relative labor costs, and current year industrial research and development.
[b]All prices are increased relative to increases in the Producer Price Index.

is not simple enough to be captured in one or two years' expenditures. Instead, it involves several previous years, with innovative results from the R&D expenditures coming on line at various times depending on many other factors. If firms can foresee years in which improvements in productivity will be low (perhaps because of the depletion of the stockpile of previous innovation), they may be induced to spend increased amounts in an attempt to build up the stockpile of innovation waiting for a chance to be implemented. Thus, the causality being detected in the data may be in the reverse direction from what one might expect. This hypothesis is further supported by the results reported in the appendix, where the coefficient on patents issued (presumably the fruition of past years' research and development) has the "correct" sign, although is not statistically significant.

The other results are much more pleasing. Both of the relative prices of inputs into the production process other than labor have significantly negative coefficients. This result fits well with a standard economic model where increases in the prices of substitute inputs cause substitution away from that input and toward labor, resulting in the use of workers with a lower marginal product, thereby lowering average output per man-hour of labor input.[3] Indeed, although the data became available too late for inclusion in this study, this conclusion can only be further substantiated by the admittedly poor productivity performance of 1979, another year of large increases in the relative price of energy. The results in the appendix also show that over an extended period of time increases in the relative price of labor also cause effects that conform to standard theory, increasing output per man-hour. The coefficient on changes in GNP indicates that there may not be economies of scale in the economy as a whole, but that there are significant cyclical effects on productivity.

The sexual composition of the workforce presents a very interesting pattern. Its inclusion is meant to control to a certain extent for the quality of the labor inputs. Such a usage should not be interpreted to mean that female workers are necessarily less productive than males. The simplest explanation of the observed result is that women entering the labor force during the period under consideration have worked for less time than the average male already in the workforce, and therefore represent lower quality human capital. In any case, the results, coupled with the similar although less significant results for teenagers reported in the appendix, suggest that a large part of the possible fall in rates of increase in gross labor productivity may be due to the shifting composition of the labor force toward relatively unskilled women and teenagers who have entered the job market in large numbers in recent years.

The final set of coefficients to be explained relates to time. In a sense these are the most important coefficients for addressing the question of whether or not there has been a downturn in the rate of growth of labor productivity after controlling for the standard economic processes represented by prices and business cycles. There does seem to be at least some indication of such a pattern. The two coefficients (on time and time squared) follow a nonlinear pattern, with a maximum reached around 1969. Thus, even after controlling for other effects (most especially the unusual year 1974, which is to a large extent picked up by the inclusion of relative energy prices), there is an unexplained and relatively significant pattern of rates of productivity growth that is consistent with the belief in a downturn. While the analysis at the beginning of the chapter has led to some doubt as to the importance of this downturn relative to the overall variation in rates of growth, it is still interesting to speculate about its cause. It should be noted that the data used for the regression analysis are only for the period from the early 1960s to the mid-1970s. As such, they miss the fact, pointed out in the first section, that the 1960s were a period of unusually high rates of growth in gross labor productivity and that the pattern looks much less unfavorable when compared with the "normal" growth rate of the 1950s.

Still, it is interesting to ask why the unusually high growth rates of the mid-1960s were not sustained in the 1970s. In this context there are some interesting, although not entirely satisfactory, factors that must be mentioned. Most studies attempt to control, wherever possible, for the quality as well as the quantity of inputs into the production process. We have done so in the above regression by including the sexual composition of the labor force as a rough proxy for the quality of human capital embodied in each hour of labor input.

Thinking of the period around 1969 or 1970, when any unexplained downturn in productivity that may have occurred seems to have begun, the primary factor that has not been included in the above analysis is a change in the quality of certain inputs. If the quality change is an ongoing and constant process, then there should be a constant bias in estimates of the rate of labor productivity growth and therefore no change in the trend over time. Hence, the factors to be sought must be ones that themselves changed in the late 1960s or early 1970s. This situation rules out the most common quality adjustments (for such factors as the quality of the labor force as measured by its average educational level), since these variables have shown rather constant time trends.

There are factors that may have resulted in a decrease in the average ability of physical capital to contribute to the production of output around 1970. In 1970 two social movements bore their fruit—the passage of legal regulations that had the power to alter substantially the type of capital spending undertaken in the United States. The year 1970 represented the peak of the environmental movement in the United States (Mills 1978), and saw the adoption of the legislation creating the Environmental Protection Agency (EPA) as well as the Clean Air Act amendments, which set strict auto emissions standards and directed the EPA to determine ambient air quality standards. Both were to be implemented on very short time schedules. In addition, Congress in 1970 passed the Occupational Safety and Health Act, giving all employers a "general duty" to provide a place of employment "free from recognized hazards" and to comply with the Act's standards of safety and health.

It is clear that both types of legislation have the potential for limiting the rate of growth of labor productivity. To the extent that there is a limited amount of saving available in the economy, the more of this saving that is required for capital expenditures mandated to clean up the air or to provide safer working conditions, the less is available for investments that increase the physical output that each worker is capable of producing. This is not to argue that the two acts were socially counterproductive. The society may well feel that the benefits of increased air and water quality and worker safety are worth sacrificing increased physical output. The "problem" comes because of the improper definition of output that has been used in calculating labor force productivity. Dirty air and dangerous work-places are negative outputs and should have been deducted from measures of physical production to arrive at a true output figure. When this correction is made, the result is that rates of growth of output, and therefore labor productivity, would diverge to a lesser extent after the passage of the two acts.

The Occupational Safety and Health Act has the potential to affect rates of growth of gross labor productivity in a manner other than to change the type of capital investments made. To the extent that compliance with the provisions of the act necessitated revisions in the structure of the work-place and the speed of assembly lines, or resulted in the addition of certain "safety" procedures to production processes, it is clear that adoption and enforcement of the act would result in the same number of workers using the same capital stock being able to produce less physical output. The result would be a fall in measured productivity in these work-places, other factors being held constant. If productivity would have risen without the adoption of the new rules and structures, then their adoption would cause a less rapid increase in productivity.

While the above shifts may well be considered to have arisen because of the definitions used and not because of actual changes in the rate of productivity growth, there may have been an actual change in the quality of labor inputs in the last ten years that might be partially responsible for the shift in productivity patterns. There are many factors that have shifted over time in the labor force. The sexual composition was controlled for above, and many of the others do not exhibit fluctuations in their rates of change and therefore should result in a constant bias.

Such a constant bias should be expected for such factors as the education of the labor force, which has been steadily increasing, resulting in an upward bias, and the relationship between number of hours paid for (used in the denominator of the productivity statistics) and hours actually worked. These two series have been continually diverging because of increases in paid vacations and holidays, resulting in a downward bias in productivity statistics. It is not clear, however, that the shift in the pattern of the amount of effort that workers expend has been of this continuous type. If it has not, then reductions in effort expended by workers may have lowered labor quality and output per man-hour.

The amount of effective labor input into the production process is composed of several factors. Most of them are explicitly measurable and controlled for in productivity studies. We can adjust the gross concept of hours of work supplied for variations in the quality of those hours arising from variations in the quality of the workers. It is much harder to adjust statistically for variations in the quality of hours supplied that arise because each worker is, in some sense, putting less into the work he or she actually does. Yet, it should be obvious that if workers have become less willing to expend effort in carrying out their jobs, then the amount of output they can expect to produce for each hour they work should fall, or rise less rapidly than it otherwise would have.

These concepts are very difficult to measure, but there is at least partial evidence that the effort component of labor supply has fallen since the late 1960s. Unfortunately, little data has yet come to light to indicate whether or not this trend was also occurring before the late 1960s and should therefore be treated as a constant bias. Intuitively, one might suspect that the social disruptions and the "counterculture" life-style of the late 1960s had a great deal to do with changing attitudes, and that the resulting decline in the work ethic may not have been a continuous one, but rather may have started, or at least rapidly accelerated, during the period under consideration.

The best evidence available concerning workers' attitudes regarding the effort component of labor supply comes from the Quality of Employment Surveys conducted by the Survey Research Center at the University of Michigan. The statement "I am not asked to do excessive amounts of work" was shown to a national probability sample of workers who were asked to consider their primary jobs and respond either "very true," "somewhat true," "not too true," or "not at all true." Table 4–3 presents the pattern of responses to this statement for the three years in which the survey has been conducted, 1969, 1972, and 1977.

Over the past decade there has been an unmistakable increase in the proportion of workers who feel that they are asked to do excessive amounts of work. The difference between each of the three surveys is statistically significant at the 5 percent level (based on the collapsed scales). This pattern is consistent with one of two explanations. Either jobs have been getting harder with respect to the amount of work that they require of those who fill them, or else people are perceiving the jobs as having become harder (that is, the standard of effort that constitutes excessive amounts of work has fallen). If the amount of work people regard as being excessive has fallen, there is every reason to believe that they would be willing to put less effort into any given job, and therefore that output per man-hour of labor input would fall.

Analysis of other questions in the Quality of Employment Surveys that attempted to measure job satisfaction, either in terms of specific aspects

Table 4–3. Effort Component of Labor Supply

Response to the statement "I am not asked to do excessive amounts of work."

	Very True	Somewhat True	Not Too True	Not at All True
1969	43.1%	31.5%	14.8%	10.5%
1972	34.2	37.0	16.9	11.8
1977	27.9	38.6	19.2	14.3

Note: All entries are percentages of respondents.
Collapsed Scales: (Very True = 4) (Somewhat True = 3) (Not Too True = 2) and
(Not at All True = 1): Mean = 3.07 (1969), 2.93 (1972) and 2.80 (1977).

of an individual's working conditions or in general, also shows significant reductions in individuals' satisfaction between the late 1960s and the late 1970s. The survey data enable the testing of whether or not these declines arise from changes in the demographic composition of the workforce or changes in the objective characteristics of jobs themselves. The data do not appear to indicate that these can be significant causes of the pattern, so once again, one is left with the conclusion that rising expections that are not being fulfilled may be the cause of decreasing satisfaction (Quinn and Staines 1979). If such is the case, it is easy to see how effort expended in the workplace, and therefore labor productivity may have suffered. Lordstown comes readily to mind.

Unfortunately, since the Quality of Employment Surveys do not begin until 1969, the year that whatever downturn there has been in rates of growth in labor productivity apparently began, it is impossible to find out from them whether the pattern of declining satisfaction or increasing belief that jobs involve excessive effort began before that date. However, a study published by the U.S. Department of Labor in the early 1970s concluded that over the preceeding fifteen years there had been no significant changes in levels of job satisfaction (U.S. Department of Labor 1974). This study was based on a large number of national surveys, but was limited by the fact that each survey included only a single-question measure of overall job satisfaction. It does appear that, pending further information, it would be reasonable to postulate that the effort component of labor supply may have fallen since 1970 in a way that it did not do prior to that date. This pattern would result in a decrease in the annual rates of gross labor productivity growth since 1970. Certainly, these results provide an interesting basis for speculation and should encourage further research.

Not all possible measures have detected such a shift. In a somewhat limited data set collected by the author,[4] there was no apparent change between 1967 and 1977 in how people rated the relative importance of their jobs, income, security, or family life in determining their subjective rating of their success. In addition, there were no significant changes in any of the various characteristics measured in the data that might influence an individual's productivity. If anything, the level of drive among members of the labor force, after controlling for demographic and educational differences, appears to have increased somewhat over that decade.

Finally, this data set shows a trend toward willingness to work longer hours and more "off time" hours (nights or weekends) during the decade from 1967 to 1977. These results remain after controlling for specific individual characteristics, including race, religion, family background, age, marital status, education, and work experience. The most important control, however, is for the sex of the respondent. Because of differences between the sexes and the shifting sexual composition of the labor force, the trend toward possible increasing willingness to work cannot be identified unless sex is accounted for in the estimating equations.

Although several results mentioned above have indicated the importance of the changing sexual composition of the labor force, care should be taken in attributing too much importance to this factor alone. The Quality of Employment Survey question regarding excessive work requirements exhibited an almost identical pattern of results for both sexes.[5] The data seem to show that women as well as men are coming to believe that they are being asked to do excessive amounts of work. Therefore, any results regarding fall-offs in labor productivity arising from this source should be independent of the shifting sexual composition, leaving that factor its primary role, discussed earlier, of standing as a proxy for the human capital stock of the labor force. Certainly the need for further research on the influence of workers' attitudes on rates of labor productivity growth is evident.

It is refreshing to be able to come to the end of a chapter and conclude that things are not as bad as we have sometimes supposed. While society should not become complacent regarding the prospects for future growth in labor force productivity, it is clear from the current research that there is no need to ring the death knell for the American economy just yet. Rates of productivity growth appear to be low only in comparison to the abnormally high period of boom economy of the 1960s. If this boom was the result of tight labor markets caused by the Vietnam War, it is not clear that we would be willing to pay such a price again for high productivity growth. It is also apparent that much of what one might call the slackening of the rate of productivity growth since the 1960s comes as a result of society's choosing other goals, at least part of whose price has been lower rates of productivity growth.[6] If America desires to clean up its air, protect its workers from on-the-job hazards, and allow previously unemployed workers with low levels of job experience to enter the labor force, who is to say that we are worse off achieving these goals at a cost of lower rates of productivity growth? There's no such thing as a free social cause.

APPENDIX

Several different sets of results could be reported to substantiate the robustness of the estimates in Table 4–2. For example, when the estimation period is extended backward to 1949, the results (with some changes in independent variables because of availablility of data or the ability to include more explanatory variables because of the greater number of degrees of freedom) become:

Dependent Variable = Change in Gross Labor Productivity

Variable	Coefficient (t Value)
Change in relative energy prices	-4.44
	(2.42)
Change in relative investment prices	-38.14
	(2.38)
Change in relative labor prices	2.01
	(1.17)
Change in the unemployment rate	-0.64
	(3.18)
Patents issued	0.058
	(1.25)
Patents issued previous year	-0.017
	(0.40)
Change in percentage of employed workforce who are female	-2.66
	(2.32)
Change in percentage of workforce who are teenaged	-2.27
	(1.72)
Change in percentage of workforce who are in the military	-0.83
	(1.16)
Time	-0.58
	(1.42)
Time squared	0.051
	(1.66)
Time cubed	0.0015
	(1.88)
Constant	4.998

$\bar{R}^2$ = 0.844   F = 6.301

COMMENT
Leonard Waverman

Professor Filer begins by examining thirty years of historical evidence to determine if there is any truth to the view that a significant reduction in the growth of labor productivity has occurred in the 1970s. He uses several statistical tests to examine whether the passage of time can, by itself, explain changes in labor productivity. He concludes that based on these simple tests "the data do not reveal an unquestionable downturn in growth of output per labor hour."

Professor Filer next turns to a more detailed examination of the causes of change in labor productivity based on the economic theory of production.

Beginning with a general Cobb-Douglas production function relating physical output to inputs,

$$Q = F\ (K,\ L,\ R) \tag{4.1}$$

where Q: output
K: capital
L: labor
R: resource inputs

Professor Filer shifts to a generalized Cobb-Douglas,

$$Q = AK^{\alpha}L^{\beta}R^{\gamma} \tag{4.2}$$

which upon totally differentiating and reorganizing leads to

$$\%\,\Delta(Q/L) = \%\,\Delta A\ +\ \alpha\%\,\Delta K + (\beta - 1)\%\,\Delta L + \gamma\%\,\Delta R \tag{4.3}$$

Equation (4.3) is not directly estimated; instead the author states, "However, at a more fundamental level, changes in amounts of inputs are the direct results (given constant technology) of changes in the *prices* of these inputs or of a change in the final amount of output." The regressions run are of the following kind:

$$\%\,\Delta(Q/L) = \%\,\Delta_{P_R}\ +\ \%\,90\,\Delta_{P_I}\ +\ \%\,\Delta Q + \%\,\Delta F + T + T^2 + D_{-1} + D_{-2} \tag{4.4}$$

where p_R is the resources price index
p_I is the investment price index
D_{-1} is industrial research and development lagged one year

D$_{-2}$ is industrial research and development lagged two years

F   is the percentage of employed workforce that is female

T   is time

Assuming cost minimization and exogenous input prices, a cost function exists that is dual to the production function. From this dual cost function can be derived the cost minimizing factor demand equations that would be of the general form

$$V_i = F(P_i, Q) \qquad (4.5)$$

From (4.5) we could derive[1]

$$\frac{Q}{V_i} = F^{-1}(P_i, Q). \qquad (4.6)$$

For labor input, equation (4.6) would relate labor productivity to input prices and output levels.

Note, however, that Filer's equation (4.3) is not of this general form (4.6). Instead, changes in output per labor input are regressed on changes in only two of several input prices: the change in output level of one input *(R&D)* and the percentage change in the workforce that is female, plus time.

To move from (4.6) to (4.3), however, is quite a leap—for a number of reasons. First, the price of capital is not used; instead only the price of investment.[2] Second, the price of labor is not included on the right hand side of (4.3). However, if the price of labor increases, we would expect less labor to be used and hence an increase in Q/L; omitting P_L from (4.3) then leads to specification error.[3] Third, there appears to be no theoretical justification to include levels of inputs (such as *R&D* expenditures) in factor demand equations. Fourth, the coefficients of equation (4.3) are difficult to interpret since the equation is not simply an input demand equation.

All this discussion is aimed at one point. The author's observation that productivity has fallen since 1969 is based on the magnitude of the T and T^2 terms in equation (4.3). Given the relative ad hoc nature of equation (4.3), I would not take this observation as conclusive proof. But then, Filer does not take these regression results as conclusive proof either, especially as they are only based on the period since 1963.

Filer does however speculate, most interestingly, as to why the high rates of growth in productivity were not sustained after 1969. I am at odds with one of these causes, namely the legislation creating *EPA* and

OSHA. Regulations that act to decrease directly output per worker of course reduce productivity. Filer, however, argues that regulations that require capital expenditure for environmental purposes reduce productivity because the nation's limited savings are channeled out of traditional capital-deepening uses. Let us take as our example the auto pollution laws that led most automobile manufacturers to install catalytic converters on new cars. Surely, aggregate measured labor productivity could *increase* if the production of catalytic converters were less labor intensive than the alternate activity it replaced (say, milk production). Aggregate labor productivity, as used by Filer, is susceptible to changes in industry mix. Regulation might change that mix so as to increase measured aggregate labor productivity. It is also, I feel, difficult to argue that the capital investments resulting from regulation were at the expense of other investments without evidence that, in this period, the demand for capital exceeded supply—increasing real interest rates, for example.

It is clear that Chapter 4 sheds light on the debate on the nature and causes of lagging productivity growth. What is needed is more research along these lines using explicit cost function analysis on an industry-by-industry basis incorporating endogenous technical change. Quite a research proposal.

NOTES TO CHAPTER

1. See, for example, Denison (1972). These are summarized in Chapter 7 of National Academy of Sciences (forthcoming).

2. To derive this result, start with the production function:

$$Q = AK^{\alpha}L^{\beta}R^{\gamma}$$

and divide through by L (labor input) to get:

$$Q/L = AK^{\alpha}L^{\beta-1}R^{\gamma}.$$

Then take the total differential of each side:

$$d(Q/L) = (K^{\alpha}L^{\beta-1}R^{\gamma})\, dA + \alpha(AK^{\alpha-1}R^{\beta-1}R^{\gamma})\, dK$$
$$+ (\beta-1)\,(AK^{\alpha}L^{\beta-2}R^{\gamma})dL + \gamma\,(AK^{\alpha}L^{\beta-1}R^{\gamma-1})\, dR.$$

Each term on the right-hand side can have a factor of $AK^{\alpha}\,L^{\beta-1}R^{\gamma}$ removed to yield:

$$d(Q/L) = [AK^{\alpha}L^{\beta-1}R^{\gamma}]\,[A^{-1}dA + \alpha K^{-1}dK$$
$$+ (\beta-1)\,L^{-1}dL + \gamma R^{-1}dR]$$

but since $AK^{\alpha}L^{\beta-1}R^{\gamma}$ is equal to Q/L and since, in general $x^{-1}dx$ equals the percentage change in x, dividing both sides by the first term on the right gives:

$$\%\Delta(Q/L) = \%\Delta A + a\%\Delta K + (\beta-1)\%\Delta L + \gamma\%\Delta R.$$

3. See, for example, Griffin and Gregory (1976: 845–857) and Berndt and Wood (1975: 259–268). Other studies can be found, but all seem to show a similar result pertaining to the substitutability between labor and energy.

4. The primary limitations of the data set are that it is concentrated in individuals who are in managerial and professional positions and are located in the southeastern United States. It might be argued that these individuals have the least likelihood of exhibiting the kind of changes being discussed, although the Quality of Employment Surveys did show a pattern of increasing job dissatisfaction at all levels, including managers. For a further description of the author's data set, see Filer (1978).

5. The collapsed scale values for the question discussed in the text broken down by sex are as follows:

	Males	Females
1969	3.07	3.08
1973	2.91	2.97
1977	2.80	2.81

6. A colleague, Joseph Berliner, points out that a similar process may be occurring in the Soviet Union, where lower rates of growth of output per unit of physical capital in recent years may well be caused by the requirement that new plants be designed in a way so as to be hardened in case of nuclear attack.

NOTES TO COMMENT

1. If production is characterized by constant returns to scale, output labor ratios are determined by input prices only.

2. The cost of capital, after Hall and Jorgenson (1967: 391–414), can be written as

$$(r + \delta) P_I$$

3. Filer states that other variables including the change in relative labor costs were "tried in various formulations that proved to be insignificant".

Part III

New Approaches

Chapter 5

Productivity:
A Psychological Perspective

Hugh J. Arnold   Martin G. Evans   Robert J. House

Introduction

Interdisciplinary research is somewhat like the weather; people are always talking about it, but we almost never do anything about it. The question this leads to is, if interdisciplinary research is so wonderful, why is so little of it being done by so few people? And, perhaps more specifically, we can ask, if economics and organizational behavior really do have something in common, why is it so difficult for us to get them together? By addressing these questions briefly at the outset we may be able to clarify differences and identify common ground, which will, hopefully, facilitate our attempted interdisciplinary interaction.

There are a number of reasons why relatively few people are doing relatively little interdisciplinary research. First, it's hard. Mastering a single discipline to the point of becoming a creative contributor to it is hard work. Mastering two disciplines and attempting to creatively integrate them is probably more than twice as hard. Second, it's dangerous. Leaving one's comfortable home turf and venturing out into an unknown and potentially threatening environment may well be discomforting and risky. Scholars, like the rest of the population, generally prefer the devils they know to the devils they don't know. Third, and perhaps most important, the development of expertise in a scholarly discipline involves both a self-selection and a socialization process that tends to reward and accentuate within-discipline homogeneity, and that is at best benign to interdisciplinary interaction. Individuals are drawn to a particular discipline because of an inherent interest in the basic questions it addresses, because their skills and abilities tend to match those required for success in the discipline, and because they feel comfortable with its methods, approaches, and assumptions (which indeed probably largely define it). Taken together, these factors (along with a number of others—such as annual conventions) often tend to produce a classic "in-group—out-group" psychology. In extreme cases one can even observe what might be called a "white man's burden" syndrome, whereby certain members of a discipline are prepared to offer their services to enlighten and "save" the poor misdirected souls in a neighboring discipline who are laboring under "false" assumptions or attempting to work on the "wrong" questions.

We eschew the role of savior. It would be presumptuous for anyone to suggest that organizational behavior and industrial psychology can, will or should "save" microeconomics. The counterclaim is obviously equally untenable. At the same time, however, there do seem to be significant areas of overlap between the disciplines; areas that, if exploited and developed, could result in fruitful new ideas and insights for disciplines. However, before drawing attention to the commonalities, the preceding discussion of impediments to interdisciplinary interaction leads us to identify some important differences between economics and organizational behavior. Hopefully, by identifying these differences we can preclude certain misunderstandings and conflicts that commonly arise.

Microeconomic theories of the firm tend to view the firm or organization itself as something of a "black box." Such theories appear to be interested in the relationship between the firm's inputs (in the form of capital, labor, and raw materials) obtained at certain costs, and its outputs (in the form of products or services) that are sold at some price. More precisely, marginalist theories of the firm are interested in explaining general patterns of relationship between changes in inputs and changes in outputs for large numbers of firms operating in competitive environments. Such theories base their analyses on a specific set of assumptions about the nature of the firm, that is, that profit maximization is the sole goal of the firm, that actual output is equal to maximum output for given inputs, and so forth. Such theories have achieved a considerable degree of success, much to the astonishment and chargrin of a number of behavioralists who criticize the theories for their implausible and unrealistic assumptions about people and firms. However, Machlup (1967) has, we feel, correctly responded to such critics by arguing that for marginalist theories such as competitive price theory, the firm is indeed no more than a "theoretical construct." No claim is made to be adequately or accurately describing the nature of the firm. Indeed, the marginalist is completely indifferent to what goes on inside the firm. The behavior of the firm or its members is simply not a variable of interest within the theory. Microeconomists who feel uncomfortable with theories embodying descriptively false assumptions might take some solace from the fact that experimental psychologists are constantly proposing and testing "paramorphic" models of human perception, attention, learning, and motivation. A paramorphic model is one that relates inputs (stimuli) to outputs (responses), while making no claim that the psychological processes hypothesized in the model are in any way isomorphic to (or adequately descriptive of) the true psychological processes occurring within people's heads. The validity of a paramorphic model is to be assessed not by the "realism" of its assumptions or hypotheses, but rather by the extent to which observed outcome agrees with the outcome predicted by the model. No doubt physiological psychologists (who actually study what goes on inside people's heads) are as appalled at some of the paramorphic models generated by the experimental psychologist as organizational-industrial psychologists (who actually study what goes on inside firms) are at some of the microeconomic models generated by economists.

Organizational behavior, on the other hand, takes as its direct object of study that which is treated as a theoretical construct by neoclassical microeconomic theories of the firm. Organizational behavior focuses upon the transformation processes within firms, how these processes are carried out, how they are organized, and how differences in intrafirm organization are related to interfirm differences in effectiveness and productivity (given identical inputs to the various firms). Rather than searching for common patterns of relationships between inputs and outputs across large numbers of firms, organizational behavior seeks to understand how and why a given firm or a given subset of firms is as productive or effective as it is in the process of transforming inputs into outputs. To adopt statistical terminology, while neoclassical microeconomic theories of the firm might be said to focus on the *common* or *shared* variance between inputs and outputs for large samples of firms, organizational behavior seeks to explain and understand the *residual* or *unexplained* variance for a given firm. It can thus fairly be said that what Leibenstein (1969) refers to as "X-inefficiency" is, in fact, an article of faith or belief for organizational-industrial psychologists. Arguments and data in support of the existence of X-inefficiency simply do not appear in books on organizational behavior since its existence is assumed. If X-inefficiency did not exist there would be no need for the books, no need for the discipline of organizational behavior, and (perhaps most threatening to us) no need for organizational psychologists.

The question we are then left with is, why should a microeconomist be interested in intrafirm processes as studied in organizational behavior? The answer is twofold. First, although marginalist theories of the firm have achieved some degree of success in finding general patterns of relationships between inputs and outputs, they are not useful for explaining the discrepancies between model predictions and observed values for individual firms or subsets of firms. The physical sciences are replete with examples of the generation of new theory from new explanations for discrepancies from the predictions of accepted models and theories. Thus, by looking within the firm for explanations of why marginalist predictions are inaccurate for a given firm, new understanding of the determinations of productivity and efficiency may emerge. Second, the neoclassical theory of the firm is restricted in its range of application. The theory is applicable to large numbers of firms in a competitive environment. As more and more industries become dominated by a relatively small number of very large firms, the circumstances for application of the neoclassical theories become more and more limited. What we appear to need increasingly urgently are theories that are applicable to relatively small numbers of relatively large firms under imperfect competition.

The above reasons for incorporating behavioral-organizational notions into the study of the productivity of the firm are especially relevant to firms in the Canadian economy. In studying the productivity of Canadian firms the research question is precisely, what are the determinants of the level of productivity of a relatively small subset of firms—a question beyond the reach of marginalist theories relating inputs and outputs. In addition, Canadian firms are relatively few in number and exist in an environment that could not be accurately characterized as "freely competitive."

In light of these considerations, our goal in what follows is to introduce and discuss several areas of research from the literature of organizational behavior that we feel may be particularly relevant to understanding the productivity of the individual firm. The conceptual framework we will follow in this discussion is depicted in Figure 5-1. In this figure, organizational decisionmaking is shown as both a determinant of and a response to the environment of the firm. As we will show, through the decisionmaking process organizations in part determine their environment and alter its characteristics. Organizations also adapt to their environment through their choice and design of formal management and organizational practices. The three practices we will discuss in some detail are organization structure, control and reward systems, and the goal-setting process. We have chosen to focus on these three practices because (1) they are rather direct outcomes of the management decisionmaking process, and (2) they have been sufficiently studied from the psychological perspective to permit some fairly definitive conclusions with respect to their relationship to productivity. The diagram also indicates our intention to address the question of how management

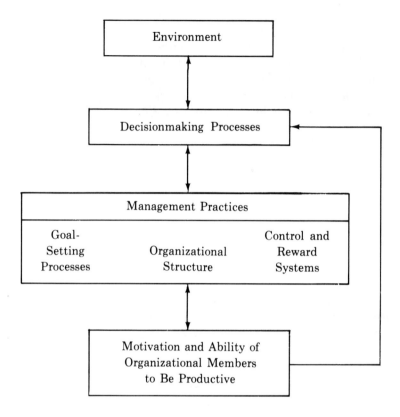

Figure 5–1. Conceptual Framework.

practices affect the motivation and ability of individual organizational members to perform their roles effectively.

In addition to modeling the downward flow of influence in the organization from decisionmaking to management practices and finally to individual responses, the diagram shows that influence also flows in the opposite direction. The individual members selectively perceive those parts of formal management practices that are most relevant to their needs and in turn exert influence on those practices according to the goals they prefer, the rewards they value most, and the directions and constraints of the organization structure that they find most acceptable. Their responses may be intended either to support or thwart the intent of the formal management practices. While these formal practices partially direct, motivate, and constrain individual behavior they also are interpreted and altered by organizational members to suit their biases and needs. Organizational decisionmakers observing such reciprocal interaction in turn modify the formal practices through the decisionmaking process.

Organizational effectiveness, as viewed here, is primarily a function of the degree of fit or congruence among the environment, the management practices, and member preferences. The decisionmaking process is viewed as the pervasive process that regulates the degree of fit among these elements. In light of this we turn first to a behavioral analysis of decisionmaking in organizations, focusing on both the nature of the decisionmaking process itself and on the types and sources of information upon which decisions are based. This discussion is followed by a review of the three management practices outlined above with special emphasis upon research evidence relating these management practices to organizational effectiveness and productivity. The final section of the chapter focuses upon the productivity and effectiveness of the individual organization member.

The outcome of this review of theory and evidence is an explanation of some of the major intraorganizational determinants of productivity from a psychological perspective rather than from an economic or technological one. Hopefully, such an explanation will help us and others gain insights about the causes of productivity. Furthermore, we hope that such an explanation will suggest testable propositions for further research on productivity.

THE DECISIONMAKING PROCESS

An organization's very existence is the outcome of a process of decisionmaking. At the outset, some individual or group of individuals must have made a decision to organize in order to carry out some activity. This initial decision would have been immediately followed by a large number of increasingly more complex decions, such as what activities are to be performed and by whom, how they are to be coordinated with one another, where and at what cost necessary inputs are to be obtained, where and at what price outputs are to be sold, and so forth. The effectiveness, productivity, and, indeed, the continued existence of an organization are dependent upon the quality of such decisions regarding the strategy, structure, design and operation of the organization.

Decisionmaking processes are critical to organizational effectiveness and productivity at another level as well. In order to be effective and productive, organizations are dependent upon the decisions of individual organization members actually to engage in the activities specified for effective performance of their roles and tasks. This is simply another way of stating that the motivation of individual organization members has a critical impact on organizational effectiveness. Psychological theories of motivation are concerned with trying to explain why people *choose* to engage in certain activities rather than others, and with what intensity and for how long they do so. Thus, a tremendous component of understanding work motivation lies in understanding how individuals make personal work-related *decisions* such as: Should I go to work on Monday or should I call in sick? Should I really work hard today or should I take it easy? Should I stay late today to finish this job or should I go home now? Should I help those people in the next department who are wrestling with that big problem or should I let them flounder? How individual organization members make decisions such as these determines their "motivation." Realistic and valid theory regarding the nature of these indivdual decisionmaking processes is essential to an understanding of how and why organizations differ in effectiveness and productivity.

Assumptions and Models of Decisionmaking Microeconomic Theory

Microeconomic theory generally contains two basic postulates regarding the nature of economic actors: first, that their goals are given; and second, that they are rational. The term rational is taken to have a very restrictive and specific meaning, namely that rational actors are maximizers. The goals to be maximized vary according to whether the economic actor is playing the role of consumer or of entrepreneur (the only roles permitted within the theory). The consumer seeks to maximize utility while the entrepreneur seeks to maximize profit. Maximizing behavior requires that the individual decisionmaker (1) consider all possible alternatives prior to making a decision, (2) consider all of the possible consequences associated with each alternative and (3) apply a system of values to the consequences in order to determine the best alternative.

Of course, economic theory did not derive these characteristics from observation of economic behavior, nor does economic research seek to confirm or deny their validity by comparing the behavior of economic actors to the implicit predictors of the postulates. Rather, the postulates are used as a basis for deductive reasoning in order to make predictions regarding things such as marginal change in firm outputs as a result of marginal change in firm inputs. To the extent that these postulates lead to derivations that subsequently result in "good" predictions of the dependent variables of interest to the theory (e.g., marginal price changes within an industry), they are "good" (useful) postulates for purposes of that theory. However, it is extremely important to keep two points in mind. First, the predictive utility of the postulates for marginalist theories tells us *nothing* regarding their descriptive validity. Second, if our dependent variables change from those of neoclassical marginalist theory to the effectiveness and productivity of individual firms or sets of firms, then the adequacy of theory will be directly dependent upon the validity of our description of the behavior of individual economic actors. In order to understand, explain, and predict the relationship between decisionmaking and productivity, we must ensure that we have a good theory of decisionmaking based upon sound knowledge of individual psychological processes.

Researchers who have turned their attention to understanding the process of decsionmaking have, in general, found little support for the postulates of economic theory, either in terms of the goals being sought or the psychological processes employed.

Utility maximization

In order to build a useful theory of consumer decisionmaking around the notion of utility maximization, the theory must contain some method for specifying, *a priori,* the components or determinants of "utility" for any particular economic actor or group of actors. Recent psychological research on decisionmaking (Janis, 1959; Janis and Mann, 1968) indicates that the notion of "utility" is oversimplified, and that in making consequential decisions individuals are influenced by (1) utilitarian gains and losses for themselves (2) utilitarian gains and losses for significant others (e.g., friends and family), (3) self-approval or self-disapproval, and (4) approval or disapproval from significant others. In addition to this need for broadening the utility function, a theory of decisionmaking based on utility maximization has no predictive or explanatory power in the absence of an *a priori* method of specify the particular outcomes to be maximized by a given actor in a given situation. In the absence of such a schema for *a priori* specification of relevant outcomes, the descriptive validity of the theory is empirically untestable and hence its explanatory value is indeterminate.

Profit maximization

The descriptive validity of the notion of profit maximization as the sole goal of the firm has been frequently attacked, first among the attackers being Simon (1964). Although the convenience of assuming all organization members to be motivated to maximize profits is appealing, it does not appear to provide an adequate description of the objectives of most or even many firm members. Organizations have multiple goals, among them are such things as market-share goals, inventory goals, growth goals, revenue goals, and so on. Characterization of the firm and its individual members as pursuing the sole goal of profit maximization is thus inadequate as a description or a basis of explanation of decision-making processes.

Rationality as maximization

Regardless of the specific goal or goals embodied in the objective function, perhaps the most tenacious and pervasive notion in microeconomic theory is that economic actors maximize something. The appeal and pervasiveness of this assumption are readily understandable in light of its ability to make tractable and soluble many otherwise intractable and insoluble analytic derivations. Nonetheless it must be concluded that as a valid description of the decisionmaking process the empirical evidence from psychological and organizational research is now overwhelming that such an assumption is untenable (Miller, 1956; Simon, 1957, 1976a; MacCrimmon and Taylor, 1976). The maximization assumption assumes degrees of omniscience and computational sophistication that human beings simply do not possess. More recent attempts to go beyond the static optimization under certainty models have similarly been called into question. Various types of subjective expected utility (SEU) models developed out of the statistical decision theory literature have recently been shown to be quite inadequate in accounting for anything beyond behavior in the simplest hypothetical experimental tasks (Tversky and Kahneman, 1974; Kunreuther and Slovic, 1978; Simon, 1978). Likewise, the attempts of game theory to deal with situations where the rationality of an action is dependent upon the actions of other rational actors have "provided no unique and universally accepted criterion of rationality to generalize the SEU criterion and exte id it to this broader range of situations" (Simon 1978:10).

Thus, the assumptions of microeconomic theory regarding individuals and indiʋidual decisionmaking do not appear to provide a valid description of how decisions are made in organizations. We now turn to a number of tneories of decisionmaking from the literature of organizational behavior and psychology that may provide us with the desired valid descriptive base, and hence serve as a starting point for understanding the relationship between decisionmaking processes and organizational productivity.

Bounded Rationality, Satisficing, and Procedural Rationality

The notions of bounded rationality and satisficing have been introduced into the literature by Simon (1957, 1976a, 1976b, 1978) in an attempt to develop a more realistic and valid picture of human rationality and decisionmaking. According to the principle of bounded rationality, "The capacity of the human mind for formulating and solving complex problems is very small compared with the size of the problems whose solution is required for objectively rational behavior in the real world—or even for a reasonable approximation to such objective rationality (Simon, 1957: 198). The principle, then, has a number of fairly immediate consequences. The first is a recognition that rational behavior occurs within the context of the simplified model of reality comprehended by the actor. Knowing that an actor has behaved in an intendedly rational fashion tells us nothing about the rationality of that behavior with regard to the real world. Understanding and predicting the behavior of the actor requires knowledge not of the objective facts of the real world but rather knowledge of the ways in which actors construct simplified models of that world, which then serve as the basis for individual decision and action. A second consequence of the principle of bounded rationality is recognition that the existence of limits to human rationality is the very reason that a need exists for a theory of organization. If there were no limits to human rationality, then all of the perfectly rational actors in an organization would always be choosing the "best" alternative and problems of organizing would be trivial or nonexistent. However, it is precisely because individuals have limited abilities to agree on goals, to communicate, to cooperate, to analyze situations, and to make decisions that organizing becomes a problem.

In applying the principle of bounded rationality to the study of organizations, Simon also introduces the goal of satisficing as a replacement for the goal of maximization. In order to maximize, a decisionmaker must generate all possible alternatives, determine all of the consequences contingent upon choice of each alternative, assign values to all of the outcomes, and finally select the "best" alternative. The principle of bounded rationality clearly indicates that such herculean mental arithmetic is well beyond the cognitive capacity of any human being. The key to simplifying this choice process is to substitute satisficing for maximizing. Rather than seeking the "best" alternative the individual seeks an alternative that is "good enough." Whereas a maximizer would require estimates of joint probability distributions, complete and consistent preference orderings of all possible alternatives, and so on, a satisficer needs none of these. In short, satisficing is within the cognitive repertoire of human beings, maximizing is not.

More recently, Simon (1976b, 1978) has extended his examination of limited rationality to draw a distinction between "substantive" and "procedural" rationality. According to Simon (1976b: 130) behavior is substantively rational when it is appropriate to the achievement of given goals within the limits imposed by given conditions and constraints. On the other hand, "behavior is procedurally rational when it is the outcome of appropriate deliberation, its procedural rationality depends on the process that generated it" (Simon 1976b: 131). Simon argues that economic theory has addressed itself only to issues of substantive rationality, and, as problems have arisen with the approach, has attempted to deal with them by broadening the criteria for substantive rationality. His position is that an adequate theory of rational behavior must account not only for "substantive rationality—the extent to which appropriate courses of action are chosen—but also procedural rationality —the effectiveness, in light of human cognitive powers and limitations, of the procedures used to choose actions" (Simon 1978: 9).

The mismatch between degrees of problem complexity and human cognitive capacities does not appear to be a minor problem to be solved by larger computers or smarter people. Recent research summarized by Simon in the areas of computational complexity and heuristic search indicates that difficulties of computation and the need for approximation are pervasive and representative rather than rare and unlikely. This in turn implies that the very basis of intelligence lies in "discovering tolerable approximation procedures and heuristics that permit huge spaces to be searched very selectively" (1978: 12).

Research summarized by Simon (1976b: 136) indicates that individuals handle complex problems by (1) using selective heuristics and means-end analysis to explore a small number of promising alternatives, (2) drawing on past experience to detect important features of the situation that are associated in memory with potential actions, and (3) employing aspiration-like mechanisms to terminate search when a satisfactory alternative is found. This line of argument ultimately leads Simon (1978) to the position that the critical scarce resource for effective decisionmaking is not information, but rather attention. Indeed, he argues that for many decisions information may be an expensive luxury since it may distract the decisionmaker's attention away from the truly important aspects of the problem situation.

What this implies for our present purposes is the need to develop a theory of the procedural rationality of organizational decisionmaking. Not only can it not be assumed that organizations make substantively rational decisions (or embody substantively rational decisionmaking systems), it further cannot be assumed that the quality of organizational decisions is primarily a function of the nature and amount of information brought to bear on a given problem. What is called for is a careful analysis of: (1) the decisionmaking process as it actually occurs in organizations, and (2) the nature of the mechanisms designed to facilitate the work of decisionmaking in organizations. By studying how organizations distribute the scarce resource of managerial attention, how they develop and implement heuristics for problem solving, how they use past experience to generate feasible solutions, and how they operationalize satisificing mechanisms to terminate search we will undoubtedly be focusing upon some of the very factors that determine effectiveness and productivity of the organization.

In subsequent sections of this paper we will either explicitly or implicitly deal with many of these issues. In the concluding section we will return to these issues and attempt to integrate our discussion around them.

Muddling Through

Lindblom (1959) has developed a description of a "successive limited comparisons" method of decisionmaking, also labeled "muddling through." The successive limited comparisons method (referred to as the "branch" method) was developed as a description of the behavior of decisionmakers faced with major policy decisions, and is contrasted with the "rational-comprehensive" (or "root") method of decisionmaking. There are some significant parallels between Lindblom's approach and Simon's position as reviewed above. The rational-comprehensive or root method of decisionmaking described by Lindblom is simply a detailed statement of the steps required for rational optimizing behavior. The argument against this method as a valid description of decisionmaking is that it is impossible for most real problems because it assumes intellectual capacities and sources of information that people simply don't possess. The method of successive limited comparisons (branch method) put forward by Lindblom as a description of "how most administrators do in fact approach complex questions" (Lindblom 1959: 81) can thus be viewed as his theory of procedural rationality. As such it is interesting and instructive to examine some of the ways in which this method departs from the substantive rationality of the rational-comprehensive (root) method.

First, while the root method suggests that the classification of values or objectives is distinct from and usually prerequisite to the empirical analysis of alternatives, according to the branch method the selection of value goals and the empirical analysis of needed action are closely intertwined. The root method of clarifying and ranking all values at the outset is argued to be impossible and irrelevant in the face of complex decisions. It is impossible because (1) actors often do not know how to rank values when they conflict with each other (as they often do), and (2) outcomes do not always have the same relative values, but change with circumstances. It is irrelevant because in practice the majority of outcomes associated with an alternative are irrelevant to a decision; attention is focused only on those outcomes whose alternatives differ. It is these marginal differences that determine decisions.

A second primary difference is in the definition of a "good" policy. For the root method, a good policy is the one that is best for achieving some objectives. For the branch method a good policy is simply one that is agreed upon by the decisionmakers. This distinction is introduced to make it possible to test the "goodness" of a policy even in the (not infrequent) absence of agreement of objectives. Although the criterion of extent of agreement as a test of goodness may seem rather flimsy, it is no flimsier than evaluating a policy against some set of objectives that in turn have no ultimate validity other than that they are agreed upon.

A third difference between the two methods is that the root method implies comprehensive analysis of all consequences of all possible alternatives, while the branch method brings the cognitive task within the grasp of real human beings by (1) restricting the search to alternatives that differ in relatively small degrees from current policies, and (2) permitting decisionmakers to ignore potential outcomes that lie outside their own particular sphere of interest and concern.

The final important difference lies in the relative reliance on theory of the two methods. Rather than the heavy reliance on theory suggested by the root method, Lindblom argues that we do not have adequate theory to address most substantial problems, and hence apply a method of comparative analysis whereby successive incremental changes permit movement toward more distant objectives.

A primary contribution of Lindblom's analysis lies in its description of a potential form of procedural rationality in organizations. Very little empirical research has been carried out using this framework to determine either (1) the generality of the descriptive validity of the model, or (2) the relationship between successive limited comparisons as a decisionmaking strategy and the overall effectiveness and productivity of organizations. Such research could well prove fruitful.

A Conflict Theory of Decisionmaking

Janis and Mann (1977) have developed what they refer to as a "conflict" theory of decisionmaking. Their theory is of particular interest since it draws into consideration some of the nonrational, affective factors that have an impact upon the decisionmaking process. Of additional interest is the fact that their theory is essentially a model of procedural rationality.

Janis and Mann begin by pointing out many of the difficulties involved in attempting to determine how well a decision has worked out. In the case of personal decisions such as career choice, the only criterion for decision quality is subjective ratings, which are notoriously subject to distortion and rationalization. In the case of organizations, it is very frequently impossible to carry out adequately controlled field experiments that permit unambiguous determination of the causal impact of alternative decisionmaking styles and structures. The solution adopted by Janis and Mann is to study the quality of the *procedures* used by the decisionmaker. They assume that decisions of high procedural quality are more likely to lead to attaining desired objectives, to be adhered to, and to be satisfying to the decisionmaker. The quality of the decision procedures employed is evaluated against seven criteria for "vigilant information processing" (see Table 5-1). These seven criteria essentially define a model of substantive rationality. The Janis and Mann theory is thus a theory of the causes and consequences of patterns of decisionmaking that cause individual actors to depart from attempts to approximate substantive rationality.

Janis and Mann characterize man as a "reluctant" decisionmaker. This characterization is drawn from a review of psychological research indicating that the process of decisionmaking evokes stress reactions in human beings (Epstein and Fenze 1965; Gerard 1967; Fleisher 1969; Mann, Janis and Chaplin 1969; Jones and Johnson 1973). The evidence indicates that regardless of the difficulty or importance of the decision, physiological measures of stress increase as an individual moves toward a decision. As one would expect, the intensity of the stress symptoms varies with the perceived magnitude of anticipated gains and losses associated with the decision. Decisionmaking is thus a source of conflict in which an individual must cope with simultaneously opposing tendencies to accept and reject a course of action. For minor decisions this conflict is often manifested in hesitation, vacillation, and feelings of uncertainty. More difficult decisions often give rise to apprehensiveness, a desire to escape the distressing choice dilemma, and self-blame for getting into the predicament of having to choose among unsatisfactory alternatives (Janis and Mann 1977: 147).

Janis and Mann's theory is designed to explain the conditions that determine whether the stress brought about by decisional conflict will facilitate or impede vigilant information processing. The basic hypothesis is that a vigilant effort to generate alternatives and to determine the most desirable requires a moderate degree of stress. Very low and very high levels of stress will result in defective coping patterns other than vigilant information processing.

The basic outline of the theory is contained in Figure 5-2. The theory characterizes the decisionmaker as responding (consciously or unconsciously) to four questions. The responses to these questions de-

Table 5–1. The Seven Major Criteria for Vigilant Information Processing

The decisionmaker, to the best of his ability and within his information-processing abilities

1. Thoroughly canvasses a wide range of alternative courses of action;
2. Surveys the full range of objectives to be fulfilled and the values implicated by the choice;
3. Carefully weighs whatever he knows about the costs and risks of negative consequences, as well as the positive consequences, that could flow from each alternative;
4. Intensively researches for new information relevant to further evaluation of the alternatives;
5. Correctly assimilates and takes account of any new information or expert judgment to which he is exposed, even when the information or judgment does not support the course of action he initially prefers;
6. Reexamines the positive and negative consequences of all known alternatives, including those originally regarded as unacceptable, before making a final choice;
7. Makes detailed provisions for implementing or executing the chosen course of action, with special attention to contingency plans that might be required if various known risks were to materialize.

Source: Janis and Mann (1977: 11).

termine first the level of stress experienced by the decisionmaker, and second the coping pattern adopted by the decisionmaker. A decision sequence is initiated by the perception of either challenging negative feedback or the existence of an opportunity. This initial perception generates some stress, the magnitude of the initial stress varying with the importance and value of the outcomes the decisionmaker associates with the situation. In response to this initial stress the decisionmaker responds to the first question regarding the seriousness of the risks involved if no change is made. If the induced stress is low and the risks are not perceived to be serious, the observed response will be "unconflicted adherence," or inertia. No search is undertaken, no alternatives are generated, no change is seriously contemplated.

If however, the stress is sufficient to result in an affirmative answer to Question 1, the decisionmaker then moves to Question 2, "Are the risks serious if I do change?" The response to this question is largely influenced by the degree of *commitment* to the current alternative. If *commitment* to the current alternative is low, the predicted coping pattern is "unconflicted change" to the first new alternative available.

Figure 5–2. The Conflict Model of Decisionmaking.

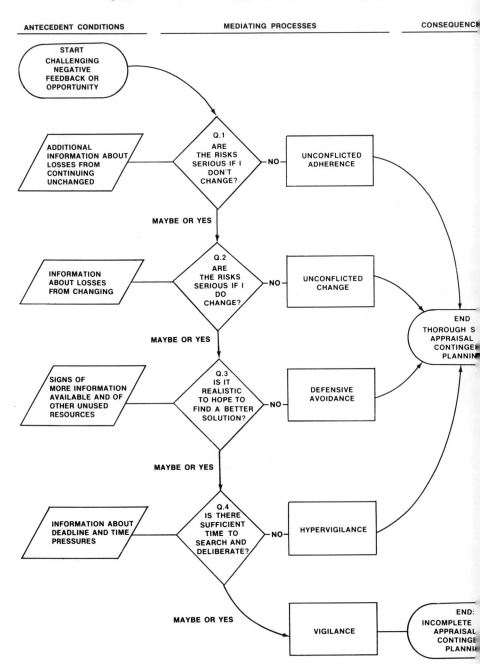

Careful search, appraisal, and planning are not engaged in. If, on the other hand, commitment to the current alternative is high, changing will be seen as risky, the second question will be answered in the affirmative and stess increases to intermediate levels.

The critical question for the decisionmaker at this point is whether it is realistic to *hope* for better solution than the current alternative (Question 3). If the decisionmaker feels there is no hope of doing better, the resulting coping pattern is labeled "defensive avoidance." Defensive avoidance is a relatively common coping pattern that can take a number of forms. Among these are procrastinating (putting off the decision), shifting responsibility for the decision to someone else (buck-passing), and bolstering (selective attention, selective forgetting, and distortion of information to bolster one's faith in the validity of one's position).

If however the decision maker does feel it realistic to hope for a better solution, the response to Question 3 is affirmative, stress remains at intermediate levels, and the decisionmaker moves on to Question 4, "Is there sufficient time to search and deliberate?" A negative response to Question 4 is likely to result in extreme levels of stress and a coping pattern labeled "hypervigilance" and characterized by frantic search, incomplete evaluation, and disjointed activity. A positive response to Question 4 results in a continued moderate level of stress, leading to a "vigilant" coping pattern characterized by thorough search, careful appraisal of alternatives, and detailed contingency planning.

Time and space obviously preclude a detailed discussion of the data presented by Janis and Mann in support of their proposed model. Data from their own research and that of others, primarily in areas of personal consequential decisionmaking, indicate that the theory holds considerable promise. The theory has not as yet been applied to decisionmaking in organizations, though such application would appear to hold considerable promise, both from the standpoint of better understanding of the decisionmaking process itself, and from the standpoint of examining the relationships between different processes of decisionmaking and the resulting effectiveness and productivity of the organization. The decisionmaking theories described above propose to explain how decisionmaking takes place. The theories proposed by Simon and Lindblom help us to understand why the assumptions of optimization do not hold. Furthermore, they specify some of the human frailties that interfere with both optimizing and vigilant information processing as described by Janis and Mann. While there is no direct data to demonstrate that vigilant information processing in organizations leads to increased organizational effectiveness, the evidence from individual decisionmaking suggests that this is the case (cf. Janis and Mann 1977). Furthermore, Filley, House, and Kerr (1976: Chapter 19) review substantial evidence that suggests that management practices that encourage vigilance in decisionmaking result in improved decision effectiveness. Thus, it can be at least tentatively concluded that the introduction of formalized decisionmaking practices and aids to vigilance (such as long-range planning, budgets, manpower estimates, etc.) will enhance organizational effectiveness. The specific nature of such aids and practices and their impact on decisionmaking and organizational effectiveness remain to be established through future research. Specifically, one might examine such issues as: Do organizations have characteristic patterns of decisionmaking? How do these patterns approximate vigilant information processing? Do they bear a relationship to overall effectiveness? How do organizations design and structure themselves to facilitate vigilance? Is vigilance itself a cause of effectivenss, or is it selective vigilance in response to serious challenges that distinguishes effective organizations? Empirical answers can be sought to questions such as these using the conflict theory of decisionmaking.

Having discussed prevalent behavioral theory regarding decisionmaking, we now turn to a review of the social science literature concerned with the use of information in organizational decisionmaking.

THE INFORMATIONAL BASIS OF DECISIONMAKING

Both trandtional[1] and newer models of decisionmaking in organizations (Simon 1976; Janis and Mann 1977) include two important building blocks in their descriptions of organizational and individual decisionmaking processes, (1) the values, goals, or preferences of decisionmaker, and (2) the factual information set available to the decisionmaker about the situation and the available alternatives.

The two givens of the classical models are that, (1) the decisionmaker is a maximizer of utility (sometimes in the case of the firm this utility is seen soley as profit, and, (2) the decisionmaker lives in a world of perfect information. The newer models treat these factors as problematic. The decisionmaker is often not a single individual but a coalition of interest groups (Cyert and March 1963), and lives in a world where information is limited, fragmentary, and costly to search for (March and Simon 1958). It is to this more complex view that we turn, in order to explore the way in which organizational factors affect the goals of the firm as a decisionmaker and the way in which decisionmakers acquire and use information.

This is not to suggest that the goals and information use and acquisition are independent of each other; the goals that the decisionmaker seeks to attain may have significant effects on the information used and sought. Conversely the information available to the decisionmaker may affect the goals he is aware of.

The Development of Organizational Goals

Classical and human relations theories of organization both postulate that consensual goals exist throughout the organization. In the classical case, this consensus is achieved through instrumental attachment of managers and employees. In other words, the owners (entrepreneurs or stockholders) purchase through the wage-bargain the commitment of organization members to the goals of the owners. In the human relations case, consensus is achieved by the organization's being formed by (and subsequently attracting) like-minded people (c.f. the documented selection procedures of nonlinear system (Kuriloff 1966), the Topeka General Foods Plant (Walton 1977), and the new Shell polypropylene plant at Sarnia (List 1978)). However, in the light of obvious internal conflict within organizations, the consensual view seems naive. Consequently, a number of theorists have developed an alternative position (Buck 1966; Cyert and March 1963; Simon 1976a; Pennings and Goodman 1977). Each states, in slightly different terms, that the agreement on overall organizational goals is tenuous; limited goal consensus is achieved as the result of temporary agreements between different organization members or stakeholders who hold goals of differing compatibility.

The actual content of subunit goals in the organization reflects the stucture of the organization and the stakeholders that each unit has contact with, or the task's facing the subunit (if it is not a boundary-sharing unit). With reference to this latter point, Lawrence and Lorsch (1967), in their examination of functional organizations, found that for both effective and ineffective organizations each subunit's goal reflected the task of the subunit; R & D reflected concerns about scientific development and application; marketing reflected concerns about customers and market share; production reflected concerns about technical and economic efficiency and cost control. Similarly Cyert and March (1963) argue that most organizations have a set of five major subgoals— each associated with different subgroups in the organization:

1. The production goal of having relatively smooth production at a particular level; this is the goal held by the production subunit.
2. The inventory goals involving a trade-off between avoiding runouts and reducing inventory costs; these goals are held by customers and budget controllers, respectively.
3. Sales goals reflecting the amount of product to be sold; this goal is held by the sales and marketing subunits.
4. The market share goal involving the maintenance of the firm's competition position; this goal is held by sales and marketing subunits and top management, whose concern is comparing the organization's performance with that of other firms.
5. The profit goal, held by top management of the organization.

This model implies two kinds of organizational differentiation—between each function and between functions and the top management group. It has been suggested by Landsberger (1961) that even these rather different goals all stem from a similar overall goal held by each group—the desire for stability and smoothness in its operations. A problem arises because of the nature of organizational interdependence. If one group achieves stability in its operations this usually causes fluctuations or constraints for another group. For example, for sales effort to be relatively constant in a state of fluctuating market demands implies that actual sales will fluctuate, the consequence being either that inventories must be built up or that the production department must vary its activities with high production in a booming market or lowered production in a slump. Alternatively, production can remain constant if inventories are allowed to fluctuate or if the sales department varies its efforts depending on the market conditions, pushing hard in weak markets, and easing off when demand is booming.

In these models, the minimal aspiration levels of each organizational stakeholder become constraints that the organization has to satisfy to ensure its continued existence. Beyond this, goals are defined by the additional resource allocation made over and above the stakeholder's minimum requirements. In addition, to the extent that others in the environment—customers, financiers, suppliers, and so on—make judgements about the organization in terms of its performance such goals become more important for the organization to fulfill.

The implications of this discussion are twofold. First, the organization goals are both the outcome of a decision process that involves bargaining between different groups with differing (but overlapping) sets of goals and the inputs to subsequent resource allocation decisions. That is, once goals have been temporarily decided upon they provide the rationale for making future decisions. The second implication is that the goals of each subunit have a dual function. First they help to focus the attention of the subunit on particular environmental sectors—hence affecting the adequacy and breadth of its search activity—the narrower or fewer the goals, the more restricted the search (see below). Second they are communicated to other subunits, and affect the decisions made by other subunits

The Use of Information

In thinking about factual information—about the environment, about the decision situation, about potential courses of action—there are two major factors that affect whether or not a particular piece of information is used by a decisionmaker. The first is simply whether or not the individual has access to the information; the second has to do with the weight placed on the information by the decisionmaker—is it believed, discounted or ignored? In other words, how is the decisionmaker influenced by the particular piece of information? These two considerations—accessibility and influence—are our major interest in this section.

On the Accessibility of Information

Any discussion of the information required by a decisionmaker logically starts with the locus of that information. Organizations are embedded in environments—technical, market, financial, and human—that they must either control or adjust to. Thus most of the information needed by a decisionmaker is to be found in the environment of the organization or in subunits that deal with various environmental sections. We shall deal more fully with the nature of environments and environmental influence on organizational design more fully later in this chapter. We should note, however, that the environment facing a particular firm can be characterized by:

1. Its uncertainty for the organization which is a function of the volatility of change (Duncan 1972).
2. The degree of heterogeneity of volatility of the specific sub-environments faced by organizational subunits (Lawrence and Lorsch 1967).
3. The degree of interconnectedness between different sub-environments.
4. Its munificence or scarcity (Child 1972b).

Many organizational analysts argue (e.g., Emery and Trist 1965) that environments are becoming more turbulent and more interconnected. Thus information needs are becoming more crucial. A two-stage survey by Wall (1974) supports this argument (see Table 5.2). Managers surveyed in 1973 reported that significantly more items of information about competition were necessary to make effective strategic decisions than managers surveyed in 1959 did. The increased interdependence among firms implied by these data is substantial. That such information is necessary is confirmed by Grinyer and Norburn (1975), who found an association between the number of pieces of information used in strategic decisionmaking and the firm's return on investment.

How do organizations acquire relevant information from the environment? The process of information acquisition is not well understood. There are a number of studies of significant information gathering roles such as those of purchasing agents (Strauss 1964) and research and development specialist (Allen and Cohen 1969). There are also more general perspectives on information-gathering activities in organizations (Aguilar 1967; Mintzberg 1973: 65-77). The main conclusion of these disparate studies suggests that at present the major information sources

Table 5–2. Competitive Information Desired for Management Decisions

Type of Information	Percent of Managers 1973	1959
Pricing	79	67
Expansion plants	54	20
Competitive plants	52	18
Promotional strategy	49	41
Cost Data	47	24
Sales statistics	46	27
R&D	41	36
Product styling	31	18
Manufacturing processes	30	25
Patents and infringements	22	5
Financing	20	6
Executive compensation	20	2

Source: Wall (1974).

for the environmental scanners in organizations are personal and concentrated among two groups—the manager's subordinates and his business associates (see Table 5-3). Similarly Allen and Cohen (1969) found the R&D laboratories relied upon technical "gatekeepers" (information gatherers and disseminators) for most novel scientific information. Furthermore these gatekeepers were involved in both keeping up with the literature and discussion with fellow scientists outside the laboratory. These findings suggest that the acquisition of information is a problematic affair depending very much on the individual scanner's place in a network of informal relationships and the extent to which he creates this network. This implies that effective scanners have to reciprocate and provide information about their own organizations to their informants.

Recently Montgomery and Weinberg (1977) have argued for a more formalized approach to strategic information-scanning and, without slighting the role of the individual word-of-mouth sourcing, have suggested a number of more formal mechanisms for scanning the environment. These are listed in Table 5-4 along with some of the informal ones. We shall explore later the individual characteristics that reduce the use of data generated from formal scanning processes.

Communicating Information

Once the information has been acquired by an individual the problem is to communicate it to the decisionmaking centers of the organization. In most organizations there is usually some distance between the decisionmaker and the environmental scanners. This means that: (1)

Table 5–3. Information Sources

	Personal		*Impersonal*	
Outside the	Customer	2	Trade publication	9
organization	Supplier	4	Newspaper	18
	Bankers	4	Other	2
	Business associates	12		
	Others	5		
Within the	Subordinates	19	Reports	5
organization	Peers	8	Scheduled meetings	3
	Superiors	1		
	Others	7		

Source: Aguilar (1967).

some time must elapse between the information entering the organizations and reaching the decisionmaker and (2) that several links in a communication chain must be completed before the information passes from its entry point to the decision maker.

The literature on organizational decisionmaking is voluminous and fragmented. No general theory of effective communications exists (Porter and Roberts 1976). Rather, there are a number of clues that point to potential barriers to the accurate and timely communication of information.

Deliberate Distortion: Pettigrew (1971) has graphically described the power of a gatekeeper in affecting the outcome of an organizational decision. By carefully controlling the flow of information between a set of suppliers and the decisionmaking body (in this case a company board of directors) the gatekeeper ensured that "his" supplier received the order for a major computer purchase. The gatekeeper used the following tactics:

1. Reluctant and tardy replies to communications from other suppliers.
2. Refusing to visit or be "wined and dined" by other suppliers.
3. Refusing to let his subordinate managers (each of whom favored a different supplier based upon their departmental interests) have direct access to the decisionmaking bodies—except when the most influential members of the body were known to be absent from the meeting.
4. Providing a biased balance of positive and negative information about "his" supplier and others' suppliers to the decisionmaking body. He did this by diagnosing the "assessed stature" (Bucher 1970) of his department with the decisionmaking body (the firm's

Table 5–4. Sources of Intelligence

Source	Example	Comments
Government	Freedom of Information Act[a]	1974 amendments have led to accelerating use.
	Government Contract Administration[a]	Examination of competitor's bids and documentation may reveal competitor's technology and indicate his costs and bidding philosophy.
	Patent filings[a]	Belgium and Italy publish patent applications shortly after they are filed. Some companies (e.g., pharmaceutical) patent their mistakes in order to confuse their competitors.
Competitors	Annual reports and 10Ks[a]	FTC and SEC line-of-business reporting requirements will render this source more useful in the future.
	Speeches and public announcements of competitor's officers[a]	Reveal management philosophy, priorities, and self-evaluation systems.
	Products[a]	Systematic analysis of a competitor's products via back engineering may reveal the competitor's technology and enable the company to monitor changes in the competitor's engineering and assembly operations. Forecasts of a competitor's sales may often be made from observing his serial numbers over time.
	Employment ads[a]	May suggest the technical and marketing directions in which a competitor is headed.
	Consultants[a]	Consultant chosen may reveal probable strategy. For example, if a competitor has retained Boston Consulting, then portfolio management strategies become more likely.
Suppliers	Banks, advertising agencies, public relations firms, and direct mailers and cataloguers, hard goods sup-	Have a tendency to be more talkative than competitor's since the information transmitted may enhance supplier's business. Can be effective sources of information on such items as competitor's equipment installations and on what retail com-

Source	Example	Comments
Customers	Purchasing Agents	Generally regarded as self-serving. Low reliability as a source.
	Customer engineers and corporate officers	Valued sources of intelligence. One company taught its salespersons to perform elementary service for customers in order to get the salespersons past the purchasing agent and on to the more valued source of intelligence.
Professional associations and meetings	Scientific and technical society meetings, management association meetings.[a]	Examine competitor's products, research and development, and management approach as revealed in displays, brochures, scientific papers, and speeches.
Consultants, management service companies, and the media	SRI International	Scenarios of alternative futures. Industry projections and analysis.
	Western Electronics Manufacturers' Association[a]	Industry financial ratios for comparison and base purposes.
	Management Horizons[a]	Retail Intelligence System
	Find/SVP[a]	Offers clients research papers of fifteen top brokerage houses.
	Stratman Systems Inc.[a]	Monitor competitors' new customer products.
	Technology Clearing House Inc.[a]	New Technology Index provides engineers with latest industrial product information.
Company Personnel	Executives, sales force, engineers and scientists, purchasing agents.	Sensitize them to the need for intelligence and train them to recognize and transmit to the proper organizational location relevant intelligence that comes to their attention.

Source: Montgomery and Weinberg (1977).
Note: The names of organizations are included for illustrative purposes only. The listing is neither exhaustive nor a recommendation by the authors.
[a]Formal methods.

executive committee) and then providing information that he wanted to be believed when the stature was high and providing information that he wanted to be discounted when the assessed stature of his department was low. (See also the discussion below on credibility and influence.)

A second form of deliberate distortion of information involves the suppression of bad news. Many individuals fail to report to others in the organization problems they are having. There is a considerable amount of research on the issue of communication between a subordinate and a superior (See Porter and Roberts 1976 for a review). Specifically, omission of unfavorable information increases (hence communication accuracy decreases) when (1) the sender does not trust the person to whom he is transmitting the information (the receiver), (2) the sender perceives that the receiver has some control over the sender's fate in the organization (i.e., has control over organizational rewards and penalties, or has high upward influence in the organization), and (3) the sender has high upward mobility aspirations. Furthermore, O'Reilly and Roberts (1974) have found similar effects of trust for communication between peers and from superiors to subordinates. A second study (O'Reilly and Roberts 1977) examines the relationship between structural characteristics of sociometrically defined work groups and communication accuracy. It was found that where groups were high on inferred indicators of trust there was a high level of perceived communication accuracy; in turn accuracy of communication was related to perceived organizational effectiveness.

These kinds of results are congruent within Argyris' (1965) views on the role of interpersonal competence (openness, confrontation, and trust) in organizational decisionmaking and the extension by Zand (1972) who argues that there exist reciprocal relationships between information disclosure and trust such that increased disclosure leads to increased trust, which facilitates further disclosure. Thus pairs of organization members are likely to get into increasing or decreasing spirals of information-sharing and trust with consequent effects upon decision-making effectiveness.

Uncertainty Absorption: A second common source of information distortion in both interpersonal and organizational communication is uncertainty absorption (March and Simon 1958). This occurs where raw data are summarized and edited prior to transmission onward. Two processes are probably involved. First, the selection of raw data from the plethora of environmental stimuli and second, the packaging of this data for transmission. In both processes, the scanner-communicator's frame of reference—or "cognitive map" (Goodman 1968)—is crucial in determining what information will be noticed and what information will be transmitted.

Dearborn and Simon (1958), Zajonc and Wolfe (1966) and Goodman (1968) have all pointed out that organizational position—functional specialty, staff, or line—and hierarchical level affect the frame of reference individuals use to scan and interpret their environments. These differences are found both in terms of aspects of the environment attended to (Dearborn and Simon 1958) and the cognitive complexity of the individual (Zajonc and Wolfe 1966; Goodman 1968). In addition, Parsons (1960) argues that at different organizational levels, organization members have different concerns. These different concerns focus the individual's attention and lead to screening and editing of information.

A number of points follow from this:

1. Organizational position creates a framework (either wide and complex or narrow and simple) from which these individuals scan the environment.

    a) Data from the environment congruent with this framework is easily assimilated and incorporated into the individual's knowledge.

    b) For individuals with narrow conceptual frameworks, information inconsistent with this framework is ignored, distorted or reinterpreted to make it consistent with the framework.

    c) Individuals with wide conceptual frameworks use inconsistent information to revise and change the framework into a new and richer conceptual framework (Harvey, Hunt, and Schroder 1961).

2. Individuals with wide and complex conceptual frameworks will use more information before aggregating and transmitting or making a decision (Driver and Streufort 1969). In addition, if they face an environment that provides them with little information, they will search for additional information (Streufort, Suedfeld, and Driver 1965).

3. Accuracy of communication is enhanced when sender and receiver share similar conceptual frameworks (either in terms of class of information attended to (Triandis 1960), or in terms of cognitive complexity (Runkel 1956)).

Weighting the Importance of Information

Once the information has been communicated to the decisionmaker, its use is still problematic. Two general factors seem to be involved: one, which overlaps somewhat the scanning and communicating processes discussed earlier, involves biases in the kinds of information stored, remembered, and used by the decisionmaker; the other involves organizational considerations that affect the weight given to information about preferences and data provided by other organizational units. We discuss each in turn.

Individual Biases: Recent research on human inference processes has indicated a number of factors that affect the weight given to a piece of information in making judgments or reaching decisions (summarized in Nisbett and Ross 1979; Tversky and Kahneman 1974):

1. Individuals have differential access to information from the environment. Therefore, each person is exposed to a biased sample of data. An example of this is the different perspectives held about the increases in corporate profits in the latest fiscal year held by businessmen and the general public. The latter are concerned about these increases because their information is simply based on the most recent figures (which are what get reported in the mass media) without being aware that in many cases, the bases upon which these percentages are calculated are at comparatively low levels (the media do not usually report these bases). On the other hand, the businessman is aware of both the current data and the historical figures, and is inclined to believe these large increases merely restore profits to the historically accepted levels.

2. Information must be stored by the individual in memory and reaccessed when needed for decisionmaking. Biases exist in that, as we have noted earlier, storage is easier when the information is congruent with the individual's frame of reference.

3. Biases in storage and recall also exist as a result of the vividness of the information. By this we mean the extent to which the information:

   a) Has emotional relevance—the more one is personally affected by the information the more likely one is to store it and recall it.

   b) Is concrete—the more specific the information and the more colorful, corroborative detail it has, the more it is likely to be stored and recalled. Additionally, information from occurring events is more concrete than information from nonoccurrences. The bids by Thompson and Weston for the Hudson Bay Co. tell us a lot about the three firms, the non-bids from Eatons and Brascan tell us little!

   c) Is temporally, spatially, and sensory close to the decisionmaker. In a recent *Economist* survey of banking there was more concern with British and West European penetration into the U.S. banking community than with recent Bank of Montreal initiatives toward entering that community.

4. After storage, a number of additional processes enhance this information's availability:
   a) When information is vivid there is often more total information stored.
   b) This increased amount of information will generate more associative networks in the individual's memory, so that more routes become open to access this information.
   c) There is a greater likelihood that vivid information will be mused upon and mentally rehearsed. This will give rise to magnifying the importance of this information for subsequent use.

These biases explain the earlier findings that boundary scanners make use of personal sources. Such sources are likely to provide information having these properties of vividness. Data from more formal sources— abstract statistics, government documents, or even company reports— lack these characteristics, and so may fail to be stored or retained for use in decisionmaking. The problem is that the grey formal data is much more likely to be an accurate representation of the actual state of affairs than is the vivid informal data and for the following reasons:

1. The classification of an observed piece of information as being representative of a particular general class of occurrences is rarely made on the basis of the prior probability of these occurences. As a result, a given piece of information may be assigned to a relatively esoteric category that it fits exactly, rather than being assigned as an infrequent member of a common category. For example, when given a description of a quiet, self-effacing person whom one is told works with people, one is likely to incorrectly categorize this individual as a social worker rather than a salesman, despite the fact that there are many more salesmen than social workers in our society. What happens is that the use of an occupational stereotype is outweighing any data based upon prior probabilities resulting from the relative percentage of the total population in each occupation.

2. The failure to be aware that biased samples are more likely to result from a small sample of observations than from a large sample whereas the larger the sample, the more likely the information represents the actual state of affairs. For example, in a real state of general economic decline, the information that a particular month's sales figures (a small sample) are very good may lead to the incorrect inference that the worst is over and it is time to plan for expansion, rather than the correct inference that this was but an aberrant bump in the sales curve, and current plans restricting output and hiring and controlling costs should be continued.

3. The tendency to erroneously infer, or overestimate the strength of cause and effect relationships because of:
   a) Relatively invalid implicit theories about them; for example, considerate leaders have productive workers.
   b) Generalizing from one or two irrelevant features of the data to make predictions of future behavior; for example, using information about the quality of a product to predict whether or not its sales will be high, without taking into account market characteristics, sales force effectiveness, and so on. This is partially a problem of the illusion that in the real world, *ceterus paribus.*
   c) Unawareness of the pervasiveness of the statistical phenomenon of regression toward the mean; for example, as a result of regression effects, unusually high and unusually low performing individuals in any given sample are likely, upon measurement at a later time, to regress toward the mean of the sample. Thus if the supervisor rewards the high performer and punishes the low performer the supervisor will conclude erroneously that the reward resulted in poorer performance and the punishment resulted in higher performance when in fact the change in performance may actually be a result of regression phenomena.

Organizational Biases: Even if the decisionmaker has available to him information from the environmental scanners, and even if this is accessible to him and is representative of the actual situation, he may still discount it. There are two reasons for this:
   1. The credibility of the information source, based on prior experience with the source—which in itself is subject to availability and representativeness biases.
   2. The power of the source: This affects whether or not the decisionmaker acts on the information provided, or considers the source's goals and values in making the decision. This process is detailed below.

Usually when power is considered in an interpersonal or organizational relationship the concern is to explain why actor A did what actor B wanted him to do (see definitions by Dahl (1957) and others). It is possible to view the issue from an information-processing perspective. This is to think of A as the recipient of information from B. This information is likely to be of two types: first, information about B's values, goals, and preferences for outcomes; second, information about the environment or other parts of the organization. Thus the question becomes: why does A give great weight to the information provided by B about his preferences, and his facts? From this perspective, the causes of B's power over A are similar to the conventional view; but the process by which A is influenced by B is transformed into an information process with A attending to and being aware of facts and values transmitted by B.

In organizational research, there are two streams of research on power and influence—the first interpersonal, the second organizational. A number of students (French and Raven 1959; Kelman 1958; Tedeschi, Schlenker, and Linkskold 1972) have argued for the existence of a set of power bases, such as reward, punishment, referent, expert, and legitimate power (French and Raven 1959). These suggested—in our terms—that individual A places great weight on the communicated (or perceived) desires and facts of individual B because individual B has some kind of control (with the exception of legitimate power) over the consequences for individual A. This can, and has, been generalized to the notion that A is dependent upon B for desired consequences occurring (Emerson 1962), thus B's power over another A is a function of the extent to which A's consequences can be satisfied by some other parties (C_1 . . . C_3). A second organizational stream of research and theory on power is also devised from a resource dependence approach. It suggests that not all organizational subunits are equally influential in determining the outcome of organizational decisions. As Hickson, Pugh, and Pheysey (1969:217–218) put it:

"In organizations, subunit B will have more power than other subunits to the extent that (1) B has the capacity to fulfill the requirements of other subunits and (2) B monopolizes this ability."

Following Thompson (1967) and Crozier (1964), Hickson, and Pugh and Pheysey (1969) argue that the crucial requirements of each subunit in an organization is the reduction of uncertainty. Thus, to the extent that each subunit copes with, manages, or reduces the uncertainty that flows from the environment to the organization, the greater the power of the subunit and hence the greater weight other subunits place upon its preferences and on the factual information it supplies.

A major impetus to the development of the theory was Crozier's (1964) observations that ability to cope with uncertainty results in an engineering unit having a large amount of power in a manufacturing organization in a monopoly situation. Similarly Perrow (1970), examining a number of firms in a more competitive market, found that marketing departments had high levels of power.

In addition, Hickson et al. suggest other variables that affect the subunit's power:

1. The extent to which the coping activities of the subunit can be provided either by other subunits or by contracting to other organizations.
2. The extent to which the subunit is connected to other units such

that its activities are either critical to the performance of other subunits or that the subunit's activities are pervasive in their impact on the remainder of the organization.

Finally they argue that these independent variables can be subsumed into the notion of control of strategic contingencies which acts as a mediating variable between these variables and the dependent variable of subunit power.

Since the theory's development, Hinings et al. (1974) found some support for their hypothesis. A number of studies reported in Pfeffer and Salancik (1978) by Pfeffer and his colleagues have explored the issue further. In doing this they assumed that a critical uncertainty for different types of organizations concerned the acquisitions of scarce resources. Thus they found that, for universities where funding was the scarce resource, the subunits (academic departments) that generated large research funds had greater influence in the university's budgetary decisions (Salancik and Pfeffer 1974). In a second study (Pfeffer and Leong 1977) of United Funds and their constituent agencies, they were able to engage in a two-way analysis—whether or not the agency was dependent on the central Fund for the major part of its reveneus, and whether or not the Fund depended on the agency for the scarce resource of prestige. In the former case, the lower the dependence (high sub-stitutability) of the agency on the Fund, the lower the power of the Fund; similarly, the lower the dependence of the Fund on the agency, the lower the influence the agency had on the Fund's decisions. The final piece of evidence is also found in work of this group (Salancik et al. in press). By examining a series of decisions whose locus of uncertainty varied, they found that subunit power in each decision correlated with the type of uncertainty that was (1) relevant to the decision and (2) coped with by the subunit.

These findings suggest that (1) when environmental subunits face and cope with uncertainty their power vis-a-vis other subunits is enhanced, and (2) such power results in a biasing of resource allocation decisions in favor of the more powerful units.

Conclusion: Information Bases of Decisionmaking

The implication of the foregoing is that the information a decision-maker uses or attends to is as much a function of (1) the decisionmaker's own selection biases, (2) the biases of those scanning the environment and communicating with him, and (3) the power of those communicating with him, as it is of the objective situation that he and his organization face.

The above discussion suggests several things organizations can do to minimize information deficiency, suppression, or distortion and thus increase the amount and accuracy of information available and attended to by decisionmakers. First, organizations will likely do well to systematically review and explicitly define what information is to be collected on an on-going basis. Such a definition should ameliorate the effects of the diverse frames of reference of data collectors and therefore provide for collection of more complete information. Also, information gatherers' and disseminators' efforts toward sharing their frames of reference should reduce the biases associated with uncertainty absorption. Such sharing is likely to result in consistency of information-coding across individuals, subunits, and organization levels.

A clear statement of the purpose to be served by the information requested by decisionmakers should also reduce the biases of uncertainty absorption because those providing the information would have better direction concerning how such information can be most effectively aggregated and presented.

Deliberate distortion and suppression of information are most likely to occur under conditions of mistrust. Such mistrust can be reduced by providing a psychologically satisfying and supportive social climate for organizational members. The dysfunctional consequences of all kinds of biases, individual or organization, can be minimized by provision of multiple sources and redundancy of information and provision for feedback to users of information.

The psychological biases associated with human information processes are likely to lead individuals to use some information selectively, although unknowingly, to reject or discount other information that may be valid and useful. These biases may be offset by making individuals aware of them through training and simulation exercises that permit the individuals to experience the dysfunctional consequences of information-processing biases. Furthermore, provision of additional viewpoints by having decisionmakers consult with others, especially others who have a different frame of reference with respect to the decision content, or providing "devil's advocates," should serve as a check on such biases to a significant extent. Finally, organization of the information and authority channels in such a manner as to facilitate lateral and diagonal communication patterns as well as vertical-hierarchical communication patterns should serve to minimize the dysfunctional effects of all the biases identified in this section.

We now turn to an analysis of three outcomes of management decisions. These outcomes are (1) the organization structure, (2) the goal setting process, and (3) the control processes employed by the organization. These outcomes were selected because there is sufficient amount of theory and empirical evidence to suggest rather definitive conclusions on how they affect productivity.

GOALS AND GOAL-SETTING

A considerable body of research has been built up over the past fifteen years on the effects of goals and goal-setting on the behavior and productivity of organization members (for an extensive review see Latham and Yukl 1975). A good deal of this research has been based upon a theory of goals and goal-setting outlined by Locke (1968). The basic premise of Locke's theory is that the conscious goals and intentions of organization members have a direct impact upon task performance and productivity. More specifically, the theory argues that the process of setting performance goals will have a positive impact on performance to the extent that the goals are (1) difficult, (2) specific, and (3) accepted by the members of the organization. A number of studies have reported strong positive correlations between goal difficulty and productivity (e.g., Stedry and Kay 1966; Zander and Newcomb 1967), indicating that setting hard goals results in higher productivity than setting easy goals. Likewise, several studies (e.g., Latham and Baldes 1975) have found a stronger effect for specific goals (such as, "operate at 95 percent load capacity") on productivity than generalized or nonspecific goals (such as, "do your best"). Finally, goal acceptance has been shown to be a necessary precondition for goal-setting to have an impact on performance. Extremely difficult goals that are perceived as impossible to attain and hence are not accepted by organization members have been found to result in lowered productivity (Stedry and Kay 1966). Thus, the general trend of research evidence from a large number of field studies of productivity in organizations supports the general theory that setting specific goals that organization members perceive as difficult but possible to attain can result in improved productivity.

In addition to the evidence regarding the direct impact of goals on performance, there is also some theory and some confirmatory evidence indicating that goals may mediate the performance effects of feedback, monetary incentives, and participation in decisionmaking. Latham and Yukl (1975) speculate that feedback may result in increased effort and performance through any of four goal-related processes (1) by inducing the person who previously did not have specific goals to set specific goals, (2) by inducing the person to raise the goal level after attaining a previous goal, (3) by informing the person that their current effort level is insufficient for attaining goals, or (4) by informing the person of ways in which to improve methods of task performance. Feedback is also likely to result in improved performance when such knowledge confirms an individual's performance expectation. Such a confirmation is likely to increase self-confidence, which in turn results in higher goal aspirations for subsequent performance.

While feedback influences primarily the difficulty and specificity aspects of goals, monetary incentives and participatory decisionmaking have an impact on goal acceptance. Monetary incentives seem to result in improved performance and productivity by increasing the likelihood that difficult goals will be accepted if valued monetary rewards are made contingent on their attainment. Participatory decisionmaking has been shown consistently to result in higher levels of acceptance and understanding of decisions (House and Baetz 1979). To the extent that decisions set difficult and specific goals, permitting those affected to participate in setting them results in higher levels of acceptance and hence increased performance and productivity.

Goal-setting processes have been introduced into a wide variety of organizations in the form of "Management by Objectives" (MBO) programs. The term "management by objectives" was first coined by Drucker (1954), though the concept was more fully developed and explicated by Odiorne (1965). MBO programs are designed to encourage organization members to systematically set specific performance goals and to regularly review performance in relation to those goals. Such programs are a subject of substantial controversy. For positive reviews see Odiorne (1965) and Carroll and Tosi (1973); more negative opinions are expressed by Levinson (1970), Kerr (1975), and Jamieson (1973). An explanation for such a mixed acceptance may lie in the extent to which a specific MBO program adequately operationalizes the critical goal characteristics of difficulty, specificity, and acceptance. Simply having organization members set goals for themselves or their subordinates does not guarantee increased productivity. However, there is an accumulating body of evidence to indicate that MBO programs that encourage and train organization members to set specific and difficult goals, and that provide members with the skills required to involve those affected in the goal-setting process can result in increased levels of productivity.

Furthermore, there is some evidence that management practices that do not include goal-setting are not likely to have an effect on employee performance. For example, job enrichment without goal-setting has been shown to result in increased satisfaction but not increased performance. In contrast job enrichment coupled with goal-setting has been shown to increase both satisfaction and performance (Umstot, Bell and Mitchell 1976). Similarly, Ronan, Latham and Kinne (1973) have shown in two studies of determinants of productivity in the forest industry that on-the-job supervision, consisting of giving instructions and explanations, providing training, using varied methods of employee payment, and being physically present at the job site, was positively correlated with employee productivity only when such supervision was coupled with goal-setting. Such supervision without goal-setting was not related to productivity.

These studies together with the results of the research by Locke and his associates suggest that goal-setting may be a necessary concomitant for any management practice to result in increased performance.

STRUCTURES AS AN OUTCOME OF ORGANIZATIONAL DECISIONS[3]

One of the major innovations in organization theory over the last decade has been increasing (though yet not conclusive) evidence that the effectiveness of an organization is in some way related to the "fit" between (1) the structure of the organization, and (2) the characteristics of the organization's context (Woodward 1958; Burns and Stalker, 1961; Lawrence and Lorsch, 1967; Child 1972a, 1972b, 1972c). By organization structure we mean the structure of the relationships between groups of functions, physical factors, and personnel (Davis 1951: 795). These relationships primarily concern individual and subunit authority, responsibility, and accountability, and determine the manner in which tasks are grouped, the degree to which decisionmaking is centralized or decentralized, and the degree to which individual jobs are fragmented into simple tasks or integrated clusters of tasks. By organization context we mean (1) the number of employees (which for manufacturing organizations is usually associated with assets and volume), (2) its technology in terms of the degree to which the production process is automated, and (3) the degree of environmental certainty or uncertainty in the acquisition of inputs (human, financial, scientific, and material) and the disposition of outputs (market).

Prevailing theory (Thompson 1967) seeks to explain the concept of fit in the following manner. The theory sees organization design as primarily a function of the organization's environment and technologies, and deals with organizations that seek to coordinate their input, technological, and output activities so that they are economical—or at least instrumentally efficient.[4] Organizations are *economically* efficient when they produce desired outcomes with minimal expenditure of resources; they are *instrumentally* efficient when their activities do in fact produce desired outcomes.

While there are no absolute measures of economic or instrumental efficiency, many organizations are required by clients, regulators, owners, competitors, or other elements of their environment to strive for a relatively high level of efficiency. Organizations therefore strive to make their technological performance as efficient as possible. Technological efficiency is greatest under closed system conditions, where all demands and requirements are predictable and controllable. However, absolute control and predictability are seldom possible, for two reasons.

First, the organization's environment is constantly changing and the uncertainty that accompanies environmental change works against efficiency. Second, the technology is often poorly understood. That is, those who perform the activities required to produce organizational products and services frequently do so without complete knowledge about what activities can most efficiently be performed and how. Examples of such activities include research tasks, artistic tasks, and tasks that require judgment rather than application of known rules and principles.

Consequently, the theory asserts that the central problem of complex organizations is coping with uncertainty. Lack of complete knowledge about the technology means organizations operating even in relatively stable and predictable environments frequently face unpredictable problems. These problems cause uncertainty, and prevent the organization's technological core from operating in an economically efficient manner.

The theory is an elaborate one, and addresses many issues that will not be covered here. We take the liberty of summarizing the essential thrust of the theory in two major propositions.[5]

1. Organizations seek to control their environments. If control of the environments is not possible, organizations seek to adapt to the demands of the environments so as to meet the economic and instrumental efficiency criteria imposed by the environments. Specifically, organizations seek to control environments by increasing their power over environmental units, and seek to adapt to environments by monitoring environmental demands and by designing structures and practices to permit effective responses to such demands.

2. Organizations seek to adjust to the demands of their technological core to permit economical and efficient coordination and scheduling of interdependent parts.

Thus, this theory is primarily concerned with how organizations control their environments and adjust their structure to adapt to environmental or technological demands.

There is a substantial amount of evidence in support of the two propositions stated above. Pfeffer and others have shown that organizations attempt to remove uncertainty in the environment by tacitly incorporating parts of the environment into the organization itself. Research has shown this is accomplished in a number of ways:

1. Through cooptation (Selznick 1949). For example, interlocking directorates are developed to provide firms with financial or legal expertise when they are dependent on the environment for financing or subject to legal regulation (Pfeffer 1972a, 1973). However, see Allen (1974) for disconfirming evidence.

2. Through mergers. Pfeffer (1972b) has shown that where a high level

of interdependency exists between industries (as measured by joint input-output ratios) firms tend to merge across industry boundaries, especially when uncertainty is high. Pfeffer and Salancik (1978) argue that at intermediate levels of industry concentration there is greatest uncertainty in the environment. When the industry is concentrated among a few firms, some informal coordination (through, say, price leadership) reduces the uncertainty; when the industry has low concentration and approaches a state of perfect competition, the market response to any firm's activities are predictable. Consequently it is at the intermediate level that uncertainty for the individual firm is at its height.

3. Through joint ventures. Pfeffer and Nowack (1976) have shown that high interdependence between organizations in two industries were associated with a high number of joint ventures. Again the association was higher when concentration was at an intermediate level (highest uncertainty).

4. Through intra-industry transfer of personnel. Pfeffer and Leblebici (1973) argue that uncertainty is reduced by setting up an intra-firm communication structure among competitors. This is achieved by developing an executive group with shared norms and values and similar patterns of response to moves made by other firms in the industry. They argued that this would be indicated by a high proportion of intra-industry recruitment, many job changes, short tenure in the firm, and short tenure prior to becoming Chief Executive Officer. Pfeffer and Leblebici (1973) found that there was a weak curvilinear relationship for the major hypotheses linking industry concentration and outside recruitment from other firms in the same industry. However, the other hypotheses were more strongly supported, that is, high uncertainty led to a greater number of job changes, less time spent in a single company, and less time in a company before becoming CEO.

The practices identified by Pfeffer and his associates illustrate some of the ways organizations seek to control their environment. By having larger boards, organizations are able to attract more contacts with sources of financing. By selecting attorneys, organizations faced with legal regulations are better able both to control the impact of such regulations and to adapt to changes in such regulations. Finally, the practices of intra-industry mergers and executive exchanges help to stabilize interdependencies, and thus make the environment more manageable.

We are arguing here that by engaging in such environmental managing activities organizations are likely to enhance their chances of survival and economic success. However, such activities may permit organizations to make inefficient use of the social resources it consumes. These mechanisms may be alternatives to engaging in productive activity. This is one more example of the violation of the classical economic model.

Organizations also adjust their structure to adapt to the environment. To describe how organizations are structured to adapt to environmental and technological demands it is useful to classify organization structures according to the degree to which they are organic or mechanistic. Organizational structures can be described and classified as relatively mechanistic or organic on the basis of a set of continua. These continua are the degree to which relationships are formally and explicitly defined, performance requirements standardized, decisionmaking centralized, jobs repetitive performance of fragmentary tasks, authority conferred on the basis of rank and position, and, finally, coordination monitored and controlled hierarchically through the chain of command rather than laterally or through self-control.

To the extent that an organization is high on these continua it is classified as mechanistic. Examples of highly mechanistic organizations are commonly found in the military, in public utilities, in government organizations, and in industrial organizations operating in very stable and predictable environments.

An organization is classified as organic insofar as relationships are defined informally and implicitly through shared norms rather than policies, procedures, and rules, performance requirements are general and vary in response to changing demands rather than being standardized, decisionmaking is decentralized and jobs consist of nonrepetitive performance of integrated composites of related tasks, authority is based on expertise rather than on rank or position, and coordination takes place laterally through self-control and team efforts rather than hierarchically through supervision and a chain of command.

The work of Hall (1963) and Burns and Stalker (1961) strongly suggests that for an organization to be effective there should be a match between the structure of the organization and its environment. When the environment is uncertain and volatile, a more organic structure is appropriate since it allows the organization to scan its environment effectively and pass accurate information rapidly to its decentralized decisionmaking units. On the other hand, when the environment is relatively stable, a mechanistic structure is appropriate for the standard rules and procedures are based upon valid precedents and the environmental situation will be relatively unchanged by the time a decision is passed back down to the operating units.

However, organizational responses to technological uncertainty appear to be moderated by organization size. Early research on the effects of technological uncertainty on organizational structure (Woodward 1958) suggested that technological uncertainty required an organic structure for effective organizational performance. More recently, the Aston group (Hickson, Pugh, and Pheysey 1969; Child and Mansfield 1972) have shown that the Woodward findings only seem to hold when the organization is small or when the examination of structure is confined to the operating units of the organization. Combining these findings with those on the effects of environment on organizational structure, Child (1975), using cross-sectional analysis, has shown that overall, as organization size increases the amount of organizational formalization and specialization (mechanistic characteristics) also increase, and at a faster rate for effective than for ineffective organizations. However, this difference was accentuated when organizations faced stable environments and attenuated when organizations faced uncertain, volatile environments. Additional support for these differences was also found by Evans and McQuillan (1977) in a longitudinal study. Over time, with growth, the organization these authors studied showed an increase in formalization; but this was more evident in departments facing a stable environmental sector than in those facing volatile sectors. While formalization increases with size, some puzzling findings vis-a-vis centralization of decisionmaking have been observed. In general, as size increases, it has been found that decentralization increases. An important question is, do major policy decisions get decentralized? The answer seems to be no. As size increases, Evans and McQuillan (1977) found that policy decisions on types of market, pricing policy, and manpower policies remain centralized. However, operating decisions, which are constrained by the formal rules, become decentralized.

The preceding discussion implies that organizations face relatively homogenous environments so that the overall organization structure can be adapted to the degree of environmental uncertainty. Lawrence and Lorsch (1967) and Thompson (1967) have shown that this is not the whole story.

1. Organizations face a multiplicity of different subenvironments: customers and clients, suppliers of finance, materials, and labor (and managers), governement and laws (all levels), and subcultures.
2. Environments vary in the extent to which each element (or the whole aggregate of elements) is stable or changing.
3. Environments vary in the extent to which the elements are closely interconnected.

Organizations deal with these fragmented environments by task-function specialization. Thompson (1967) has argued theoretically that organizations create specialized units to deal with relatively homogeneous components of the overall environment. Lawrence and Lorsch (1967) take a more pragmatic view. They argue that the structuring of the organization and its specialized functional subunits (R&D, production, marketing) must reflect the nature of the environment. They conceive of the environment in terms of (1) the degree of variability within each subenvironment and the heterogeneity of variability between subenvironments (leading to structural differentiation between subunits so that each subunit's orientations and practices are designed to deal with the variability of the subenvironment), and (2) the degree of interdependence between subenvironments around the basic competitive issue, which should be reflected by the patterns of integration or coordination required within the whole organization.

In addition, the difficulty of integration and hence the number of integrating mechanisms required, that is, rules, hierarchy, liaison people or teams, and matrix structures, is a function of the level of differentiation in the organization. Where environments are heterogeneous in terms of variability, the subunits in effective organizations will be differentiated. High differentiation requires a large number of integration mechanisms. Where environments are homogeneous, subunits of effective organizations will be undifferentiated and few integration mechanisms will be necessary. Thus ineffective organizations may have either too much, too little, or inappropriate differentiation or integrating mechanisms.

In summary, in designing an organizational structure, the manager must consider four contingencies (1) the level of certainty or uncertainty in the environment, (2) the degree of homogeneity or heterogeneity in the environment, (3) the technology of the production systems in the organization, and (4) the size of the organization. Environmental uncertainty and unit or process production systems suggest the use of organic structure; environmental certainty and mass production procedures require the use of mechanistic structures. Heterogeneous subenvironments or production systems require complex integrative coordination systems. Large size requires the use of formalized but decentralized structures.

CONTROL AND REWARD SYSTEMS[6]

Of major importance to the quality of management decisionmaking and the behavior of organizational members is the exercise of management control. In addition to informal control through personal supervision, control is exercised through one or more formal systems. Control systems are used for management decisionmaking, planning, corrective action and for motivating organizational members. To be used effectively such control systems must produce valid information for decisionmakers and valid feedback for employees. In this section we will present conclusions drawn from organizational research concerning the characteristics of control systems and the organizational conditions that promote the generation of valid data and induce functional organizational behavior.

The literature on organizational control systems usually differentiates between externally imposed control and that generated internally by an individual. For both types of control to be effective, they must be based upon valid data. In this section we shall outline the conditions under which valid data can be generated and then go on to discuss internal and external control processes.

Data Validity: Control systems produce invalid data when valid data are difficult to collect or when organizational members are motivated to report invalid data. Several characteristics of the data partly determine whether they are likely to be valid when reported by organizational members. First, the more objective the data the less easy it is to be falsified. Data that are specific and concrete can be verified and therefore leave little room for falsification. If such data are also of sufficient importance that they significantly affect organizational performance, then any falsification and its source will eventually be identified. Consequently, data that meet the requirements of objectivity and organizational importance are less likely to be falsified than data that are subjective and unimportant. Another factor that determines the validity of data produced by control systems is the ease with which the required data can be gathered. Organizational members who are responsible for collecting and reporting the data must be able to do so without significant inconvenience to themselves or interference with other work they are expected to perform. Data that are not, or cannot, be collected by organizational members, or that they can only collect at significant personal cost, are likely not to be collected or to be replaced by unreliable estimates or, in some cases, by deliberately falsified information.

As discussed, there are a host of events in organizations that result in distortion and suppression of information. To the extent that these events occur in conjunction with the gathering of control system data, the data are likely to be invalid.

Extrinsic Control

Control systems are frequently used to induce extrinsic motivation—that is, motivation depending on anticipation of a desired reward or feared punishment. Lawler (1976) argues that control systems intended to induce extrinsically motivated behavior often induce bureaucratic behavior. Bureaucratic behavior is defined as behavior that is called for by the control system but is dysfunctional as far as the generally agreed upon goals of the organization are concerned. Such behavior occurs because individuals are usually motivated to report data and respond to control systems in ways that will reflect favorably on them, even when such behavior is dysfunctional to the organization.

Control systems can be effectively used for extrinsic motivation only when the control systems and the conditions under which they are administered meet a rather severe set of requirements. If these requirements are not met the control system is very likely to produce both invalid data and bureaucratic behavior. The requirements are:

1. The individual whose behavior is to be controlled values the rewards, views the punishments as aversive, and is not alienated by the system.

2. The behavior and the outcomes measured by the control system constitute all behavior and outcomes necessary and sufficient for effective performance. If the control system measures only some of the behavior and outcomes, individuals are likely to attend to those that are measured and neglect those that are not. For example, when individuals are measured in terms of quantity of production they tend to neglect quality aspects of their work and to attempt to maximize the amount of output produced.

3. The data are not easily falsifiable (see above).

4. The standards are seen as reasonable and attainable by those who will be evaluated against them. This is most likely to occur when those whose performance is measured have had an opportunity to influence the level at which the standards are set, or when the standard-setter is perceived as having a high degree of expertise and legitimacy. When these conditions are not met it is likely that individuals will falsify data, abuse equipment, and neglect non-measured but important activities.

5. Organizational goals are clear and are accepted by organizational members. When goals are unclear or not accepted individuals tend to suboptimize by focusing on personal or subunit goals.

6. Organizational members identify primarily with the larger organization rather than with their own organizational subunit. Primary identification with one's subunit constitutes a psychological force toward suboptimization because individuals who have primary identification with the subunit tend to perform in a manner that will make the subunit be evaluated positively by other members of the organization.

7. Organizational members have trust in the person administering the control system.

The above requirements for the effective use of control systems to induce extrinsic motivation are very constraining. Such systems are not likely to be useful except when jobs are highly structured and desired outcomes and behavior are objectively measurable and therefore specifiable in advance. Such jobs are most frequently found in mechanistic organizations and then only at the lower hierarchical levels.

Intrinsic Control

Control systems designed to induce intrinsic motivation are required when activities and outcomes to be controlled cannot be concretely specified in advance. Under such conditions the control systems need to be designed to facilitate self-control rather than control by others. While self-control and intrinsic motivation can be enhanced by control systems that meet the requirements stated above, they do not need the information completeness and unfalsifiability requirements. Information completeness and unfalsifiability, though desirable, are not required under conditions where people are intrinsically motivated. Intrinsically motivated individuals are more likely to attend to all aspects of the job required to do it well, and are less likely to falsify information because they themselves will be the primary users of such information.

If a control system is to be intrinsically motivating, the information it produces must meet five additional requirements. These are:

1. The information must be fed back directly to the individual whose behavior it measures. It is on the basis of such information that the individual controls his or her own behavior (rather than on the basis of directions from others).

2. The goals are perceived as challenging yet attainable with significant effort. Challenging, difficult goals are more intrinsically motivating then extremely easy or extremely difficult goals. Attainment of extremely easy goals is not a source of pride. Attainment of extremely difficult goals is usually viewed as so unlikely that they are not intrinsically motivating.

3. The measures used are seen as reasonably valid and objective. Data produced with the control system are used primarily for the purpose of feedback about performance. If the data are not viewed as reasonably valid and objective they are not likely to be used for corrective action.

4. The goals are valued in themselves rather than for their instrumentality for extrinsic rewards. For example, goal attainment may be valued because of pride in work or because such attainment is a source of feedback about the individual's competence.

5. Continued goal achievement is sustained by extrinsic rewards over the long run. That is, individuals who attain challenging goals out

of intrinsic motivation are rewarded over the long run by recognition, remuneration, and promotion.

The above conditions are most likely to occur when the organizational members are allowed to participate in and influence the design of the control system, the goals, the standards, and the data to be collected. As Lawler has pointed out, several organizational conditions

. . .that favor the establishment of an effective extrinsic reward system also favor the creation of self-control and intrinsic motivation. One obvious implication of this conclusion is that certain kinds of organizations simply are not in a position to effectively control the behavior of their members. Ironically, it is in those organizations that were developed to use external contol over the behavior of their members (that is, autocratically run bureaucracies) that find themselves unable to use control systems well. They were never designed to use self-control, and the external control which they were designed to use cannot operate without significant side effect (Lawler 1976:1284).

INDIVIDUAL PRODUCTIVITY: A SOCIAL LEARNING THEORY ANALYSIS[7]

Decisionmaking, organizing, goal-setting, controlling, and rewarding all affect the productivity of organizational members. The processes through which these practices affect individual productivity are largely psychological. In this section we attempt to explicate these psychological processes. The starting point of our discussion is the assumption that the motivation and performance of individual organization members are necessary, though not sufficient, conditions for organizational productivity. In line with the conceptual framework presented at the outset, our focus here will be primarily upon the ways in which management practices influence organizational members' motivation and ability to produce. Social Learning Theory (SLT) will be used to provide a theoretical basis for the analysis of such practices in terms of their implications for individual productivity. We now turn to a brief overview of the essential elements of Social Learning Theory (Bandura 1977).

Social Learning Theory: A Brief Overview

SLT asserts that individuals develop hypotheses about the relationship between their own behavior and future consequences on the basis of their experience and observations. To the extent that the hypotheses are correct their future performance will lead to expected results. Individuals are hypothesized to act on these hypotheses (expectations) when they perceive that they have the ability to behave in the manner required (efficacy expectations) and when they perceive that such behavior will result in the desired outcome (outcome expectations). These two kinds of expectations and their relationships among persons, behavior, and outcomes are diagramed in Figure 5-3.

SLT asserts that individuals learn behavior and choose to engage in it on the basis of their expectations and the value they place on the outcomes they expect. Outcomes can be divided into three components: (1) the intrinsic satisfaction one gains from engaging in particular behavior (the intrinsic valence of behavior, IV_b), (2) the intrinsic satisfaction one gains from successful accomplishment of goals, (the intrinsic valence of goal accomplishment, IV_a), and (3) the satisfaction one gains from the extrinsic rewards for engaging in behavior or accomplishing goals (the valence of extrinsic outcomes, EV).[8] These expectations and outcomes can be viewed as cognitions that represent the individual's generalizations about cause-effect contingencies in the environment. According to SLT such cognitions are formulated (learned) through two sets of processes: (1) response consequence processes and (2) modeling processes. In addition SLT asserts that motivation to engage in learned behavior results in part from response consequences and modeling but to a greater extent from a third process, the self-regulation process.

In the immediately following sections the process of learning from, and the motivational implications of, response consequences and modeling will be described. Then the motivational process of self-regulation will be outlined. Finally SLT will be used as a framework to analyze managerial practices as determinants of individual productivity in organization.

Learning by Response Consequences

Response consequences impart information and serve as motivators for future action. By experiencing different outcomes to their actions individuals develop hypotheses about which responses are most appropriate in various settings. This information serves as a guide for future action. "Accurate hypotheses give rise to successful performances, whereas erroneous ones lead to ineffective courses of action. Cognitions are thus selectively strengthened or disconfirmed by the differential consequences accompanying the more remotely occurring responses" (Bandura 1977: 18).

Response consequences perform a motivational function in that they create expectations that certain behavior or levels of performance will result in valued outcomes, avoidance of negatively valued outcomes, or no outcomes at all. To the extent that the outcomes that are cognitively associated with behavior are valued either positively or negatively by the individual they take on motivational force.

Figure 5 – 3
Diagrammatic Representation of the Difference
Between Efficacy Expectations and Outcome Expectations

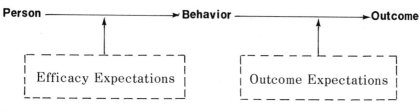

Source: Bandura (1977:79)

Learning Through Modeling

Learning through modeling (observational learning or learning through verbal instruction) is governed by four component processes. The first of these, the attentional process, determines what one selectively observes from modeling influences in environment. The individuals with whom observers deal, their interpersonal attraction, the salience and complexity of the behavior of models, the observational abilities of the observers, and their perceptual sets affect what features they abstract from observation and how they interpret what they see and hear.

The second component process involved in modeling concerns symbolic retention in memory of activities that have been observed. Observed activities are transformed into visual or verbal images that serve as guides to performance. This process is referred to as symbolic coding. In addition to symbolic coding either mental or motor rehearsal or actual performance of observed activities serve to enhance retention. Individual ability to represent events symbolically or verbally, frequency and number of repeated exposure to modeled behavior, and opportunity for rehearsal determine what will be retained in memory.

The third component of modeling involves the conversion of symbolic representation into appropriate behavior. This conversion process consists of imagining the behavior to be enacted, enactment, and refinement on the basis of informative feedback. This conversion process thus requires practice and refinement of behavior in response to feedback in order to achieve the desired response pattern.

The fourth process involved in observational learning is the motivational process. Information about response consequences obtained through observation is used to form both efficacy expectations and outcome expectations. These expectations, together with the value the individual places on outcomes serve to motivate the individual to engage in or avoid modeled behavior. Individuals model behavior they value and behavior they observe to be rewarded and avoid behavior that they disapprove of and behavior they observe to be not rewarded or punished. Thus the behavior of high status, expert, previously rewarded, and interpersonally attractive individuals is more frequently modeled by observers than the behavior of individuals who do not possess these characteristics.

Self-Regulation

Modeling and response consequences serve to guide learning and motivate individuals to engage in learned behavior. Self-regulation, the third process described by social learning theory, is primarily a motivational process concerned with maintaining behavior once it is learned. This process explains why behavior is commonly performed in the absence of immediate external reinforcement and in the absence of observation of such reinforcement for models. In the absence of immediate external reinforcement some behavior is maintained by anticipation of its consequences, but most is maintained by the process referred to by Bandura (1977) as self-regulation. This process is also called self-management or self-control. According to Thorsen and Mahoney

A person displays self-control when in the relative absence of immediate external contraints, he engages in behavior whose previous probability has been less than that of alternatively available behaviors (Thorsen and Mahoney 1974:12).

Self-regulation serves to support short-term activities that are directed toward long-term achievement under conditions where short-term activities are not reinforced by the immediate environment but long-run accomplishments are. Manz and Sims illustrate the process using a long distance runner as an example:

Imagine that this individual offers himself self-praise contingent upon each mile he runs during this training. Then, if he goes on to win a gold medal in a marathon, he has received an external consequence contingent on his performance. Self-praise served as an internal consequence and was part of the self-control process which helped to manage the training behavior. The winning of a gold medal was an external consequence resulting from the effective self-controlled training. It should serve to reinforce such self-controlling behavior in the future. In the absence of long-term external reinforcement for the self-controlling behavior, such behavior is not likely to be continued (Manz and Sims 1979:8).

Self-regulation consists of several subprocesses. These are:

1. Establishment of specific goals and subgoals. Motivation is maintained by anticipation of long-term goal achievement and assessment of progress in terms of subgoals. "Self-motivation is best maintained by explicit proximate subgoals that are instrumental in achieving larger future ones. Subgoals help to create present inducements for action, while subgoal attainments provide self-satisfactions that reinforce and sustain one's efforts along the way" (Bandura 1977:162). "Strength of self-inducement varies curvilinearly with level of discrepancy between standards and demonstrated competence: relatively easy goals are insufficiently challenging to arouse much interest, moderately difficult ones maintain high effort and produce satisfactions through subgoal achievements, while goals set well beyond one's reach are discouraging" (Bandura 1977:165).

2. Establishment of standards of performance regarding the quality, quantity, time, and expense criteria by which goal accomplishment is to be judged. Such standards specify the criteria for self-administration of reward.

3. Establishment of environmental conditions that serve to maintain intended behavior. This is accomplished in several ways. For example, individuals can in many instances select the environments in which they intend to work. Many individuals, over the long run, have substantial job mobility and if this is recognized can, through the process of careful search and trial and error, place themselves in jobs where stimulus patterns and reinforcements are consistent with their values and abilities. Further, once on a given job individuals can alter their environments physically (working in libraries or other secluded places, closing their office doors, rearranging their desks so as to minimize distractions) and socially (answering phone calls only at limited times, arranging to be in places where they will be visible to those who administer rewards, insuring their performance output is called to the attention of rewarders, informing others of their own values and expectations).

Individuals are also capable of cognitively transforming their environments to suit their purposes. For example, by focusing on selected aspects of the environment individuals can ignore otherwise distracting noise, noxious odors, or offensive visual images. Such selective attention significantly modifies the impact of stimuli on behavior (Mischel and Moore, 1973), and influences what can be learned and thus later ability to perform (Bandura 1971a, 1971b).

4. Self-control of thought processes. Individuals also maintain their behavior by controlling their thought processes. By imagining the rewards and punishments associated with effective and ineffective performance individuals are able to influence their own behavior in the same manner as when such rewards and punishments are externally

administered. "These covert activities serve to maintain goal-directed work until the performance matches or exceeds the person's terminal standards" (Mischel 1973: 274).

Thought processes can also be changed through administration of rewards and punishments to self, contingent on the kind of thoughts engaged in. "In this process, constructive lines of thought are enhanced by making self-reward contingent on their occurrence; trains of thought that are subjectively distressing or behaviorally disruptive, such as self-derogations, infuriating or vexation ruminations, obsessions, and hallucinations, are reduced by contingent self-punishment or supplanted by rewarding alternative cognitive activities" (Bandura 1977:180).

5. Provision for evaluation of the adequacy of behavior. One can consciously choose to regularly obtain information with respect to quality, quantity, time, and expense parameters of performance, or to ignore such information. This information serves as a basis for comparing performance with established goals. Such comparisons serve both on informational and motivational function. They inform individuals of the appropriateness of their behavior and allow them to administer rewards and punishments to themselves contingent upon accomplishment of previously established goals.

Individuals differ in degree to which they provide and use information in the environment for feedback purposes. Some individuals seek out information that can be used for feedback purposes but that is not readily apparent to others. Some individuals also construct information-gathering systems for feedback and control charts in order to ensure that feedback information is tabulated so as to evaluate performance against pre-established goals. Thus, individuals can transform their environments by selectively attending to data that can be used as feedback information.

6. Self-reinforcement contingent on goal accomplishment. Self-reinforcement takes the form of either self-evaluative reactions or tangible self-administered rewards and punishments. Self-reactions include feelings of pride or shame over one's performance, satisfaction or guilt, self-praise or criticism. Tangible rewards or punishments vary widely in form, depending on the individual's preferences and resources. One can reward oneself by taking a break, performing an enjoyable activity, or purchasing or consuming a desired commodity. One can punish oneself by working extra hours, performing an unenjoyable act, or denying oneself desired food or commodities.

A Social Learning Theory Analysis of Management Practices and Productivity

The analytic scheme described by Social Learning Theory provides the principles by which management practices relevant to individual productivity can be analyzed. To illustrate, let us consider an organization to be a set of roles for a group of individuals whose behavior jointly results in the accomplishment of goals they could not accomplish individually.[9] Following Vroom (1964) we consider each role as consisting of a set of one or more functions to be performed by the individual. As Vroom states:

These functions represent effects which the role occupant is expected to produce on his (work) environment and they represent the basis for inferring the effectiveness of his performance.

In the context of his role, the role occupant is exposed to a variety of situations, S_1 S_2 . . . S_n, each possessing different stimulus properties. To each stimulus pattern there are one or more *functional* responses that can be made by the role occupant, i.e., responses which produce the required effects on the environment. The specific responses that are functional often vary from one stimulus pattern to another, i.e., S_1 calls for R_1, R_2, etc. . . . by definition, the more consistently the role occupant performs responses functionally appropriate to the stimulus the more effective his performance (Vroom 1964: 73).

In terms of productivity we are interested in arranging the environment of the role incumbent in such a manner that its stimulus properties will be reflected in effective role performance.

Viewed in this manner, one aspect of the problem of understanding the determinants of productivity within an organization concerns how environmental conditions can be established that cause members to learn and be motivated to perform functional responses to various patters of stimulation, that is, R_1 to S_1, R_2 to S_2, and so on. A second aspect of the problem concerns when it is more useful to encourage individuals to engage in self-regulation rather than rely on environmental influences to guide their behavior.

Concerning the first aspect of the problem, establishing organization conditions that cause members to learn and be motivated to perform functional responses, SLT suggests several tentative guidelines that can be applied to the design of management practices in order to induce functional role behavior and productive performance on the part of organizational members. From the SLT perspective, management practices (goal-setting, organization structure, control and reward systems, etc.) would be predicted to result in productive behavior to the extent that such practices generate high efficacy expectations and high outcome expectations associated with functional role behavior for individual organization members. Our two tentative guidelines hence focus upon the impact of management practices on these expectations.

Guideline 1: Efficacy Expectations

Management practices should induce individuals to form expectations that they are capable of engaging in functional role performance.

Our review of SLT would indicate that efficacy expectations can be influenced primarily by modeling processes. Hence, Guideline 1 has the following corollary implications for the design of management practices:

C1.1—Behavioral Modeling
Management practices should permit individuals to observe the behavior of others that is appropriate to effective role performance.
C1.2—Verbal Modeling
Management practices should convey to individuals the information necessary for them to form correct hypotheses concerning what behavior is appropriate in their role (i.e. functional role behavior).
SLT also implies the need for the design of management practices to take into account the need to induce individuals to attend to the information provided via modeling in the face of competing information with which they are confronted.

Guideline 2: Outcome Expectations

Management practices should induce individuals to form expectations that functional role behavior will be enjoyable in itself (IV_b), result in the accomplishment of work goals that are valued (IV_a), and result in the attainment of desired extrinsic rewards such as pay, promotion, recognition, etc. (EV).

Outcome expectations can be influenced both via modeling and via regulation or response consequences. Hence, the following corollary implications of Guideline 2 are stated:

C2.1—Behavioral Modeling
Management practices should permit individuals to observe that functional role behavior is rewarded by the organization.
C2.2—Verbal Modeling
Management practices should convey to individuals accurate and complete information regarding outcomes contingent upon functional role behavior.
C2.3—Response Consequences
Management practices should be designed such that:

a) individuals obtain positively valued intrinsic (IV_b and IV_a) and extrinsic (EV) outcomes contingent upon functional role behavior.
b) individuals are not punished for testing the accuracy of their behavior hypotheses.
c) individuals obtain nonthreatening feedback in order to refine their behavior.
d) individuals obtain positively valued outcomes for engaging in preliminary practice (rehearsal) of functional role behavior.

The second issue about which we should provide guidance concerns when self-regulation by subordinates should be encouraged. When environmental demands are stable and predictable and task technology is well understood, it is a relatively straightforward task to design management practices consistent with the above guidelines. However, when environmental demands are unstable and uncertain and technology is poorly understood, such management practices are extremely difficult to design. Under these latter conditions organizational members are likely to learn and be motivated on the basis of the unique expectations and values that they bring to the situation, and the uncontrolled and unpredictable aspects of the environment to which they are exposed. Thus, under conditions of contextual uncertainty, behavior of organizational members is ordinarily likely to be uncontrolled, uncoordinated, and unpredictable. Furthermore, the use of conventional management practices is not likely to be effective in remedying this situation because such practices cannot be designed to meet the requirements suggested by SLT in the above guidelines. How then can this dilemma be resolved? SLT suggests an answer—coordinated self-regulation within the context of organic management practices.

As we have shown, conditions of contextual uncertainty call for organic management practices. However, in addition to organic structuring, management practices that model, develop, and reward self-regulation are also needed. Under such conditions the management practices can be predicted to induce productive performance on the part of organizational members to the extent that self-regulated behavior is encouraged and coordinated with the pursuit of organizational goals.

There are several reasons why self-regulated behavior, when adequately coordinated, will result in effective performance. Self-regulation serves as a "substitute" for management. It maintains behavior without the support or control of immediate supervision. Successful accomplishment through self-regulation is more satisfying to individuals because it enables them to take credit for their own success rather than attribute their successes to others. It permits individuals to make immediate use of feedback rather than rely on others as intervening transmitters of feedback. Furthermore, it permits individuals to select the information that is most meaningful and acceptable to them from feedback. To the extent that feedback is accurate, corrective action based on relf-regulation is likely to be more timely and less costly. Finally, self-regulation generally results in higher performance. "Those who influence their own behavior by contingent self-reward attain higher levels of performance than those who perform the same activity but receive no reinforcement, or are rewarded noncontingently, or observe their own behavior and set goals but do not self-reward their successful efforts" (Bandura 1977: 144).

We suggest that encouragement of self-regulation by managers through modeling and instruction should improve organizational performance of subordinates when such performance is difficult to control externally. Peformance is often difficult to control externally because the immediately relevant information necessary to administer contingent rewards and punishments is likely to reside in the heads of the people doing the work and not to be accessible to their superiors. When roles of organizational members require them to assume personal responsibility for goal formulation and attainment, take independent initiative, function autonomously with little guideance or control from superiors, respond to crises or rapidly changing and unpredictable environmental stimuli, and create and use their own feedback self-regulated performance is likely to be more effective than performance controlled externally by superiors or by organizational policies. Thus, entrepreneurial roles, service roles, sales roles, and roles requiring significant analytical mental operations are likely to be best performed by individuals who actively self-regulate their behavior.

Management practices can be predicted to induce productive self-regulated performance to the extent that the following questions about such practices are answered in the affirmative:

1. To what extent are the overall goals of the organization and the organizational subunit communicated to organizational members? Such goals are important to induce individuals to engage in self-regulation because without knowledge of organizational goals individuals cannot intelligently establish subgoals for themselves consistent with the organization's goals.

2. To what extent is long-range goal achievement reviewed and rewarded by the organization? Self-regulation is maintained by the instrumentality of subgoal achievement to longer range goal achievement. Long-range goals need to be reviewed and rewarded to coordinate goal achievement among individuals and subunits and to maintain the motivational value of subgoal achievement.

3. To what extent are the performance standards that individuals use to measure their achievement consistent with organizational criteria of productivity? Without some assurance of consistency

between performance standards and organizational criteria individuals are likely to suboptimize in the interest of their own goals and at the expense of the organization's goals.

4. To what extent are individuals allowed the freedom necessary to establish the environmental conditions required to maintain intended behavior and to administer self-reinforcements contingent on goal accomplishment? Such freedom would require individuals to have substantial control over when and where they work, when they take breaks, and the schedule by which they complete specific tasks.

5. To what extent is information made available to individuals so that they can evaluate their own performance without reliance on formalized control and feedback systems? Are individuals free to request information they perceive as useful in evaluating their own performance? Is there agreement between individuals and higher level managers concerning the appropriate use of such information?

6. To what extent do higher level managers encourage self-regulated behavior on the part of organizational members by instruction and modeling?

7. To what extent is the degree to which an individual engages in self-regulated behavior used as a criterion for approval, salary increases, promotion, and other tangible rewards administered by the organization?

CONCLUSION

In this chapter we have attempted to explain some of the major intraorganizational determinants of productivity from a psychological perspective. In so doing we intended to explain some of the *residual* or unexplained variance in productivity over and above the *common* or shared variance ordinarily explained by microeconomic theories. This residual variance occurs because of factors that are unique to indiviual firms. We have argued that some of the factors that are unique to any firm are its decisionmaking processes and management practices. An understanding of these processes and practices and their effects thus leads to an understanding of part of the residual variance in individual firm productivity.

The management practices we chose to analyze in this chapter, goal setting, organizational design, control and reward systems, decision processes, and their impact on individual motivation were selected because there is sufficient theory and empirical evidence about them to permit rather definitive conclusions to be drawn. Behavioral scientists have also studied other management practices and psychological phenomena that have implications for firm productivity. Some of these are: job-task design, leadership, selection, compensation, development, and inter-and intragroup conflict. A select set of these practices and phenomena could serve equally well as the content of a monograph or book addressed to the psychological determinants of productivity. Our purpose in selecting the practices we did select was to illustrate how a psychological perspective might provide additional insights to those provided by economists. Hopefully, we have accomplished this goal.

COMMENT
John Kervin

Chapter 5 represents a significant departure from the main thrust of this volume, which concerns macro-level factors that influence productivity growth at national, sector, and industry levels. Arnold and his colleagues are interested in the firm—in particular how decisionmaking at the level of the firm affects productivity. They begin by discussing the concept of the firm, and explain how an organizational behavior approach asks different questions and makes use of different explanatory variables from the traditional microeconomic analysis. They also suggest that an organizational behavior approach may provide economists with new understanding of the determinants of a firm's productivity.

In undertaking this goal—providing new insights for economists—they cut a very broad path. The chapter includes a lengthy treatment of theories of decisionmaking in organizations. Then three particular areas of managerial decisionmaking are examined for their potential effects on the productivity of the firm: structuring the organization and its work, controlling and rewarding the activities of employees, and setting goals for individuals and subunits of the organization. Finally, the chapter concentrates on questions of productivity at the individual (as opposed to firm) level in a section examining motivational methods from the point of view of social learning theory.

Faced with such a broad range of topics and not many pages, I am going to limit my comments to two areas: (1) the relationship of organizational decisionmaking to the general problem of lagging productivity growth, and (2) the relationship between organizational decisionmaking and productivity within the firm.

While it is clear that organizational decisionmaking is intimately related to productivity through a number of mechanisms, including the three discussed in this chapter, it is not clear that it is related to the current problem of lagging productivity growth. The difference is between the micro and the macro point of view. Any of a number of changes in a firm's decisionmaking practices might be expected to increase its productivity, for example, initiation of specific decisions about performance goals for a given subunit of an organization. A decrease in this kind of decisionmaking activity would tend to result in a decline in that organization's productivity. However, there is no evidence of a *general* trend of this nature that would account for an overall decline in productivity growth in any industry, sector, or nation. We do not see that fewer shared decisions about goal-setting are being made generally, or that organizational decisionmaking is resulting in structures that are less responsive to environment and technology, or that organizational decisions about rewards and control are being based on increasingly invalid data. In short, decisionmaking within organizations themselves does not seem to account for lagging productivity growth. (Chapter 5 does, however, refer to analysts, for example, Emery and Trist (1965), who believe that changes in the environment are adversely affecting the quality of management decisions. Such changes could conceivably be related to declining productivity growth.) As a result, it appears that we cannot look to factors of this kind for policy recommendations that get to the causes of the current trend.

But this conclusion does not mean that attention to organizational decisionmaking is irrelevant to our interests. Even though the causes of lagging productivity growth may not lie in this area, the chapter implicitly suggests that effective ways of countering decline in productivity growth can be found in organizational decisionmaking. In other words, in the absence of a cure we can treat the symptoms. If we can improve the quality of the decisions managers make, we can counteract to some extent our productivity problems.

To pursue a course of action along these lines we need the answers to several questions. First, what kinds of decisionmaking practices should firms and managers be following in order to increase productivity? Second, what are the current decisionmaking practices compared to the known optimum? And third, how can we bring about improvements in management decisionmaking that will have maximum impact on productivity?

To answer the first question, we need to build on the already considerable literature on managerial decisionmaking in two ways. First, more theoretical and empirical work is needed to tie decisionmaking explicitly to productivity. At present, most studies speak of decisionmaking "effectiveness" which is either left vague or defined in ways not directly relevant to productivity (e.g., return on investment). Second, since much of the existing work deals with the *structure* of decisionmaking (e.g., where in the organization decisions are made—Burns and Stalker, 1961; Woodward, 1958), further attention should now be paid to the *processes* of decisionmaking and their relation to productivity.

A large part of Chapter 5 deals with the cognitive dimension of the decisionmaking process in the discussion of the work of Simon (1976a, 1976b), Janis and Mann (1977), and others on the problems of rationality in decisionmaking. This work seems to apply more to individual decisionmakers than to those in an organizational context. However, the model of a single decisionmaker is rarely valid with respect to organizations. The organizational decisionmaker must take into account not only the goals of the firm, but also his own, and those of other individuals and subunits within the firm since their motivation is important to the organization's functioning. In addition, the decisionmaking process itself may be carried out by a group or committee that will vary in the extent to which decisions are made or affected by the group leader. For these reasons the work on decisionmaking processes has focused on the social aspects and the cognitive aspects. The chapter devotes less attention to social aspects of the process but does deal briefly with goal consensus in organizations and information-filtering by individuals and subunits whose interests are involved. It seems to me, however, that in dealing with productivity the social aspect is not only more important than the cognitive, but more likely to lead to workable prescriptions for organizational decisionmaking to improve productivity. I will have more to say about this below, but for now let us examine the remaining two questions for which answers are needed if we are to undertake decisionmaking improvements to counter lagging productivity growth.

The current state of management decisionmaking is a topic of considerable interest in management journals, and numerous studies and surveys have been carried out to assess how well management is "managing." Unfortunately, very little of this is tied to satisfactory measures of productivity. Thus while we may have some intuitive feeling for what constitutes good and bad decisionmaking in a given firm, we have little in the way of systematic evidence to show how different processes of decisionmaking directly affect productivity in different situations, and we cannot be sure that we are even measuring decisionmaking itself in relevant ways. As a result, following the theoretical and empirical work linking decisionmaking and productivity, we are in need of much better survey data to determine the nature of management decisionmaking these days, and whether structures and processes of decisionmaking are appropriate to the technology and other characteristics of the firm.

Armed with the answer to that question, we might then turn to the third: how can we make improvements in organizational decisionmaking so as to maximize productivity? Once we know what works best, and what is presently being done, we will be in a position to narrow the gap by establishing training programs for decisionmaking. The easiest place to apply the results of decisionmaking research would be in business schools. However, such an approach not only misses the crucial population—current management—but ignores the socializing effect that organizations have in "overcoming" the business school training of recent recruits to management ranks. As a result, attention will have to be paid to ways of encouraging decisionmaking processes that maximize productivity among those who are currently making organizational decisions. I do not expect this to be an easy task; human beings can become as married to means as to ends. A change in the decisionmaking process is a major change of means, and it will take more than guarantees of greater productivity to bring about that change. But the attempt must be made if management practices are to counteract the effects of lagging productivity growth.

To summarize, the implications to be drawn from Chapter 5 with respect to lagging productivity growth focus on responses to the problem rather than analyses of its causes. These responses culminate in training programs that, guided by sufficient theoretical and empirical work, attempt to bring about management decisionmaking appropriate to the nature and context of the firm.

The second topic I want to discuss is the link between productivity of the firm on the one hand and the social aspect of organizational decisionmaking on the other. This chapter leads me to believe that a reconceptualization of this link could have a number of benefits: refinement of existing organization theory, fruitful hypotheses about the productivity of firms, and useful prescriptions for improving productivity. What I want to do in the rest of this brief commentary is to suggest a direction for the task of rethinking this link between productivity and decisionmaking.

Chapter 5 discusses the three predominant approaches to organizational decisionmaking. They are the structural approach—best described by the "organic-mechanistic" distinction of Burns and Stalker (1961)—the cognitive approach—for example, Simon's (1976) "satisficing" as an alternative to rational models of decisionmaking, and the social approach—of which Vroom's (1974) work on participation in decisionmaking is a good example. These approaches all offer different explanations for lower productivity. In the structural model, decisionmaking structures may not match production technologies. In the cognitive model, decisions may be made without sufficient knowledge of alternatives and implications. In the social model, conflict among the parties to a decision may result in actions that are not optimal for productivity.

If we want to examine the ways social conflict in decisionmaking is related to productivity, it seems reasonable to begin by redefining productivity in terms that are congruent with our approach, that is, the social aspect. The most commonly accepted definition of productivity is "output per unit input." However, as well as producing the products or services for which they were established, organizations also give rise to a number of intangible *social outputs;* for example, the job satisfaction of individual employees, the reputations of up-and-coming junior executives, or the vengeance one department supervisor takes on another for some unredressed wrong of the past. These social outputs can be roughly grouped into three categories based on their relation to the firm's product or service production. Positive social outputs will augment the product-service output of the organization. For example, a production manager may reorganize his department to enhance his own reputation for innovativeness in the firm. Negative outputs will decrease the product-service output. An example is the department head who withholds vital information from a meeting so that a decision that might adversely affect his department's autonomy will not be made. Neutral social outputs will be unrelated to the firm's product-service output. It is clear that the greater the proportion of negative social output, the more adverse the consequences for a firm's productivity.

Having defined productivity in social terms (that is, the feelings and actions that comprise social outputs arise from social-emotional interactions), we can now link it to organizational decisionmaking. This linkage is achieved by considering as social outputs the consequences of goals held by individuals and subunits of the organization. Such goals were implied in the examples used above. It is important to note, however, that goals themselves are not necessarily congruent or incongruent with the firm's product-service objectives. The key is the social output that results from a goal. A single goal may result in a number of potential social outputs, only some of which might hinder the goals of the larger organization. For example, the production manager mentioned above is interested in enhancing his own reputation. In this case, this goal results in social output congruent with the organization's goals. On the other hand, a sales manager with the same goal might strive to increase sales but reach the point where the firm cannot keep its commitments, and its reputation and future sales suffer as a result. The department head whose concern is his department's autonomy has a goal that leads to action incongruent with the organization's product-service goals.

In any organizational decisionmaking situation, we can be sure that a number of goals are present as hidden agenda items (if they are not already made explicit!). These are the goals of the individuals and subunits involved in or affected by the decision. The decision to be made will have both product-service and social output consequences. We can therefore classify the decision in two ways—as to whether or not it satisfies the individual and subunit goals, and as to whether or not the resulting social outputs of the decision are congruent with the firm's product-service goals. (Both of these are, of course, actually matters of degree. The dichotomies are used here for the sake of simplicity.) The result is a four-part design of organizational decisionmaking consequences shown in Figure 5-4.

Figure 5—4

Consequences of Organizational Decisionmaking

Social Outputs

		Congruent	Incongruent
Individual and Sub-Unit Goals	**Satisfied**	High Morale and Productivity	Productivity Declines
	Not Satisfied	Morale Declines	Morale and Productivity Decline

If individual or subunit goals are satisfied and the social outputs of the decision are congruent with the firm's product-service output, then an optimal decision has been made. On the other hand, if goals are not satisfied and the social outputs are incongruent, then both morale (because of unsatisfied goals) and productivity (because of negative social output) decline. The other diagonal represents the two intermediate cases.

This simple model of goals and outputs, even in its present state of underdevelopment, suggests a number of interesting implications. For example, it helps explain why high morale and high productivity are not necessarily related. As many studies of work groups have shown, these groups may make decisions (such as holding production rates at a certain level) that increase the morale of the group, but work against the larger productivity goals of the company.

The model also suggests that good decisionmaking involves taking into account individual and subunit goals and finding decisions that will satisfy those goals as well as lead to positive rather than negative social output. Such a view also suggests some of the techniques by which optimal decisionmaking is achieved. Bargaining is one; some goals are traded off with others. Another is influence; some people are persuaded to assign lower priority to some of their own goals.

Another implication worth exploring is the degree of "sharing" of decisionmaking power. Vroom (1974) distinguishes among autocratic, consultative, and group models of decisionmaking, all of which have different implications for the satisfaction of individual and subunit goals and the congruence of social and product-service outputs.

One of the most interesting implications of this particular model is that collective bargaining between union and management can be seen as decisionmaking in which parties to the decision have individual and subunit goals. This is not only true of union and management bargaining across the table, but also of the decisionmaking about priorities, sanctions, concessions, strategy, and tactics that takes place within each negotiating team. Effective bargaining results in a decision (the collective agreement) that maximizes the congruence of social outputs and product-service outputs, and that maximizes the goal satisfaction of individual negotiators and the units they represent.

The issue of industrial democracy and worker participation in decisionmaking is certainly relevant to this conceptualization of productivity and decisionmaking. The introduction of workers to the boardroom means that additional, and potentially more conflicting, interests are interjected into the immediate decisionmaking situation. Certainly this has been a major concern of many who oppose moving in the direction of industrial democracy. Its proponents argue that it is better to have such conflicting interests involved right from the start rather than to encounter their negative social outputs after a decision has been made.

Finally, this model of decisionmaking brings us back to our initial topic—lagging productivity growth. Using this model we can speculate how social changes in the environment of the firm may have led to less productive decisionmaking. It is safe to say that in the last decade or two we have witnessed in North America and in the western industrialized world generally a rise in alternative concerns and lifestyles. The importance of leisure, the protection of the environment, greater emphasis on time with friends and family, and a growing distrust of the purely achievement orientation—all represent other goals that individuals bring with them into the work-place. Some refer to this phenomenon as the decline of the work ethic, but I think it is more fruitfully seen as the rise of other competing ethics. As these goals are brought into the decisionmaking situation, the individuals involved have a broader range of goals to be satisfied, and thus congruence of social outputs with the firm's product-service outputs is more difficult to achieve. As these other interests become more pervasive, productivity increases are increasingly harder to attain. The result is increasing difficulty in maintaining the previous patterns of productivity growth.

In summary, my comment briefly posits a linkage between social aspects of organizational decisionmaking and productivity. This linkage also suggests, in a speculative way, how decisionmaking affects productivity growth—not through changes internal to the decisionmaking process in firms, but in ways in which the social environment affects the nature and quality of those decisions.

COMMENT
Shlomo Maital

Hugh Arnold, Martin Evans, and Robert House (henceforth, AEH) have provided us with an exceptionally useful and informative road map of those areas of organization behavior that relate to productivity. In our efforts to deal with what Albert Rees has termed "the great productivity lag"—to collar the culprits, and construct some cures—their chapter will hopefully break down some of the suspicion with which economics regards other social and behavioral sciences, even those with which it maintains uneasy diplomatic relations. In responding to the challenge Noah Meltz and I placed before them, AEH have undertaken the formidable task of learning the terminology, assumptions, theories, and methods of economics, and have reviewed for us, in a lucid and understandable way, those parts of the literature of individual psychology that impinge upon economic efficiency.

Past and Future:　AEH define the focus of organizational behavior as "processes (of transforming inputs into outputs) within firms, how these processes are carried out, how they are organized, and how differences in intrafirm organizations are related to interfirm differences in effectiveness and productivity." There are strong reasons for believing that such processes have had a great deal to do with productivity growth in the past, and will become even more important in the future.

John Kendrick has reminded us that "informal incentive and innovative activity, including the myriad small technological improvements devised by plant managers and workers, was the chief source of technological progress in the nineteenth century, and is still significant". What work climate must be created to restore these individualistic productivity gains to their rightful prominence? AEH offer some useful prescriptions.

Recent U.S. Department of Labor projections indicate that the fastest growing sectors with regard to employment will be the service sector, particularly private medical care and business services. By 1990 two workers in every nine will be employed in services, compared with about one in every eight during the late 1950s. As work becomes increasingly white-collar in nature, the attitudes, perceptions, and feelings of workers and managers will necessarily become a central consideration.

Information, Incentives, Structure: Despite its length, Chapter 5 is in fact quite terse, ignoring (for lack of space) such major areas as job-task design, leadership, selection, compensation, development, and inter- and intragroup conflict. AEH begin by examining the decisionmaking process and the use of information in that process. They list seven major criteria for vigilant information processing, including taking into account unfavorable information and examining the consequences of decisions, and list ways in which to minimize the distortion, suppression, and deficiency of information.

In discussing goals and goal-setting, they examine the structure of organizations in an uncertain environment, comparing "organic" and "mechanistic" structures and arguing that technological uncertainty requires "organic" structure. After drawing a distinction between extrinsic and intrinsic motivation, they state the requirements for effective use of control systems to induce desirable, extrinsically motivated behavior (rewarding quality as well as quantity, making sure that goals are clear and accepted, and insuring that the individual values the rewards he is being offered, among others).

Next, AEH turn to social learning theory—which posits that people's choices depend on their expectations regarding the outcomes, and the value of those outcomes to them—and use it to study managerial practices and their effect on individual productivity. In particular, they examine in detail "modeling", or observational learning, which is useful in inducing individuals to believe that they can perform well.

Much labor is self-regulated in nature. AEH conclude by presenting a list of questions regarding productive self-regulated performance, with affirmative answers indicating efficient practices. These questions relate to communication of goals to members, rewarding achievement of goals, and provision of adequate information.

Every page emanates solid common sense. I would expect that the reaction of many nonpsychologists will be that AEH belabor the obvious. Of course workers must be rewarded for functional behavior and goal achievement. Of course they require understandable, relevant information. Of course the presence of admired, constructive role models is helpful. One might respond that there are two kinds of "obvious" facts—those that are right and those that are wrong. All of the prescriptions AEH cite have been most carefully researched and shown to be empirically valid.

The Economics of Behavior: In fairness to economics, there is an "organizational behavior" literature within conventional economic theory. To cite just a few references: Marshak and Radner have devised a theory of "teams"; Hirschman's theory of voice, exit, and loyalty discusses the three options available to an individual operating within an organization; Beckman has written on optimal hierarchical structure; Reiter has studied the role of information processing in the theory of the firm; and Mirless has analyzed optimal reward structures. This body of work highlights what I believe is the major difference between economics and psychology—not *what* each discipline studies (recall that Lionel Robbins' now standard definition of economics calls it "the science which studies human *behavior* . . .") but *how.* The vast majority of AEH's references contain empirical findings that test directly hypotheses about individual or group behavior. The economics literature cited above is predominantly theoretical and mathematical, bursting with untested hypotheses and conjectures.

Have Management Practices Deteriorated? AEH do not, of course, attempt an organizational behavior explanation of lagging productivity growth. To do so would require both (1) a clear statement of what effective managerial practices are, and (2) a demonstration that such practices are less adhered to in recent years. AEH attempt (1) but not (2). It would be interesting to canvass top-flight managers themselves and pose the question of whether less able management has something to do with the productivity slump. Meanwhile, it is fascinating to speculate about the role of organizational behavior in understanding what Donald Daly has described as "the greater gap between actual practice and best practice technology in Canada, compared with the United States", and, perhaps even between the United States and Japan. Professor Daly finds it "hard to imagine a more difficult task than trying to pick the winners among Canadian companies," a sentiment most stockholders would no doubt share. Can AEH's criteria for effective organizations help us pick winners *ex post,* or even better, help develop ones *ex ante?*

X-Efficiency: Despite AEH's best efforts, the seam along which organization behavior and economics is welded remains a rough one. Economics seeks aggregate relationships among labor, technology, intermediate inputs, capital, and physical outputs for whole economies, large or small sectors, and sometimes individual firms. Organizational behavior experts focus on organization effectiveness and study "the degree of fit among the environment, the management practices and member preferences." As AEH suggest, organizational behavior seeks to understand the unexplained variance between conventional inputs and outputs, while economics focuses on the shared variance. Harvey Leibenstein, in a *Fortune* interview, has suggested that the unexplained variance is perhaps larger than we might have thought, estimating that the amount of slack in the average firm (the gap between actual and maximal output for given inputs) is about 20 percent. This "X-inefficiency," as he terms it, is the very mortar from which organizational psychologists make their bricks. It stems from the indisputable fact that wage-earners hold "incomplete" contracts, in that they are told what payment they are to receive, but not how much effective effort they are to put forth. Once effort, rather than labor hours, becomes our focus, the path to the literature of organizational psychology becomes much more inviting.

If it is indeed true that "productivity depends on how work is organized and on the motivational elements within the work place," as Leibenstein argues, then words like motivation, organization, reward, structure, incentive, self-regulation, and autonomy must find their way into the economist's working vocabulary. Toward this end, AEH have made a splendid start.

Notes to Chapter 5

1. See Edwards (1954) for a review.
2. See Latham and Yukl (1975) for a review of this evidence.
3. his section is drawn largely from Filley, House, and Kerr (1976).
4. Not all organizations seek such efficiency. Some family-owned business, for example, place higher value on family control than on their instrumental performance. Other organizations, such as political parties and churches, are primarily concerned with preserving and disseminating certain moral convictions.
5. While these propositions are consistent with the theory, they hardly do justice to the precision with which the theory deals with the specific sources of uncertainty. For a detailed appreciation of the theory, consult the original work.
6. This section draws heavily from Lawler (1976) and Lawler and Rhode (1976).
7. This section is based primarily on Bandura (1977) and Mischel (1973).
8. This division of outcomes into IV_a, IV_b and EV is based on House (1971).
9. The use of roles as the unit of analysis for understanding performance effectiveness, or productivity, of individuals within organizations was originally suggested by Vroom (1964).

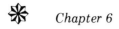 *Chapter 6*

X-Efficiency, Intrafirm
Behavior, And Growth

Harvey Leibenstein

INTRODUCTION

In the usual analysis of growth there are frequently two types of considerations: the growth of inputs, and the introduction of innovations. In this chapter we will focus on a third aspect of the problem, one that is normally ignored. We shall focus on the utilization of inputs, and on the relation between input utilization and innovation. While the main emphasis will be on the determination of the quantitative and qualitative aspects of effort in the production process, we shall argue that these elements are very much related not only to the utilization of all inputs, but also to the motivational environment that determines the introduction of innovations.

Our approach will be somewhat roundabout. To start with we will present (1) a different approach to the microeconomic process (i.e., X-efficiency theory), (2) the argument that a free rider problem exists in production and hence a well defined production function is lacking, (3) that variability in effort leads to variability in the utilization of inputs (which in turn implies variable growth rates with constant saving rates and constant purchased inputs), and (4) we will stress that the motivational environment both inside and outside the firm must be looked at as sources of growth.

DISCRETION, FREE RIDERS, AND THE PRODUCTION FUNCTION

In my recent work, I have attempted to develop a microeconomic theory, called X-efficiency theory, that is more general than the traditional model and that includes the existing theory as a special case. Table 6-1 indicates the basic postulates and variables.[1]

Units

In traditional theory, households and firms are the basic decisionmaking units. While a contractual relation between workers and firms is presumed, the objectives of firms are assumed to be identical with the objectives of individual firm members. In short, much of the theory is couched in language that suggests that groups behave as if they were individuals. It leaves unanswered the issue of how individuals are related to economic decisionmaking units that operate as a group. Under X-efficiency theory the basic decisionmaking units are individuals, even in the case of multiperson firms.

Effort

We assume that individuals who are members of a firm are paid on a time basis, operate under incomplete contracts, and can exercise some discretion with respect to the degree of effort they put forth in their work. Effort is a fairly complex and significant variable that includes such discretionary aspects as the *choice of activities,* the *choice of the pace* at which activities are carried out, and the *quality* with which they are carried out. Since in this system the firm does not control the effort levels of the individuals, it cannot necessarily minimize costs. The deviation between the optimal levels of effort from the firm's viewpoint and the actual levels that individuals are motivated to put forth determines the degree of "X-inefficiency" in the system.

The idea of X-efficiency contrasts with allocative efficiency, which is the sole efficiency notion in the conventional theory. In that theory, since firms are presumed to minimize costs, efficiency depends only on the allocation of resources to decisionmaking units. But if effort is to some degree a discretionary variable, then inefficiency can also arise because of insufficient effort levels.

Interpersonal and Agent-Principal Relationships

Since motivation is extremely important in determining effort levels, we have to take into account interpersonal interactions, especially peer group interactions, which determine the system of approval and disapproval, which in turn influences the effort level. At the same time, the distinction between principals and agents is extremely important in such contexts, since if effort is a variable there is no reason to presume that the interests of the agent and the principal are identical. Most work is

Table 6–1. Comparison of X-Efficiency Theory with Neoclassical Theory

Components	X-Efficiency Theory	Neoclassical Theory
1 Units	Individuals	Households and firms
2 Contracts	Incomplete	Implicitly assumed complete
3 Effort	Discretionary	Assumed given
4 Agent-principal relationships	Differential interests	Identity of interests
5 Inert areas	Important variable	None
6 Behavioral	Selective rationality	Maximization or minimization

carried out by agents, but there is no reason to assume that the agent puts forth the same degree of effort that the principal would under similar circumstances.

Inert Areas

The concept of inert areas is akin to that of inertia. Individuals are presumed to choose effort positions (a set of related effort-level options) in interpreting their jobs. The basic idea is that when an individual has been in an effort position for some time, he will not shift to a new position —even though there may be a gain achieved thereby. Why individuals possess inertia is another matter. We may try to rationalize the phenomemon by assuming the existence of an inner inertial cost, that is, the "cost of moving" from one effort position to another that dominates the perceived gain.[2] Thus an individual may find himself stuck within his inert area, even though apart from the inertial cost, superior effort positions may exist from his viewpoint.

Behavior

The basic behavioral assumption behind the theory is selective rationality. That is, we assume that people work out a compromise between the way they would like to see themselves behave (internalized standards of behavior acquired through background or environmentally determined standards or ethics), and the way they wish to behave in the absence of constraints of any sort (which we might describe as behavior controlled only by one's id).[3] A central notion in economic and other contexts is that behavior involves pursuing opportunities subject only to constraints, such as living within one's income plus credit or, indirectly, such as the degree to which one wishes to pursue an opportunity. Contexts contain opportunities and constraints. Under selective rationality, an individual need not pursue an opportunity for gain to a maximum degree subject to constraints if this runs counter to his standards of behavior. But he has to show concern for the constraints and opportunities to some degree.

The cost of ignoring constraints and opportunities is a feeling of pressure. This pressure may arise in part from ignoring the consequences and in part from the desire to behave in accordance with one's internalized standards (or ethic). For example, if someone does not pay the bill for a service, he may fear that the service will be cut off. In some cases the internal pressure involved may not be sufficient to induce the individual to pay the bill on time. Internalized standards will be different for different individuals. In this particular context some will pay bills immediately. Others may have such a low degree of constraint concern that they will not have a sense of mounting pressure until service is about to be discontinued. Similar considerations may help to explain differential degrees of absenteeism on the job.

Of equal importance are *external* pressures on the individual such as peer approval and disapproval, authority approval and disapproval, and sanctions of various sorts. Thus, the fear of peer disapproval or peer sanctions may result in a different effort level from that a person would choose on his own. Most people will deviate from maximizing behavior most of the time. However, external pressure may be strong enough to induce a normally nonmaximizing individual to behave in a maximizing manner or approach maximization. Also some unusual personalities may maximize most of the time. Some nonmaximizing patterns of choice may be according to (1) an ethical rule, (2) a behavioral convention, (3) habit, or (4) partial calculation. In a later section we shall indicate how these ideas may be summarized in terms of a lexicographic or hierarchical preference ordering.

Given these assumptions, we can now show that a free rider phenomenon exists with respect to the determinants of labor productivity. This follows from the postulates that contracts are incomplete and that effort is a discretionary variable. Consider the case in which the incompleteness of contracts means that employees know the wage they are to receive, but their responsibilities or work activities are either unstated or imperfectly alluded to. Each worker is better off in some more general sense if he is a member of a more rather than a less successful firm. However, if the size of the work force is large, say, over a thousand workers, then each worker is aware that his contribution, and his alone, is not significant in determining the firm's success or failure. As a result, each worker is in a position where he would like to see workers in general do their jobs effectively, but he has no special motivation to do his particular job effectively. This is similar to the classic free rider problem, within which it is desirable for every individual to contribute to a common outcome, or to pay for some common service (e.g., national defense), but each individual is not motivated to make that contribution, or to make as large a contribution as would be required.

By itself the free rider problem would make it impossible to obtain a well-defined production function. Under this scheme there is no clear relation between inputs and outputs. The degree to which any particular worker contributes to output is not determined. As a result, it is necessarily the case that the purchased labor units combined with other inputs are consistent with a wide range of outputs. Hence we cannot have a well defined production function. Of course entirely apart from the free rider problem we can see that this would follow just from the existence of discretionary effort, if the choice of the effort level is not completely controlled by either the contract or the management. We shall see that this argument is strengthened if we consider differential agent-principal interests.

To see what is involved suppose that the effort set for an individual is decomposed into specific effort activities e_{ij} where i indicates the specific activity, and j indicates the quality with which the activity is carried out. If an activity is not chosen, then it would have a quality index of zero. The nature of the choice problem is indicated in Figure 6-1 below. The abscissa indicates the range of activities, and the ordinate indicates the effectiveness of activities from management's viewpoint—essentially the quality j. The horizontal line marked ME represents the maximum

Figure 6–1. The Nature of the Choice of Effort Problem.

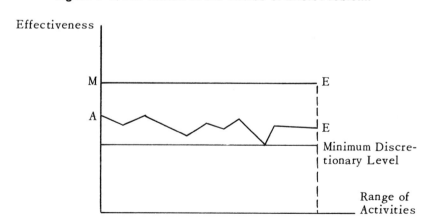

effectiveness boundary. Thus choices below ME do not result in cost minimization. The line AE indicates one possible actual choice made by the employee. As long as the choice is above some minimum discretionary boundary (below which the employee might be fired), then one could readily see that there are wide variations of effort effectiveness possible.

We should keep in mind that in most firms the managers are not the owners. Thus many multi-employer firms are run by agents who have their own interests and are not primarily or entirely motivated to carry out the interests of the principals. Since most firms are hierarchically structured, there will be effort discretion for each management level so that there is no one-to-one relationship between what it is that top managers want to see done, and the actual activities at the bottom. In other words, the actual relations will depend on a discretionary span at various junctures in the hierarchy. Indeed it may take extreme and unusual pressure, so to speak, on the part of somebody at a top level to get exactly the kind of results that the person would like to have from employees at the lowest level.

Of course, effort choices are indeed made. We will consider in a later section how this takes place. For present purposes, we ought to keep in mind that employees need not maximize utility in order to determine their own effort level. Their actual choice, given some experiments, which is not likely to involve a sequence of somewhat random effort choice trials, is indeterminate, since the choice would be different if the sequence of initial on-the-job events that determine the choice was also different. However, we will go into this matter more fully later as we consider the determinants of effort choice more fully.

THE PRODUCTIVITY PROBLEM: A GAME-THEORETIC VIEWPOINT

If effort is a discretionary variable, then we want to consider the options available to management and to workers in determining effort. These elements can be posed in terms of a game-theoretic problem. Furthermore, it seems likely that in many contexts the strategic game involved falls into the Prisoner's Dilemma classification. To see this let us shift immediately to a possible game situation under which both management and employees have certain options. We will view it as a two-person game, although later we can relax that particular assumption.

Assume that there are three basic types of options availabile to employees. These fall under the rubrics: (1) cooperate with management as much as possible, (2) cooperate with mates, and (3) maximize personal interest gains. The three options open to managers are (1) offer the highest anticipated return based on maximum loyalty from employees, (2) offer payment in terms of a peer group standard of work, and (3) pay the least and ask for the most effort. The options are illustrated in Figure 6-2 below, with possible rewards in terms of utility in the boxes along the diagonals.

We now turn to compare some of the possibilities. We see that the combination E1M1 is obviously the best solution for both employees and employers. It is clearly the cooperative solution. Nevertheless, it is not the solution that will be chosen if each party attempts to maximize separately. In the case in which each attempts to maximize separately we obtain the Prisoner's Dilemma solution. This is the one that results if employees choose E3, and management chooses M3. It can also be shown that the normal maximizing incentive would lead to this solution. The situation in which employees choose E3, whereas expecting management to choose M1, is of course best for the employees. However, whether or not this can come about depends on how management chooses. Thus employees may feel worse off if they choose the cooperative solution E1, but management chooses M3. Hence, we see that for employees E3 is the dominant self-interest solution, irrespective of which one management chooses. In other words, E3 is superior to being worse off when management chooses M3, and involves the best situation when management chooses M1.

Exactly the same maximizing self-interest strategic reasoning holds for management. If management chooses M3, that is their best choice given that employees choose E1. On the other hand, if employees choose E3, management is better off with M3 than they would be with M1, since E3M1 is the worst situation. Hence, given the options involving M1M3 on management's side and E1E3 on the employees' side, we see that individualistic self-interest behavior leads them to the Prisoner's Dilemma Solution, which is worst for both.

It is possible that a non-Prisoner's Dilemma solution can be worked out if there is a high degree of trust on both sides, and a strong awareness of their mutual dependence. Nevertheless, it is difficult to see how this would be worked out without some third party intervening. The free rider aspect of effort choice situation would usually work against such a solution.[4] Trust may not be enough given employers' individualistic interests. No matter what management does, there is nothing to prevent employees from shifting toward the discretionary level that is worst for management, and vice versa.

Of course, in each category in the payoff matrix there is a continuum of possible employee effort standards, and of management options. Let us now look at the problem in terms of a two-state peer group standard, as indicated in Figure 6-3. Within itself, this is also likely to lead to a

Figure 6–2. Management and Employee Options.

Management Options

		M1	M2	M3
Owner-Management Choices / **Employees' Choices**		Maximize Sharing Gains with Workers	Accept Peer Work Standard ―――― Nonsharing	Get Most from Employee ―――― Pay Least
E1	Cooperate with Owner-Managers	Optimal Cooperative Solutions 20 / 20		Best for Owner 30 / 3
E2	Cooperate with Mates Only		Peer Group Standards of Work Nash Equilibrium Solutions 7-15 / 7-15	10 / 4
E3	Maximize Personal Gains	Best for Employee 3 / 30	4 / 10	Worst Prisoner's Dilemma Solution 5 / 5

(Employee Options on left axis; Management Options across top)

Prisoner's Dilemma situation, for managers prefer the lower wage irrespective of the effort standard, and employees prefer a lower effort level, irrespective of the wage. Trade union intervention may create an exception to this. A trade union can through its contractual arrangements attempt to promise a high wage in return for a relatively high peer group standard. Hence, roughly the same situation holds with respect to the alternatives under a given peer group standard as existed previously for widely different effort levels. We note that the third-party intervention of a union can prevent the gradual atrophy of the general standard and working conditions towards the Prisoner's Dilemma situation.

Figure 6–3. Management and Employee Options

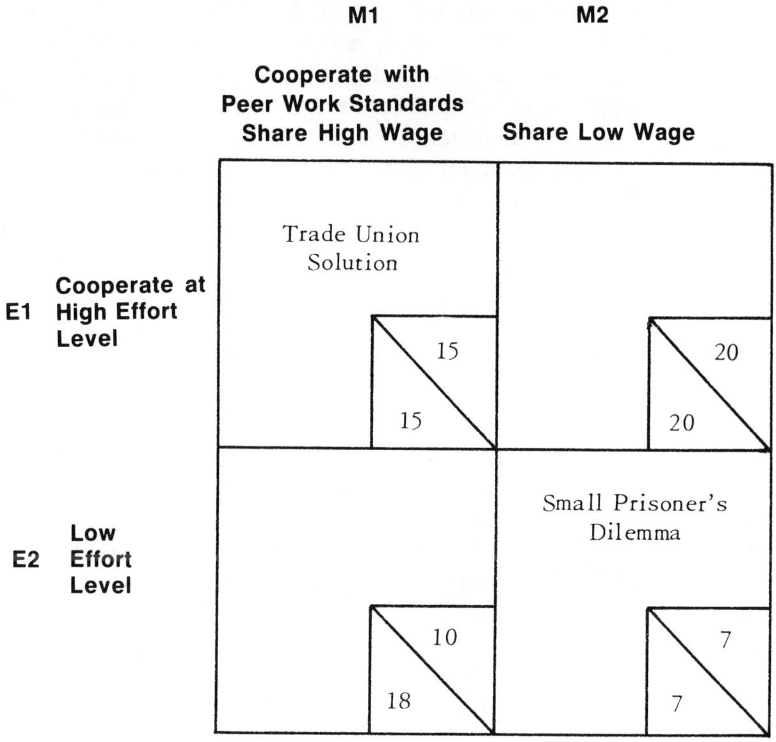

	M1 Cooperate with Peer Work Standards Share High Wage	**M2** Share Low Wage
E1 Cooperate at High Effort Level	Trade Union Solution 15 / 15	20 / 20
E2 Low Effort Level	10 / 18	Small Prisoner's Dilemma 7 / 7

Unionization can lead to this result, but it need not. Up to this point we have not attempted to specify what actually occurs, but have only attempted to indicate the game-theoretic nature of the problem.

CONVENTIONS AS DECISION ELEMENTS

A minimum amount of reflection should suggest that adhering to convention is a major way of deciding things in many areas of life. One simply has to think of the importance of language and reflect that all word usage is simply a matter of convention. In fact convention not only determines the meaning of words but also in many cases, their emotional content. The existence of swear words is a case in point.

We can also look at convention as a type of game-theoretic problem within which one individual has to coordinate his choices with that of another, or a great many others. Consider the case of choosing the side of the road on which one drives a car. In the payoff matrix (see Figure 6-4) we look at the problem from the viewpoint of individual A as against individual O (standing for others). Both A and O have to decide whether to drive on the right or left side of the street. Clearly the payoffs will be high if they both choose the same sides, and it will be disastrous for A if he chooses the opposite side. Also it is immaterial to A whether he drives on the right or the left side as long as O also chooses the same side. Once a decision is made for the same side it will be in equilibrium since it is desirable for all parties to choose the same side. Obviously there is clear advantage in having a convention for on what side people should drive.

In the next payoff matrix (see Figure 6-5) we make one slight deviation from the previous one: the payoff is in two parts. The first part represents the intrinsic value of choosing the same side, and the second part represents obtaining the approval or avoiding the disapproval of other individuals. This helps us see the point that conventions will frequently be followed even if it does not pay to do so.

In Figure 6-5 we consider whether a person should choose a queuing convention or not. Obviously, as the utilities are indicated, it makes sense for individuals to choose a queuing convention over always attempting to break the queue. The utilities are listed with a plus (+) sign between them. The first number deals with the utility attributed to queuing. The second number in the first box, +5, indicates that individual A receives five utiles from the approval or lack of disapproval of others. This implies that even in situations where queuing does not make sense, and hence the intrinsic value of queuing (10 utiles in box 1) drops to zero, the individual may still abide by the convention if others are around. In other words, this suggests that conventions might persist after their intrinsic usefulness disappears.

Note that some individuals will not go the wrong way up a one-way street, even though they are certain that there are no other cars going in the opposite direction, if there is a bystander on the sidewalk observing them. In some cases the convention will have become internalized into an ethic, and the individual will not go the wrong way on the one-way street even if no one else is there. Another example is jay-walking. In cities where jay-walking is strongly enforced, city residents will not jay-walk when no one else is around, although strangers will frequently do so.

Another aspect to keep in mind about conventions is that in some cases the convention is followed even though there are unpleasant aspects associated with it. Consider the case of choosing the place to meet. Suppose A does not like Joe's Bar but he knows that B frequents Joe's Bar. Rather than not meet at all with B, A goes to Joe's Bar. In fact it is possible for a group to develop meeting places that the majority of the members who meet there in fact do not like.

Figure 6–4. Payoff matrix.

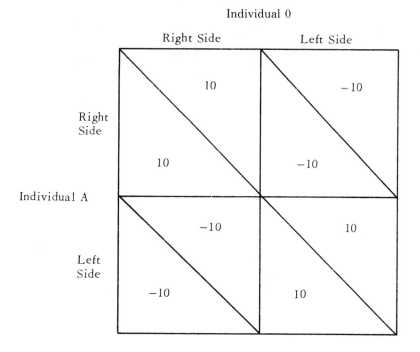

Individual 0

One final point we wish to make is that conventions can overcome Prisoner's Dilemma difficulties if adherence to the convention is strong enough. For instance, if there is a high degree of trust in certain commercial relations, then very little policing is necessary. Contracts are automatically enforced, even in situations in which it may pay for everybody acting as an individual to lie to each other. For instance, in the diamond brokerage business most deals are consummated with a handshake, despite the fact that there are considerable possibilities for fraud.

LEXICOGRAPHIC ORDERINGS, ETHICS, CONVENTIONS, AND EFFORT CHOICES

One way of organizing some of our ideas about conventions and nonmaximizing behavior is to attempt to interpret all these matters in terms of a lexicographic preference ordering. Consider the case in which the ordering has three stages in the lexicographic hierarchy, (1) convention, (2) partial calculation, and (3) full calculation. In this case the individual will behave in the conventional way if a convention covers the

Figure 6–5. Payoff Matrix.

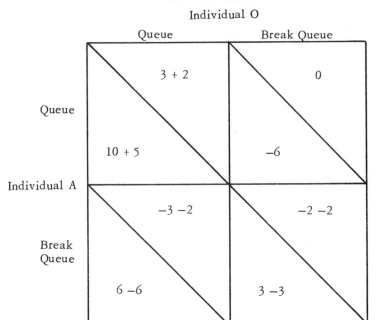

Individual O

	Queue	Break Queue
Queue	3 + 2 / 10 + 5	0 / −6
Break Queue	−3 −2 / 6 −6	−2 −2 / 3 −3

situation. However, in some cases there are disadvantages to behaving according to some convention. If the disadvantage or cost is too great, the person shifts to the next stage in the ordering to partial calculation. If the cost (or disadvantage) of partial calculation appears too high, then he shifts to full calculation. However, these switch costs may bear no relation to the way a maximizing person would behave. Thus, for the average individual the switch cost, so to speak, from one stage in the lexicographic ordering to the next may be considerably higher than maximizing behavior would call for.

Now let us return to the problem faced by an individual who joins a firm. He has to choose his effort level. Let us keep in mind the game-theoretic view of the problem as illustrated above. His interaction with fellow workers may lead him to discover that there are conventional bounds within which effort is put forth. Thus he can readily "solve" the effort-choice coordination problem, assuming he wishes to coordinate his activities with the preferences of his peers, by choosing an effort level that fits within the conventional standard. This is illustrated in Figure 6-6 below, within which the conventional standard is indicated by the bounds C_1 and C_2. The much wider bounds indicated by I_1 and I_2 represent the inert area.

Figure 6–6. Effort Level Choice.

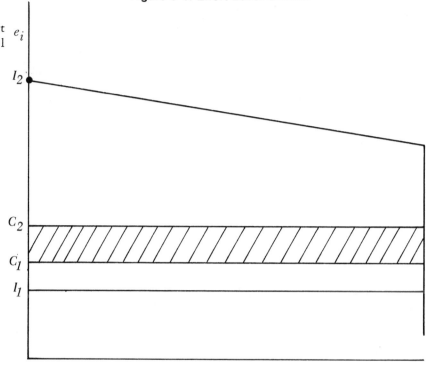

We have to distinguish between rules and conventions. Rules in themselves are not conventions since individuals may choose to disregard rules. Furthermore, conventions involve a desire for coordination with others, in some sense. For example, individuals may treat the meaning of words as conventions, but may treat many grammatical rules simply as rules that frequently may be disregarded. Conventions have a mutually enforcing element to them. For example, in some cases union rules may indeed become effort-choice conventions, but it is possible that identical rules established arbitrarily by employers would be ignored. Nevertheless, it seems likely that work rules worked out between the union on behalf of the union members, and the employer can become (but need not), at least initially, effort conventions.

Now let us look a little more deeply into the lexicographic ordering. Consider the one indicated in Figure 6-7. All lexicographic orderings are essentially hierarchical. The components fall into two categories, those that are individualistic (I), and those that we will refer to as being

Figure 6–7. Structure of Lexicographic Ordering.

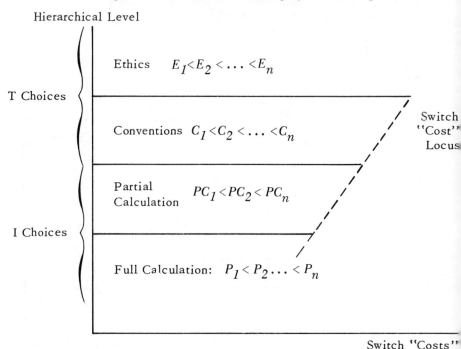

Hierarchical Level

T Choices

Ethics $E_1 < E_2 < \ldots < E_n$

Conventions $C_1 < C_2 < \ldots < C_n$

Switch "Cost" Locus

Partial Calculation $PC_1 < PC_2 < PC_n$

I Choices

Full Calculation: $P_1 < P_2 \ldots < P_n$

Switch "Costs"

transindividualistic (T). Thus, maximizing utility (i.e., fully calculating behavior) without regard to the concern of others is an individualistic component. The same is true of partial or incompletely calculating behavior. However, to follow a convention is to go beyond calculation (consideration of the preferences of others). The same is true of any ethic such as a work ethic. Thus, we visualize the process of the effort-level choice as follows: He chooses a work ethic if one exists; if not, he attempts to discover the conventional level, or the conventional effort bounds, and he fits his level within these bounds. Some of these elements may be interrelated in the sense that the convention must not go counter to the work ethic, and the same may be true for some types of individual calculations. However, for present purposes, we will ignore these complications.

IMPLICATIONS FOR GROWTH

On the basis of the payoff matrix in Figure 6-2, the outcome will depend on whether the management-employee relationships and their strategic choices result in cooperative or noncooperative solutions in some sense. Without introducing work ethics or conventions as choice procedures, it is likely that a Prisoner's Dilemma solution will result. This is the case in which employee effort is lowest in order to maximize personal gain. Simultaneously management attempts to pay least and obtain most from employees. All of the solutions are likely to operate as self-fulfilling prophecies and hence are likely to become stable low-level effort conventions. A pre-existing convention of peer group cooperation will result in an intermediate level of effort, provided management respects the peer group standard and offers to reward such a standard in some sense. In other words, directly or indirectly, group incentives are introduced.

The completely cooperative solution is likely to occur only when a high work ethic is combined with a maximum employee welfare ethic by management to support it. This may be approximated in the Japanese firm. The extent to which this solution is stable would depend on the degree of stability of the weaker of these two ethics. It is also worth noting that the peer group standard can be broken down into a continuum of solutions depending on peer group cohesiveness and the degree to which management takes the peer group seriously. We can also decompose peer group standard possibilities into a game that may also contain a Small Prisoner's Dilemma solution.

It may be useful to consider various aspects somewhat more fully. It is easy to show that from a macroeconomic viewpoint the higher the effort level the higher the growth rate, if we consider the effect of effort on output, and the effect of output on the capital-output ratio. Thus,

$$\frac{K}{O} = \frac{K}{L} \cdot \frac{L}{O} \qquad (6.1)$$

where K is capital, O is output or product, and L is labor. It seems clear that as output rises, the labor-output ratio falls, and hence the capital-output ratio increases. It also follows from the standard growth equation indicated below that the lower the capital-output ratio, the higher the growth rate.

$$G = \frac{S}{O} \cdot \Big/ \frac{K}{O} = \frac{S}{O} \cdot \frac{O}{K} \qquad (6.2)$$

where G is the growth rate and S is savings.

The interest in all of this is in part related to fear of technological unemployment, which results from the introduction of labor-saving technology. There is a seeming paradox in the general situation. The lower the effort level in the combined employee-management choices, the greater the employment obtained from a given stock of capital. At the same time the lower the effort level, the greater the incentive to substitute labor-saving technology as capital is replaced. All of this fits, and indeed strengthens John R. Hicks' induced innovation hypothesis. Hicks speculated that induced innovations must on the average be labor-saving. We can see how this will influence choice of technology and the resulting degree of potential technological unemployment.

Does it make sense for employees to attempt to maintain low effort levels in order to avoid being displaced by technological innovations? It may appear to workers on specific jobs that the lower the effort level, the more laborers that are required for a given amount of capital. Hence, from such a short-run viewpoint it would appear that low effort levels protect jobs. However, we will show that, from a macroeconomic viewpoint, this is unlikely to be the case. Jobs may be protected if employees resist both the introduction of technical change in the firms in which they work, and directly or indirectly in competing firms. By indirect competition we have in mind firms that produce substitutes for the commodity in question.

The equation below (6.3) indicates the ratio of technological unemployment determined by replacement of the existing capital stock by improved capital, assuming a constant capital stock.

$$\frac{U}{L} = \frac{\Delta K^*}{K} \cdot L_s \qquad (6.3)$$

where U stands for the new technologically displaced, ΔK^* stands for the capital that is replaced in a given year, and L_s stands for the labor-saving ratio per unit of *new* capital. It indicates in ratio terms how much less labor is required with the new capital than with the old. Clearly the ratio of capital replaced will depend on the physical durability of the capital, and the extent to which new capital is more productive than the old capital. If capital lasts twenty years, then the amount replaced will be 5 percent per year.[5] The labor that is replaced depends on the nature of the new capital. For present purposes let us assume it is one-fifth less than the labor utilized with the previous capital for the same effort level. Thus, the amount of technologically unemployed labor is 1 percent. This implies that an increase in the capital stock of 1.2 percent will re-employ the technologically displaced labor. The rate of savings S*/O required to do this is indicated in the formula in (6.4), which in turn depends on the capital-output ratio.

$$\frac{S^*}{O} = \frac{K}{O} \left[\frac{\Delta K^*}{K} \left(L_s + L_s^2 \right) \right] \qquad (6.4a)$$

Also,

$$\frac{S^*}{O} = \frac{\Delta K^*}{O} \left(L_s + L_s^2 \right) \qquad (6.4b)$$

Assuming that the capital output ratio is 3/1, this will imply that 3.6 percent of national product will be required to absorb the technologically unemployed. Furthermore, the lower the capital-output ratio, the lower the percentage of income needed for unemployment absorption.

An interesting case to consider is the one in which the effort level for the old technology is the same as it is for the improved technology. Now it should be clear that from (6.4b) that the capital replacement rate is not likely to change very much if the effort level is the same in both cases. If anything, a higher effort level will increase the efficiency of the old technique compared to the new one, since labor contributes more under the old technique. In any event, since the capital-output ratio falls as X-efficiency increases, employees as a group are safer in retaining an opportunity for a job under high effort levels compared to low effort levels.

Clearly the essence of the problem is that macro considerations suggest that employees are better off with high effort levels, but employees concerned about specific jobs may correctly feel that they are better off with lower effort levels. We have here a fallacy of composition problem and a free rider problem. Thus managerial arrangements that associate jobs and prerequisites with specific skills will result in resistance to productivity improvements, and are likely to motivate toward low effort levels. On the other hand, the sort of situation that is assumed to exist in the Japanese firm, in which the job is associated with firm membership and not with a particular occupational category, is likely to lead to higher effort levels (i.e., a cooperative game-theoretic solution) and a lack of resistance to the introduction of productivity increasing innovations.

Reducing the resistance to innovation is a significant element in increasing the growth rate. But the innovation problem should not deflect our attention from the main points of this chapter. The intrafirm choices (of the intrafirm options) made by managers and employees determine the effort level and the productivity level, which in turn determine the capital-output ratio. Clearly, the greater the effort level, the lower the capital-output ratio, and for a given savings rate, the greater the growth rate.

At the core of our argument is the idea that productivity depends on how work is organized and on the motivational elements within the workplace. This view is especially relevant in light of the fact that over time there is a tendency for work to be organized in larger and more interdependent organizations. As firm size increases firms become bureaucracies. Also as firm size increases, the cash nexis between the demand for the products of effort and the supply of effort becomes attenuated. It is this attenuation that gives rise to the free rider problem, and the connections between free rider elements, effort choice, productivity, and growth.

The analyses in this paper only scratch the surface of the growth problem. The transition from the micro-micro elements to macro considerations is too abrupt. A more refined analysis would have developed these issues in a number of easy stages of gradual aggregation. Also, among the considerations that should have been treated are the relation between education increases and effort choice, and the increase in services as a ratio of GNP and the relative effort-choice range for services versus manufacturing. Especially important is the growing importance of government as a provider of services and productivity and its connection to the problems of bureaucracies. The sort of analysis presented above could easily have been applied to the problem of the factors that determine the degree of bureaucratic efficiency.

COMMENT
Donald J. Daly

This chapter continues an area of research interest of the author that goes back about twenty years, namely the relations between people within organizations, and their differing goals and reactions to organizational carrots and sticks. These differing reactions can lead to either conflict or cooperation.

The theory developed departs strongly from the simplifying assumptions of neoclassical economic theory of the firm, and this chapter discusses half a dozen differences. However, it does not discuss any similarities or differences between his ideas and those that have been developing from psychologists and sociologists who have been working and publishing in the same area in recent years. I will return to this point at the end of my comments.

In earlier articles and books the author has applied his theories of X-efficiency to the production function of the firm and industry (which is much more indeterminate than in neoclassical production theory); costs and cost curves; competition, monopoly, duopoly, and monopolistic competition; productivity growth over time in individual industries and countries; productivity and cost differences between countries; inflation; and management (Leibenstein 1976: 29-47, 200-272). This is clearly a wide range of applications and the contribution warrants careful consideration.

An important theme in this chapter is the importance of individual motivation and involvement in an organization, and the degree to which individual's goals and behavior correspond or conflict with their peers and superiors in the organization. I regard this as a central area in any discussion of productivity and cost performance for two reasons. One reason is that labor is a major cost factor for the typical firm (as measured by value-added cost, i.e., excluding the costs of purchases from other firms and industries). This is reflected in the share of labor income in net national income. For the United States, for example, labor compensation amounted to 68.3 percent of *gross* private national income (Christensen and Jorgenson 1973: 249). The Denison studies put the labor share of nonresidential business *net* national income at about 80 percent in the United States for the 1960-68 period and the labor share is comparably high for Canada, the eight countries in northwestern Europe, and only slightly less for Japan (Denison and Chung 1976:29). As these income shares are broadly comparable to the contribution of labor to output, this is an important factor to analyze and understand in any broad assessment of productivity growth.

It is also important to study the role of labor and the degree to which it is used effectively or ineffectively within the firm. Neoclassicial theory of the firm assumes maximum output for a given combination of inputs, or minimum costs to produce a given input, *in the absence of constraints in the markets for inputs and outputs* (my emphasis). An important theme in Leibenstein's work has been empirical evidence from the market and other sources that contradict those assumptions, and a theoretical framework that opens up the process of interaction within the firm that neoclassical theory assumes away.

Thus I feel that Professor Leibenstein is dealing with important topics for both economists and behavioral scientists who are interested in how the modern firm operates and influences productivity levels and growth.

There are three topics I would like to discuss: (1) the interpretation for the lower levels of productivity and higher costs in Canadian than U.S. manufacturing, (2) estimates of the gains from free trade for Canada, and (3) the theory for intrafirm behavior covered in Chapter 5. The first two topics were important aspects of the 1966 paper that have been central in his later work related to the firm (Leibenstein 1966).

In 1974, output per man-hour in U.S. manufacturing was about 25 percent higher than in Canada, with the differences for some industries being substantially higher than that (Frank 1977). In interviews some years ago, we had examples of individual products whose output with the same labor and capital would triple if they could attain the U.S. length of run. These are examples of higher cost and lower output per man than in the United States, and where the firms were fully aware that average costs per unit would be lower. These are examples of product-specific economies of scale, but the firms felt that *lower* profits would result from the achievement of *higher* productivity. Although long-run average and marginal costs would decline with higher volume and longer runs, there was no financial gain from higher profits. The high cost position limited sales to the small domestic market, and the marginal revenue curve was falling more sharply than the marginal cost curve in the current situation (Daly 1975; Daly and Globerman 1976). A key reason for the persistence of the product diversity and less than minimum efficient scale is the presence of tariff and nontariff barriers to trade in Canada and other countries. Business managers follow a corporate strategy that they know leads to persistent lower productivity levels, as specialization and longer runs would give *lower* profits if each firm tried to specialize on its own.

This interpretation builds on neoclassical price theory, but incorporates modern cost theory and the influence of project diversity and product-specific economies of scale. Elements of Professor Leibenstein's views on X-efficiency are still relevant, but there is still room for the neoclassical tradition to clarify the influence of constraints on the productivity performance of the firms and industry. Profit maximization need not lead to high levels of productivity within the constraints faced by Canadian manufacturing.

A second theme in the 1966 paper was the negligible values of the estimates of allocative inefficiency on GNP. The estimates were drawn from studies by such authorities as Harry Johnson, Arnold Harberger, Tibor Scitovsky and L.H. Janssen (Leibenstein 1966). All of these authors estimated the cost of the tariff to the consumer only (essentially the small consumer surplus diagram). This procedure implicitly assumes that the production conditions in the tariff-protected industry would be the same with and without the tariff (a standard assumption in the Hecksher-Ohlin-Samuelson trade literature of recent decades). What the contribution of a number of Canadian economists has done is establish that this concept is downward biased, as the cost of the tariff should also include the production costs of the domestic tariff (together with allowance for the tariff revenue in other countries in certain circumstances). When these considerations are allowed for, the estimate of the cost of Canadian and U.S. tariffs amount to 8.2 percent of real GNP in Canada in 1975 (Wonnacott 1975a, 177; Daly and Globerman 1976: 18-30; Economic Council of Canada 1975). This is a conceptually correct and appropriate estimate of the cost of tariffs to Canada, but far higher than the frequently quoted references given in the 1966 paper. The practice of assuming no change in production conditions from the presence or removal of tariffs continues to be widely followed by a number of studies (Bergsman 1974, Mussa 1974).

Any estimate of the costs of just one source of allocative inefficiency of 8.2 percent of GNP is going to be relatively large for manufacturing (which amounts to about 25 percent of the employed labor and gross domestic product). Many of the symptoms of X-inefficiency are inevitably going to be apparent within individual firms and industries in Canadian manufacturing, and affect organizational slack, openness to change, selection and promotion of management, gaps between current and best practice. My own thinking about these issues has tried to incorporate some of the notions pioneered by Professor Leibenstein, but with a recognition that allocative inefficiency is also important in Canada and other small market economies that are partially insulated by tariff and nontariff trade barriers from lower cost world suppliers.

This chapter develops some notions of the reactions of individuals to various game strategies, and various payoffs to participants. Some of the illustrations are interesting, but it isn't difficult to see that drivers going in opposite directions will get into difficulty if they are both on the same side of the street!

Professor Leibenstein discussed some of the literature on organizational analysis in his 1960 book (Leibenstein 1960: 119-262). However, his most recent book *Beyond Economic Man* and this chapter put more reliance on the theory of games and strategy choices facing individuals. Chapter 5 cites more than one hundred references, with 85 percent of them published since 1960. Could economists move ahead faster in the long run from the other disciplines than trying to build our own theory and accumulate evidence for those theories? My preferences would be closer to Professor Maital based on cooperation with behavioral scientists interested in productivity rather than a go-it-alone approach. Perhaps Professor Leibenstein can expand on his research strategy and correct me if I have misinterpreted his recent emphasis. Should we put more emphasis on finding solutions to problems than on developing more theories?

Professor Leibenstein mentions Japanese practices, but suggests they may be unique to Japanese culture. A recent paper by Charles McMillan suggests some convergence among managerial styles in different countries, and a recent study suggests that the application of tender loving care by Japanese managers to employees in the United States has led to positive effects on both morale and productivity.

NOTES TO CHAPTER

1. For a more comprehensive view of these ideas see Leibenstein (1976) Chapters 5-10, and Leibenstein (1975: Chapter 2).

2. The "cost of moving" is an individual psychological cost. It is part of personality (A truly maximizing individual would not have such costs since utility would be ascribed only to goods, services, and work activity, and kept separate from whatever the inner feeling may be that makes an individual sluggish or reluctant to change).

3. The use of a Freudian term does not in any way imply that this is a Freudian analysis.

4. The exception is the stylized Japanese firm that gives lifetime tenure very early and receives very high degrees of loyalty from employees. But this involves a very special *ethic* on the part of both management and employees—one that may be unique to Japanese culture.

5. We include in our assumption of durability the degree to which the greater productivity of new capital increases obsolescence of old capital.

Note that S^*/O is not the savings-output ratio; it is only the savings rate required to avoid technological unemployment arising from the introduction of labor-saving capital.

* *Part IV*

Remedies

Chapter 7

Remedies for Increasing Productivity Levels in Canada

Donald J. Daly

The central portion of this chapter will concentrate on an interrelated series of measures for raising productivity levels in Canada. Although the primary emphasis is on suggested changes in government policies, the effective implementation of those policies will require the active support of the private sector.

It is important to be explicit about the economic goals that are the objectives of policy, that can also be used as criteria to assess whether those goals are being achieved. It is also important to be explicit about the framework used to analyze productivity performance, and the problems that the policy proposals are designed to correct. This introductory discussion can be relatively brief, however, as these topics have been well explored in earlier literature.

ECONOMIC GOALS

For our purposes, the goal of real national income per person employed will be emphasized. Real Gross National Product at Market Prices will be emphasized, although Net National Product would be preferable since it would allow for any differences in capital consumptions. Such a measure emphasizes the real output and productivity aspects of economic performance, rather than the welfare aspects, but the rates of change over time are broadly similar for both measures (Nordhaus and Tobin 1973: 509–564).[1] There do not seem to have been studies of the differences, if any, between productivity-oriented as contrasted to welfare-oriented measures of performance between countries. However, the differences within the industrialized countries and between the in-

223

dustrialized and the less developed countries are so large that I doubt if the broad conclusions would be affected (Kravis et al. 1975: 170–183; Kravis, Heston, and Summers 1978b: 1–29, 1978a: 10).

Such other economic goals as low unemployment, price stability, and balance of payments equilibrium will not be explored systematically. However, successful productivity performance can help achieve those other goals, and can also reduce the potential conflicts between goals. For example, higher rather than lower increases in output per person and per man-hour can reduce the price pressure for given rates of increase in wage rates. Furthermore, high levels of productivity internationally can help improve the competitive position of individual industries (for given exchange rates and wage differences). This is particularly important for a small country like Canada, but the United States also should give far more consideration now than in the 1950s to the competitive position of manufacturing industries in such countries as Japan, Germany, and the developing countries.

FRAMEWORK FOR DIAGNOSING THE PROBLEMS

There has been a considerable amount of research in the 1960s and 1970s on economic growth and productivity changes—both over time in individual countries, and comparatively between countries. A common objective in many of these studies is to try to identify the major factors that have contributed to the high rate of economic growth that most industrialized countries have experienced over the postwar period compared to long-term historical experience. Other studies have tried to identify major differences between individual contries. Some studies have gone on to use the results obtained to make estimates of potential output in the future. Some studies have examined the implications of their results for future government policies (Denison 1962; Daly 1968: 75–93; Christensen, Cummings, and Jorgenson 1978: 234–238).[2]

Although there is a continuing debate about some aspects of methodology, there is also broad consensus on many important points. Most of the researchers initially use the shares of national income accruing to the main factors of production (labor, capital and natural resouces) in order to combine measures of the main factors of production into a measure of total factor input. For most countries, and most time periods since the Second World War, the results show smaller increases in total factor input than in real income over comparable periods. The difference is the increase in total factor productivity. The number of studies that go further, and try to identify the various possible sources for the increase in total factor productivity is small, however. Although this additional step is difficult, it is important and very useful in forming initial views of topics requiring more intensive research.[3]

Research on economic growth accounting in Canada from 1950 shows that the increases in labor and capital inputs and increases in real output in relation to total factor inputs have been more rapid in Canada than in the United States. The increases in output in relation to total factor input in Canada have been more than in the United States, but less rapid than in Japan and most of the countries in northwest Europe (excluding the United Kingdom) (Walters 1968: 151–164; Denison and Chung 1976; 39–45; Christenson, Cummings, and Jorgenson 1978: 226, 231). If research stopped at this point, one would probably draw the same conclusion that Denison drew for the United States—that it would be very difficult, if not impossible, to raise the growth rate appreciably. If work had stopped there, this chapter could not have been written. But Denison has pioneered by applying the same methods developed for comparisons over time to comparisons between countries.

Further work has gone in two directions. At the level of the economy as a whole, comparisons of real income differences between countries have been made. When the methods in *Why Growth Rates Differ* were applied to comparisons between Canada and the United States, it became possible to look at Canada in the international perspective of the eight Western European countries and Japan. The application of economic growth accounting methods to comparisons between countries at a point in time as well as comparisons over times makes the analysis more fruitful than the reliance on only one type of comparison.

A further step is to supplement the national comparisons between countries with some *industrial disaggregation.* Such comparisons can be made for only some of the major industry groups thus far, but they do include the major commodity-producing industries, manufacturing, mining, and agriculture. The results to date are dramatic in that they point up significant contrasts between individual industries in Canada and comparable industries in the United States and Japan; it is to be hoped that research will be continued along these lines in the future (West 1971; Frank 1977; Daly forthcoming a; Yukizawa 1977; Daly forthcoming b)

Most of the other chapters in this volume emphasize changes over time, and there is only limited discussion of remedies for correcting lagging producitivity growth. Although this chapter emphasizes producitivity levels in Canada, considering both causes and remedies, any steps that raise productivity levels in Canada would also raise the rates of productivity growth.

THE SOURCES OF LOWER PRODUCTIVITY LEVELS IN CANADA

What can be said about the level of real output per person employed in Canada compared to that of the United States? It is clear from Table 7–1 that the level continues to be lower in Canada on both a per person employed and a per capita basis. The estimates are lower on a per capita basis than on a per person employed basis in Canada as a smaller proportion of Canada's total population is in the labor force (reflecting both a lower participation rate for women, and a relatively larger number of young people) than in the United States.

In considering possible reasons for the lower level of real output per person employed, one would initially want to check the levels of total factor input per person employed in the two countries. Data for 1960 are given in Table 7–2 and indicate that the level of total factor input per person employed is almost the same in the two countires. The higher level of land and natural resources per person employed in Canada reflects the high level of natural resource availability compared to any other industrialized country. The level of inventories and nonresidential structures and equipment per person employed is *higher* in Canada than in the United States, which makes Canada the most capital-intensive country in the world. On the other hand, the level of education input is lower, reflecting the lower proportion of the labor force that has completed university and high school. Table 7–2 shows the contribution to differences in net national income per person employed between Canada and the United States.

The major conclusion from this table is that almost none of the differences at the time could be associated with differences in total factor inputs per person employed, and almost all the differences were associated with differences in the levels of output in relation to total factor input.

Would these results be modified by subsequent data revisions? Dorothy Walters reworked the results on growth over time to incorporate some later revisions, but did not redo the level comparisons. The revisions raised the level of national income in Canada in the later years, and increased the level of investment and thus the stock of capital, but they would not affect the main conclusion.

Developments since 1960 increase the level of capital stock per person employed more in Canada than in the United States. For example, the level of capital stock per hour worked increased 1.7 percent per year from 1960 to 1973 in the U.S. while the comparable increase in Canada was 2.3 percent per year, or about one third more (Frank 1977: 113). The level of capital stock per person employed and per hour was thus about one-sixth higher in Canada than the United States by 1973.

Table 7–1. Comparisons of Gross Domestic Product

(Percentages of U.S. Quantities, Canadian Market Price Weights)

	Year	United States	Canada
GDP per person employed	1970	100.0	84.8
	1976	100.0	93.2
GDP per capita	1970	100.0	82.0
	1976	100.0	86.8

Sources: The estimates are based on relative prices in Canada and the United States for 1965 in Walters (1968: 260). Figures for 1970 and 1976 are updated from OECD, (1978) and Department of Finance (1978).

Table 7–2. Contribution to Differences Between Canada and the United States in Net National Income per Person Employed

	Canada, 1960 (U.S. = 100)	Contribution to Overall Canadian-U.S. Differences, 1960
Net national income per person employed	81.7	18.3
Input per person employed	98.9	0.7
Labor quality	100.0	—
Hours worked	103.8	-2.8
Age-sex composition	102.2	-1.6
Education	94.3	4.4
Capital	90.5	1.3
Dwellings	94.5	0.2
Foreign investments	-241.2	2.0
Nonresidential structures and equipment	107.3	-0.7
Inventories	107.8	-0.2
Land	124.0	-0.6
Output per unit of input	82.6	17.6

Sources: Walters (1968: Tables 73 and 75, 109 and 111). The methods follow those used in Denison and Poullier (1967).

Consideration of some of the major factors contributing to the higher level of capital stock per person employed must take into account that (1) the industrial structure contains a somewhat higher share of capital intensive industries (such as mining, smelting, and refining), (2) the small population thinly spread over a wide geographic expanse leads to heavy overhead costs in transportation and communication, (3) there is favorable tax treatment on depreciation of capital costs, (4) there are the larger real costs to having water, sewers, and building foundations below frost-level and to insulation and double windows, and there is greater seasonality. These factors tend to lead to a higher stock of capital per person employed, without a comparable increase in real output.

The comparisons thus far have emphasized Denison-type comparisons of the sources of real income per person employed—the only comprehensive level comparisons that have been made between Canada and the United States. However, some other studies of economic growth put more emphasis on the contribution of factor inputs to growth and less on their contribution to increases in output in relation to total factor inputs than Denison does.[4] This is not the place to continue that debate, but one point is interesting. The earlier study by Jorgenson and Griliches and later studies by Christensen, Cummings, and Jorgenson put considerably higher income share weights on the contribution of capital than the Denison-type studies. For example, Dorothy Walters used a weight of 12.8 percent for nonresidential structures and equipment in 1960–62 for Canada, compared to 10.2 percent for the same period in the United States. However, the value share of capital input for 1960–62 in the United States was 40.0, and 44.6 for Canada in the Christensen, Cummings, and Jorgenson study (1978: 218). The use of these higher weights for the contribution of capital would suggest a level of national income per person employed of about 6 percent higher in Canada than in the United States in 1973 from higher levels of capital stock per person employed. This tends to reinforce the conclusion suggested earlier that the major reasons for the real income differences are associated with differences in the levels of output in relation to total factor inputs, rather than low levels of input per person employed. These data provide little support for the view that further increases in the capital stock per person employed are needed to increase productivity levels in Canada, but emphasize the importance of more efficient use of both labor and capital.

CANADA'S COMPARATIVE ADVANTAGE

Most of the empirical research on economic growth accounting has gone on rather independently of the work in international trade, in such fields as the structure of trade flows, the gains from trade, the effects of tariffs and other barriers to trade, and the theory of comparative advantage. Some of my own research has attempted to integrate these two areas, with special emphasis on the comparisons between Canada, the United States, and Japan. Let me illustrate the gains from linking international trade and economic growth accounting with some applications of results from economic growth accounting to comparative advantage.

The theories of comparative advantage emphasize differences in relative prices between countries as a major determinant of commodity trade. One country will exchange products with low relative prices in that country for products with relatively high prices. When there are differences in the structure of relative prices between countries, both countries can produce some products at lower prices that they can exchange, and both countries can be better off. Even when the basic structure of consumer tastes and preferences are similar in different countries, differences in relative prices can occur and persist due to differences in supply conditions. The Hecksher-Ohlin-Samuelson tradition of relative cost theory in relation to international trade would emphasize the presence of different supplies of the various factors of production and differences in factor prices between countries as a determinant of international trade flows. These theorists have usually kept their models simpler by assuming constant returns to scale and similar production conditions for the same industries in different countries. Theorists in the Ricardian tradition also emphasize differences in relative prices as a determinant of commodity trade flows but emphasize *differences* in productivity levels for the same industries between countries as a determinant of trade flows (Daly 1976).

With the existing data on intercountry differences in factor supplies and productivity levels it is possible to assess the relative strengths and weaknesses of different countries and examine the implications for comparative advantage. For example, it is widely recognized that Canada is extremely well endowed with natural resources—land, mineral resouces, forests, water resources, and so forth widely scattered over a very large land area. On the other hand, the population density is one of the lowest in the world. Some comparisons with other industrialized countries are shown in Table 7–3.

Canada's favorable resource endowment is clearly shown. The quantities of arable land per person employed in Canada are more than twice the U.S. level, and more than forty times the Japanese level. (Important differences in climate and rainfall affect both the types of products grown and the yields per acre and per farmer.) Mineral production is also relatively more important in Canada than in any other country shown. On the basis of twenty major minerals, mineral production per person employed in Canada was more than double the U.S. level, about eight times larger than in Europe and almost fifty times larger than in Japan (Daly forthcoming b).

Canada is also the most capital-intensive country in the world, as indicated in Table 7–2 above, and by the evidence referred to there that

Table 7–3. Land Area and Mineral Production per Person Employed (U.S. = 100)

	Land Area Per Person Employed		Value of Mineral Production Per Person Employed (U.S.$)	
	All Land	Arable Land	Denison List	Expanded List
Canada (1970)	1036	218	181	222
United States	100	100	100	100
Northwest Europe (1960)	13	20	26	26
Japan (1970)	6.4	5.2	3.7	—

Sources: United States and Europe: Denison and Poullier (1967: Table 14–2, 184); Japan: Denison and Chung (1976: 258) and Walters (1968: Table 64, updated to 1970 with sources as described on pp. 233–34).

the levels of capital stock per person employed have increased more rapidly in Canada than in the United States during the 1960s and 1970s.

On the other hand, the available evidence indicates that the level of formal education in the labor force is lower in Canada than in the United States and Japan. Furthermore, less complete evidence suggests that business organizations and governments provide less in-house training for management and employees than takes place in the United States and Japan. These two countries are now the two most important export markets for Canada, amounting to more than $40 billion, or three-fourths of Canadian exports in 1978. The proportion of the labor force with training in science, engineering, and business is less in Canada than in the United States.

To summarize, Canada's strength in factor supplies lies in natural resources and reproducible capital facilities, while her relative weakness is the level of formal education.

Although the data on productivity level by industry in Canada and other countries are incomplete, there are some interesting and important contrasts. For example, in 1970 the level of output per person in mining were more than 60 percent higher than in the United States. However, the level of agricultural output per person was lower in Canada than in the United States—65 percent of the U.S. level in results by Auer, and 74 percent by Hayami and associates (Auer 1970: 63; Kravis 1976: 28). The mining sector, clearly one of Canada's strengths both in terms of relative supplies and productivity level, has been a declining share of world trade for some decades and is not a large share of the labor force or national income even in Canada, however.

Manufacturing is an important factor, as it has been a growing share of international trade, and a fairly important part of the labor force in most industrialized countries. Employment in manufacturing has declined absolutely in a number of major industrialized countries since the 1960s, with the declines being less in Canada than other countries (Daly and Neef 1977; 11–17). Canada has had a lower level of output per person and per man-hour in manufacturing than the United States. Considerable differences exist in the levels of output per person and per manhour in individual industries, but the level for total manufacturing was almost 30 percent lower than in the United States in 1976 and 1977. These statistical estimates are broadly consistent with earlier company interviews in representative secondary manufacturing industries, and a large number of term papers by full and part-time students at York University, many of them with first-hand experience in the companies studied. The differences in productivity that emerged in both the interviews and statistical studies were large and widespread. These productivity differences are especially significant when average hourly earnings and wage rates in Canada have moved above the average for U.S. manufacturing. There has been some narrowing in the productivity differences between the two countries since the mid-1950s, but such narrowing has been more than offset by increases in earnings. Labor costs per unit of output have increased more in Canadian currency than have occurred in the United States. These differences in productivity level, in wages, and in costs have been reflected in the large merchandise trade deficit in manufactured products that Canada has experienced, and is also a partial factor in decline in the value of the Canadian dollar that has taken place over the last two years.

The existing pattern of comparative advantage is bound to affect the structure of Canadian trade in the years immediately ahead, as existing distributions of natural resources, capital facilities, education level of the labor force, and productivity levels can change only slowly. For the longer term, however, more dynamic changes in comparative advantage can occur and can be encouraged, but the balance of the paper will consider longer term measures to increase productivity levels in Canada.

REMEDIES TO INCREASE PRODUCTIVITY LEVELS IN CANADA

This section will emphasize governmental policies for raising productivity levels, emphasizing the scope for federal policies. A number of interrelated policies will be necessary, as no single policy would be adequate on its own. Changes in the policy environment must also associated with changes in corporate strategy and corporate practices. Any changes in government policy must be associated with changes in corporate behavior on the supply side to be effective and be reflected eventually in the levels of real national income per person employed. This discussion will deal not only with policies that would raise pro- ductivity levels in Canada, but also with alternative measures that are sometimes put forth that would work in the contrary direction in my opinion.

Tariffs and Other Barriers to Trade

Earlier discussion has identified manufacturing as an important sector (amounting to more than 20 percent of the Canadian labor force in 1971), in which output per man-hour was appreciably below the currently prevailing level in the United States. These data are inconsistent with the assumption that individual plants and firms will maximize output for a given combination of factor inputs. It is also clear that Canadian firms and plants have quite a high level of capital facilities (although not necessarily as modern as in the United States), that the average plant size is not much below that in the United States, and that smaller plant size does not necessarily lead to substantially higher costs per unit. Canadian firms are consistently familiar with U.S. practices, and the high degree of foreign ownership and control would permit Canadian subsidiaries to be completely knowledgeable about the differing practices in the plants of the parent firm.

The major factor in the lower productivity levels in Canadian plants is the presence of a significantly higher degree of product diversity in the production schedules of plants in Canada than plants in the same industry in the United States. This analysis puts much more emphasis on product diversity as a factor in cost and productivity differences than plant size, a shift in emphasis in the literature on industrial organization (Scherer et al. 1975; Gorecki 1976; Daly 1975, 1978a: 9-26, 1976b: 87-97).

A major reason for this marked degree of product diversity is the presence of tariffs and other barriers to trade in Canada and in Canada's major trading partners. For example, a firm in Canada could decide to produce an item in Canada rather than import it if the effective tariff rate was sufficiently high to make domestic production somewhat lower in cost than importing the item. When a large number of producers decide to do this, the result is a high degree of product diversity and a lowered productivity level in Canada, but profit levels need not be any higher, as long as there are no significant barriers to entry. Canadian manufacturers end up with high production costs per unit of output, and sales are then limited to the smaller domestic market with 22 million people. Manufacturers in other industrialized countries, on the other hand, have access to larger markets on a free trade basis that amount to

215 million people in the United States, 265 million in the enlarged European Economic Community and 110 million in Japan. Manufacturers in large markets can take advantage of economies of scale that lead to higher levels of productivity, while there are neither the incentives or the competitive pressure to attain the same results in the smaller protected market.

It is easy to check this interpretation that reductions in tariffs and non-tariff barriers to trade by Canada and Canda's major trading partners would lead to specialization and a narrowing of the productivity gap between Canada and the United States. The reductions in tariffs approved under the Kennedy Round in 1967 was the largest tariff reduction of the postwar period, and these reductions were phased in over a period of years. In addition, the Canada-United States automotive agreement permitted free trade between producers of autos and parts. The range of models of cars and trucks produced in Canada was sharply reduced, wage, price, and productivity differences narrowed, and international trade in both directions increased sharply. The productivity differences in many other industries also diminished. From 1967 to 1978, output per hour has increased more than 50 percent in Canada, but less than 30 percent in the United States. The productivity gap had narrowed to about 25 percent in 1978 from 38 percent fifteen years earlier. The increased specialization in individual firms and industries has been reflected in relatively larger purchases of materials in relation to both gross and net value of output.

Reductions in tariffs and non-tariff barriers on a multilateral basis will encourage further product specialization in Canada. Trade in manufactured products would increase in both directions, but Canada would have to sell a larger volume of a more limited number of manufactured products abroad to take full advantage of the cost reductions associated with greater specialization. R.J. Wonnacott has estimated the increased real GNP to Canada from a Canada-U.S. free trade area as 8.2 percent of GNP in 1975. In commenting on this magnitude, he has said, "Not since the last depression has there been a Canadian policy that offered such a substantial economic benefit" (Wonnacott 1975: xxii). This is a gain from free trade that is substantially larger than had been estimated for other countries (Harberger 1959; Leiberstein 1966; Daly and Globerman 1976; Daly 1978b). These other countries had lower ratios of trade to GNP, and no other estimates have included an allowance for changed production conditions and economies of scale as the Wonnacott estimates for Canada have.

The latest multilateral round of tariff reductions under the General Agreement on Tariffs and Trade are in their final stages, and the latest offers have been made available to the U.S. Congress for formal approval. If these proposals are approved by the participating countries, the basis will have been laid for an important further reduction. This would lead eventually to bringing the productivity levels in manufacturing in Canada toward the U.S. levels, similar to what has taken place over the last two decades with the reductions under the Kennedy Round and the Canada-United States automotive agreement.

One of the concerns frequently expressed about further tariff reductions in Canada (and elsewhere) is the potential adjustment costs during the transition, especially on the employment side. These risks and costs during the transition are frequently exaggerated in the Canadian situation. My opinion is based on three factors of special importance for Canada.

1. On the production side at the level of the firm, the earlier discussion has emphasized the key role of the greater degree of product diversity in Canada as a major factor in the lower level of productivity (and associated higher cost). There is nothing easier for a firm to do than to drop the high degree of product diversity and specialize more and shift to longer product runs. It would be substantially more difficult if firms had to shift to a radically larger plant size, or to a world-scale national corporation size quickly in order to achieve higher levels of productivity. The emphasis on product diversity thus leads both to estimates of greater gains from tariff reductions *and* an easier adjustment process on the production side.

2. Marketing is another important area that has not yet had a comparable degree of analysis in the context of tariff reductions. However, the large degree of foreign ownership would be of assistance for domestic subsidiaries, as they could easily sell the longer runs that would be produced in the subsidiary through the existing distribution system of the parent. In this context, it should be noted that past studies of subsidiaries can rarely find evidence of explicit limits on export sales of the subsidiaries (Safarian 1966: 186, Table 22; Government of Canada 1972: 164, Table 29), (Britton and Gilmour 1978: 92, 104-108, 110-111), despite frequent assertions to the contrary Canadian-owned firms would have to develop foreign markets for the longer runs assoicated with specialization, but plants in Ontario and Quebec would only have to sell to a few adjacent U.S. states within three or four hundred miles of their plants to attain a market comparable to the domestic market spread over 4,700 miles from Vancouver to Halifax. In a number of industrial markets for intermediate products, wholesalers buy from a variety of manufacturers to provide the variety that larger Canadian firms produce within the firm. If their costs come down to

the U.S. level, they could compete on the same basis as existing firms and plants of a comparable size.

3. Existing data from a variety of sources suggest a higher degree of labor turnover on an industrial and regional basis within Canada than takes place in the United States—which is usually regarded as a highly mobile population. This tendency, together with a higher rate of labor force growth in Canada, should make it easier for labor market adjustments to take place by attrition and turnover than in other labor markets with less growth and less mobility. There may still be some exceptions to that generalization, such as the clothing and textile markets in the province of Quebec, for example.

This interpretation is consistent with a number of empirical studies of the employment adjustments in Canada associated with tariff reductions under a variety of assumptions. Even with pessimistic assumptions about reorganization of industry and stimulative government policies of expediture increases and tax reductions, the transition employment adjustments were relatively small (Economic Council of Canada 1975: 166-170).[5] These studies stand in marked contrast to the predictions in one study of "a devastating scenario" in which "it seems inevitable that a large number of Canadian businesses both large and small would fail" (Britton and Gilmour 1978: 153).

It should be recalled that a floating exchange rate would provide a degree of flexiblity during the transitional period, if that became necessary. The decline in the value of the Canadian dollar of almost 20 percent between 1976 and the opening months of 1979 has already provided a significant degree of moderation in the degree of price competition from imports. The change in the exchange rate that has taken place has been far larger over the last two or three years than any tariff reduction that might finally be approved from the current GATT negotiations, and any reductions would be phased in over an eight-year period.

This assessment of the ease of making the necessary adjustments to reductions in tariffs and other barriers to trade in Canada and elsewhere recognizes that there are risks in moving to lower tariffs, associated with the large gains suggested earlier. It is important that governments have policies in place to facilitate adjustments in uncompetitive sectors where management seems unable to get productivity up to an internationally competitive level. Adequate internal demand can facilitate the shift of resources from regions and industries providing low incomes and limited employment opportunties to expanding sectors; such shifts slow down during periods of slace demand. Other policies for retraining workers and financing moving expenses to new jobs are also desirable (Daly and Globerman 1975: 61-67; Economic Council of Canada 1975: 165-186).

Such policies are desirable to facilitate such shifts that may partially be associated with the tariff changes, but also to meet the concerns of both labor and management who want to be protected by the tariff and other barriers from the pressures for change and adaptation.

The Production and Adoption of New Technology

Most of the studies on economic growth conclude that technological change is an important factor in the increases in real output per man-hour input. Research and development in both the private sector and the government sector is one element in that technological change. Another element is the speed at which new technology is adopted. A further factor is the international transfer of technology, an area that is particularly important for a relatively small and open economy like Canada. A brief summary of these points for Canada will provide a background for considering policies to raise productivity levels in Canada.

It is important to recognize that Canada does relatively less technological innovation than other industrially advanced country even allowing for the number of industrial employees and the size of manufactured exports in Canada compared to other individual countries (Daly and Globerman 1976: 109). Much of the support for a more active policy of government support for research and development is based on evidence of this kind on the limited amount of R & D in Canada.

There are, however, a number of reasons why management in the private sector has been reluctant to spend large amounts on research and development. A variety of professional skills and specialized equipment are normally necessary for a research and development team to provide a minimum mass. The initial research and development costs are only a small part of the total innovative process—5 to 10 percent of the total cost is a widely quoted figure (Daly and Globerman 1976: 108). These costs (both for the initial research and development and total innovation costs) are going to be less if spread over a large market, and there is probably also less risk in a larger market. There are also a number of studies that indicate that the international transfer of technology is relatively easy to accomplish. Canadian firms (both Canadian-owned and subsidiaries) would frequently find it cheaper to buy technology than produce it within Canada.

The evidence on the diffusion of technology indicates that Canadian plants are slower at adopting new technology than plants in the same industries in the United States and elsewhere. An earlier study indicates that new synthetics were first produced later in Canada than in some of the other large industrialized countries (Daly and Globerman 1976: 83-98; Hufbauer 1966).

A number of suggestions that would encourage technological change as a part of raising productivity levels within Canada can be made in light of the above analysis. For one thing, it is important to put high priority on the fast adoption of new technology in Canada. There is currently a greater gap between actual practice and best practice technology in Canada than in the United States. Any measures that can encourage a narrowing of this gap would tend to raise productivity levels in Canada. Specialization and rationalization associated with lower barriers to trade would encourage such tendencies. Rapid adoption of existing best practice can be important in raising productivity levels and encouraging economic growth. It is likely that the X-efficiency emphasized by Harvey Leibenstein would be even more important for Canadian than for U.S. firms.

In considering research and development, the costs are bound to be lower on a per unit basis if they are spread over long runs, rather than over short runs. For Canada, this suggests that it would be appropriate to emphasize areas in which Canada has a comparative advantage in world markets. International competitiveness in production and marketing is critical, as these are normally the major factors in business costs. On the other hand, research and development expenditures are normally only a small part of total business costs. If research and development is emphasized in those sectors where Canada can compete in world markets, those costs can be spread over the larger world markets and further strengthen the competitive sectors.

If research and development is undertaken domestically in manufacturing products where Canada's productivity levels are already low by international standards, this would further accentuate the low productivity, high cost situation of Canadian secondary manufacturing. The real economic situation is not changed if part of the costs are born by the taxpayer (whether in the form of subsidies or special tax treatment for R & D expeditures). Furthermore, if R & D projects that are successful technically are not adopted by Canadian plants, there is no general gain to the Canadian consumer. There are some examples of projects that have been subsidized by the Canadian taxpayer that end up being produced initially in Japan rather than in Canada.

Those who are broadly familiar with science policy discussion and legislation in Canada will realize that actual policies have been considerably different from what they would be if raising productivity was the goal. The Technical Information Service of the National Research Council provides assistance for the technical development of medium and small industries. Their budget of $1.9 million 1977-78 is woefully small, but it is almost the only federal government organization in Canada with the basic objective of increasing the productivity of

Candian manufacturers through better utilization and faster adoption of existing technology (Britton and Gilmour 1978: 181). On the other hand, the federal government was paying about $140 million to Candian industry for research and experimental development by the early 1970s (Daly and Globerman 1976: 106), and the shift to tax incentives for research and development in the November 1978 budget was expected to cost about $50 million per year. These subsidies and tax incentives for research and development normally only cover the *initial* costs of the whole development process, which normally amount to only 5 or 10 percent of the total process.

If the interests of the consumer and high productivity were the goal of government policy, the support would be for the total innovative activity (including its commercial implementation) rather than just the research and development costs.

When government policies emphasize only the research and development stage, with no support for commercial implementation, and negligible support for faster adoption of new technology, it appears doubtful that they can have much positive impact on productivity. The primary beneficiaries of current policies are the limited number of professional and scientific staff involved in research and development. These occupations receive incomes 60 or 70 percent above the average for all occupations in Canada, but were only a small part of the employed population in Canada in 1971(Daly and Globerman 1976: 110-111).

Foreign Ownership and Control

The earlier discussion has pointed out that levels of real output per person and per man-hour are lower in Canada than in the United States. There are, however, some differences in productivity levels within Canada. Value-added per person employed in U.S.-controlled establishments tends to be fairly consistently higher than in Canadian-controlled establishments in the same industry. For eighteen major industry groups, the unweighted arithmetic mean was about 25 percent higher in the U.S.-controlled establishments (Daly 1978a: 20).[6] U.S.-controlled plants also pay higher wages and have large profits in relation to both sales and assets than Candian plants (Statistics Canada 1978b: 52, 53; Safarian 1969: 82). Since Canadian plants tend to produce a smaller range of products than U.S. plants, the lower productivity levels in Canadian establishments cannot be explained by greater product diversity.

Subsidiaries have extensive dealings with their parent and affiliated companies on exports, imports, and managerial services. It is possible that transfer pricing policies could lead to an underreporting of profits and value-added in the subsidiary, but there is almost nothing in the public domain on this point. Insofar as this did happen, the levels of net vanue-added per employee in U.S.-controlled establishments could be understated relative to the Canadian-owned establishments.

It is possible that the smaller size of Canadian establishments may be a factor in the lower level of net value-added per establishment, but differences in plant size do not seem to have been as dominant a variable in costs and productivity as the extent of diversity.

A recent study by D. MacCharles contains data on the costs of certain managerial services and knowledge production in firms in the same industry and asset size groups. These costs were relatively higher in smaller Canadian firms than in U.S.-owned firms in the same industry and asset size group in relation to both sales and net value-added. The level of net value-added per employee was typically higher in foreign-owned plants than Canadian-owned plants in the same industry and asset size group (MacCharles 1978).[7]

These results would suggest that policies designed to limit or check the operations of subsidiaries in Canada would tend to depress productivity levels. It seems preferable to get Canadian-owned plants up to the performance level of the subsidiaries, rather than penalize efficiency.

Management Education and Recruitment

Earlier evidence and discussion has pointed out that Canadian plants and firms in manufacturing are frequently not producing a maximum amount of output for given levels of factor inputs, and that one cannot explain the differences in performance on the basis of inputs of capital and natural resources. There are larger gaps between current and best practice in Canada than in the United States. These differences in adoption of technology do not reflect lack of knowledge of the technology or difficulty in getting access to it. There is less competitive pressure to adopt new technology in the small, protected Canadian market, and also there is likely to be less potential gain in doing development work or introducing new products and processes in a small market.

COMMENT
Mieko Nishimizu

I claim none of the professional credits or personal attributes that make one an expert on Canada, and therefore feel quite inadequate to comment on Professor Daly's paper. In particular I should like to refrain from assessing in detail each of the "remedies" proposed in this paper, since the task requires an extensive knowledge and understanding of how the Canadian economic system works at a disaggregated level. I would like to comment instead on the overall analytical framework of this paper.

It is not entirely clear from this paper why one needs to worry about the level of productivity in Canada. The paper paints a rather pessimistic picture of Canada through various international-level comparisons of output and factor inputs. The author combines a 1960 aggregate level comparison between the United States and Canada with growth rates of output and input for the subsequent years, and indicates that the difference in output per capita (to use the term loosely) between the two countries is mostly due to the difference in the level of total factor productivity and not to the difference in capital intensity of production. This does not imply, however, that Canada lies below its own production frontier. The author also refers to evidence of lower average labor productivity in some of the Canadian industries compared to the United States, and concludes that "the data are inconsistent with the assumption that individual plants and firms will maximize output for a given combination of factor inputs." This is a rather dangerous conclusion. Relative prices may differ, capital intensity of production may differ, or level of technology may differ between the U.S. and Canadian industries. Lower labor productivity does not imply that Canadian industries are not doing their best. The author also draws on comparisons with other countries such as Japan to deepen the color of pessimism. This, again, is quite dangerous, as countries may differ in the types of growth paths they are on at any point in time. The pessimism about Canada may thus be misleading, or perhaps may even be erroneous. One can't simply shoot Canada down just because it is not "doing" as well as the United States.

Although it is not explicitly stated and no supporting data are offered in the paper, I suspect that the source of the worry and pessimism may lie in the reduction of the *rate of change* of labor productivity in recent years. If not, it should be. An economy can grow only as fast as the rate of expansion of its productive resources and the rate of technological progress. One national objective is to maintain the growth of an economy close to the potential per capita output path with a reasonable unemployment rate and price stability. Assuming that fiscal and monetary policies do their job well on the demand side, the rate of change of the potential per capita output path is determined by the rate of growth of labor force and productivity in the long run. The *level* of the potential output per capita at any point in time is determined by the economy's saving rate and capital intensity of production. The pressing question we face is whether the observed decline in productivity *change* is a cyclical phenomenon or one that will persist in the long run. We cannot offer any policy prescriptions without having answered this question; and the level of productivity at a given point in time takes on a secondary importance.

Let us follow Kaldor, and sort out some of the important regularities and trends in the economic growth performance of Canada since World War II. The rate of growth of output has been remarkably steady at about 5.1 percent per year for the period 1947–73. The trend growth rate of labor input seems to have accelerated from about 1.1 percent (1947–1960) to 2 percent (1950–1973), so that changes in output per unit labor input declined from average 4 percent per year to 3.1 percent per year. The rate of growth of capital stock has slowed down significantly from 6.8 percent (1947–60) to 4.9 percent (1960–73), but remains above that of labor input. Thus capital labor ratio has been increasing, but the rate of change has slowed down from 5.7 percent to 2.9 percent.

The recession since 1973 swung Canada off this trend, but all indications suggest Canada will return to the decelerating trend path. If the decline in the rate of growth of productivity is cyclical, that is, if Canada is somehow off its full employment growth path in the short run, the question is how to bring the economy back to the full employment path. The relevant policy prescriptions would then be the set of stabilization policies on the demand side of the economy. The Council of Economic Advisors in the United States has already made up its mind that the similar decline for the United States is not cyclical. But of course there are others who disagree.

The state of the art of growth theory and the stock of our empirical knowledge about growth process might be called dismal. But we do know enough to identify Canada as being on an intermediate-run growth path, based on the observed pattern of economic growth for Canada. That is, Canada is tracking its full employment growth path *on average* and gradually approaching a long-run growth path. The rate of change of that path for Canada is of moderate magnitude, and declining as it nears the long-run path. We must then ask the following two questions: (1) What determined the rate of change of the intermediate path? and (2) must Canada be stuck with the long-run path (with even lower rates of change) once it reaches that state? The former for an optimist, and the latter for a pessimist.

The gradient and hence the time duration of the intermediate path depends on the elasticity of output growth rate with respect to growth rate of capital stock. Assuming a good behavior of the demand management and for a given saving rate, the higher the elasticity the steeper the path. And it is the nature of technological change that determines the elasticity and hence suggests alternative policy prescriptions. This is precisely where we benefit from the contributions and continuing effort made by Denison, Jorgenson, Kendrick, Solow, and others. If technological change is neutral and disembodied, the return from policies that encourage human and nonhuman capital accumulation is smaller than the return from policies that affects those elements in the Hicks-neutral black box for a given percentage change. If technological change is embodied in capital, the expected return from policies that stimulate investment—such as investment tax credits and favorable depreciation schemes—is relatively high. This, by the way, seems to be the position taken by the Congressional Joint Economic Committee of the United States as indicated by the Committee's Annual Economic Report (March 1979). If technological change is embodied in labor, the payoff of policies that raise quality of labor is greater. Certainly, disembodied factor-augmenting technological change would reduce the effectiveness of these policies appreciably.

Canada, and any other country for that matter, need not be stuck with the long-run growth path. Greater investment rate will do the trick, getting a nation off one long-run path and climbing up to another with larger gradient. And it is precisely here that a concern for the level of productivity takes on its importance. Unfortunately, the policy control variable then is the economy's saving rate. Policy instruments that affect the society's intertemporal preference are indeed quite limited. Perhaps Western industrialized countries have much to learn from the behavior of the Japanese government, which acts as the ultimate financial intermediary for the private sector.

Professor Daly seems to suggest that Canada is perpetually inside its production frontier. If the claim is indeed true, it is a very serious problem. But we do know very well that it is a rather difficult task technically to substantiate the claim empirically. Till then, I remain unconvinced. I do not mean to suggest that the remedies offered by Professor Daly are irrelevant. Not at all. Execution of policies itself does eat up some of our scarce resources. It is important to note that the choice of optimal policy prescriptions depends critically on the nature of the economic growth path, the nature of technological change, and the society's preference between the present and the future.

COMMENT

John Vanderkamp

Whereas the theme of this volume deals with lagging productivity growth, Donald Daly's contribution is concerned with productivity levels. This is a safer topic. Lagging productivity growth may turn out to be a nonproblem after we have finally figured out what business cycle pattern we are in, and after Statistics Canada revises the data. But there is no doubt that Canadian productivity levels have been below those in the United States for some time.

Daly starts off by reciting a number of well-known facts about the factor endowments of the Canadian economy. He concludes that the difference between Canadian and U.S. real income is associated with differences in total factor productivity and cannot be attributed to differences in input ratios. He then takes up the main explanation for these differences in productivity put forward by Canadian economists over the last few decades. Ultimately the Canadian tariff structure is responsible for excessive product diversity and short production runs that result in lower labor productivity.

The remainder of the paper consists of a discussion of possible remedies. Not suprisingly, policies related to tariffs (and non-tariff barriers to trade) receive the lion's share of the attention. Next comes technology policy, followed by a brief comment on foreign ownership. Finally, management education and "Policies of Nationalism," a title designed to encompass the recommendations of the Science Council of Canada, complete the list. As I am on the whole in agreement with the tenor of Daly's discussion I shall restrict my comments to three points that deal with the three most important policy areas.

First, in his discussion of tariff policies Daly makes the claim that the narrowing productivity gap between Canadian and U.S. manufacturing industries over the last few decades can be directly attributed to the greater openness of the Canadian economy. In particular, the Kennedy Round of tariff reductions and the Canada-U.S. automotive agreement are given most of the credit for closing the productivity gap. This argument certainly fits with Daly's theoretical approach, but some hard-nosed evidence on this issue would have been useful. There must be enough variation in the experience of different Canadian manufacturing industries over the last few decades to provide some econometric evidence on the quantitative importance of these two events. The impact of the automotive agreement has been studied by a number researchers, but the impact of the Kennedy Round may be of even greater significance since it is being followed by the Tokyo round and possible further GATT negotiations. If the Kennedy Round led to significant improvements in our productivity levels without great adjustment pains, then our policy stance in GATT and other places might well be more positive.

Second, in the section on technology policies Daly appears to be arguing that present government policies that emphasize general research and development in part through general tax incentives may not be fostering productivity growth. He suggests that Canadian policy should stimulate research and development in "areas in which Canada has a comparative advantage in world market." Moreover he suggests that government policies should emphasize not only the R&D stage but also commercial implementation of best-practice technology. This approach would appear to require knowledge of where Canada's comparative advantage will be in the future. In other words, it would mean that the Canadian government would have to pick the winners in the sense of potential market size for the industries' products. Elsewhere Daly has been rather critical of the idea that governments can pick the technological winners. Now, it may be easier to emphasize comparative advantage than to pick technological winners. But the problem is that technological developments may provide a self-reinforcing comparative advantage. For example, should Canada stimulate the development of submarine tanker technology, since the exploitation of arctic oil and gas may well create a sizable market for this form of transportation? Or alternatively, should Canada foster the design and development of STOL aircraft when the domestic and world markets might be quite large if the development is successful?

Third, in the final section Daly criticizes the nationalistic policies advanced for almost a decade by the Science Council of Canada. I do not wish to support the Science Council's views and I share Daly's objection that the "goal of technological sovereignty" is a fantasy. On the other hand, because of its size government has a very important influence on technological developments. When the Canadian government's decision to open an additional frequency range for CB radios is heralded as having a major impact on our technological capabilities in communications then it is not really possible for the government to adopt a neutral technological stance in many of its decisions. In other words, it may be possible to adopt the goal of fostering technological capability as a secondary policy objective in government purchases and regulation decisions. To illustrate this point let me pose some questions. In view of the recent debate surrounding Canada's purchase of fighter aircraft, would we have received less defense per dollar if the government had continued to support a version of the AVRO Arrow? Should the government take a leading role in adopting regulations to facilitate the development of fibre optics? The decision to build a large diameter pipeline apparently favors the technical capacities of Canadian steel mills, and the question is, should this be a factor in the decision? Under the auto pact the Canadian government has considerable powers of persuasion, and why should it not attempt to persuade U.S. auto companies to shift a significant proportion of research and design activity to Canada? These questions are not intended to be purely rhetorical but to illustrate the point that governments have an important effect on the development of technological capacity, whether they are prepared to admit it or not. And if this is true, it may be better for the Canadian government to formulate a comprehensive and coherent policy in this area.

Notes to Chapter 7

1. See Nordhaus and Tobin (1973: 509–564), especially Tables 1 and 2: 518–520.

2. Christensen, Cummings, and Jorgenson (1978) give illustrations without attempting to be comprehensive.

3. Research in Canada that has been initiated to examine in more depth some of the questions raised includes work on rates of return to education and the role of education in economic growth, economies of scale in manufacturing, the role of tariffs in Canadian cost and productivity performance, science policy, the mining industry, and management recruitment and performance. Most of these studies have involved comparisons with other countries.

4. See the various articles by Jorgensen and Griliches and Denison in the May 1972 issue of the *Survey of Current Business*. The 1967 article by Jorgenson and Griliches estimated that increase in U.S. real output in relation to total factor inputs from 1945 to 1965 at 0.10. Christensen, Cummings, and Jorgenson (1978) revised the estimate for the same time period up to 1.05, a major change. Their estimates of total factor productivity for the United States and Japan continue to be lower than the estimates by Denison for approximately the same time periods. For some comparisons see Daly (1978b: 234–235).

5. For other estimates of employment adjustments for Canada see Cline et al. (1978a: 125; 1978b).

6. Based on statistics Canada Catalogue 31–401: *Domestic and Foreign Control of Manufacturing Establishments in Canada, 1969–1970.*

7. Also from unpublished notes from the author.

8. For examples of these views, without attempting to be comprehensive, see Britton and Gilmour (1978), Gilmour (1978), M.J. Gordon (1974), M.J. Gordon (1978:46–56), W.L. Gordon (1978), Levitt (1970), Watkins (1978:87), Rotstein (1974), and Science Council of Canada (1979). For regular comments from this point of view, see both the news and editorial pages of *The Toronto Star*. The new Canadian Institute for Economic Policy is expected to emphasize this point of view.

9. Examples of this analysis would include Breton (1974), Daly (1979a), Daly and Globerman (1976), Globerman (1978:34–45), Palda (1979), and Wonnacott (1975: 536–547).

Chapter 8

Remedies For The Productivity Slowdown In The United States*
John W. Kendrick

INTRODUCTION

Looking ahead to the 1980–90 decade, the growth of real business product is projected at about 3.4 percent a year, assuming no major new policies are adopted to promote productivity.[1] This projection implies that productivity growth will accelerate modestly to 1.8 percent a year, up from the 1.4 percent of 1966–76, but still well below the 2.9 present average for the 1948–66 subperiod. The chief factors behind the improvement are expected to be changes in labor quality, as shifts in the age-sex mix become favorable, and volume-related factors, assuming high-level employment in 1990. However, continued declines in the average quality of natural resources, negative effects of interindustry shifts of factor inputs, and possibly a bit slower rate of advance in technology will prevent a significant resurgence of productivity growth.

In our view, a positive program to release the dynamic forces of the private economy could raise the rate of growth of total factor productivity back to the 2.8 percent a year experienced in the two decades prior to 1966, and the rate of increase in real business product to 4.8 percent. The centerpiece of the program would be the pursuit of macroeconomic policies, including significant reductions in business income tax rates that would raise the net rate of return on investment by about 2 1/2

---

*This chapter is an edited version of Dr. Kendrick's testimony before the Joint Economic Committee of Congress in June 1978 and before the Subcommittee on Science, Technology, and Space, Committee on Commerce, Science, and Transportation, U.S. Senate, April 1978.

percent (back closer to that of the mid-1960s), resulting in an increase in the proportion of income saved and invested by about 2 percent. This would not remove the biases against saving and investment now present in the U.S. tax system, but would offset them sufficiently to have a marked stimulative effect. It would be further enhanced by the increase in business confidence engendered by adoption of measures to facilitate the operation of the enterprise system.

Specifically, I would urge reduction of the corporation income tax and expansion of the investment tax credit to cover structures as well as equipment. But this is not enough. Macroeconomic policies should be pursued to permit a further widening of before-tax profit margins closer to those of the 1960s. And in 1980 business taxes should be pared further by reducing the double taxation of dividends and permitting firms to price-index their depreciation allowances to reflect replacement costs of plants and equipment. Other policy options are available, as discussed below.

The increase in tangible investment, embodying new technology, would also help speed up creation and application of advances in knowledge. In view of the high rate of social return on R&D, however, we recommend additionally a tax credit or other subsidy for privately financed R&D, and a substantial increase in government R&D outlays in selected areas, including basic research. These measures could increase the contribution of technological progress to productivity by 0.5 percent —back to the rate experienced prior to the mid-1960s when the ratio of R&D to GNP began to decline sharply.

There are other policy options available to promote education and training, health, factor mobility, and economic efficiency, and improve the net effect of governmental activities on unit real costs of business. The impact of these measures will be reinforced by wider opportunities for economies of scale, increases in rates of utilization of capacity, and a more stable economic growth rate.

In the following sections I set forth a program of policy measures that I believe could accelerate the growth of total factor productivity by 1 percent over and above what it would otherwise be. I begin with a discussion of measures to promote tangible investment.

TANGIBLE INVESTMENT

Policies to promote tangible investment and thus the rate of growth of real stocks and inputs of structures, equipment, inventories, and developed natural resources would obviously accelerate the growth of real product per unit of labor input and per capita. Real product growth would be favorably affected by the faster rate of diffusion of new technology, reflected in a declining average age of the fixed capital stock. Also, the acceleration in tangible capital formation would have a positive effect on R&D spending and other intangible investments that are part and parcel of the invention-innovation process.

The key policy lever for stimulating business investment is the after-tax rate of return on investment, increases in which influence expected rates of return favorably, as well as enlarging internal sources of funds. In this connection it should be observed that during the most recent eight-year period, 1970–77 inclusive, adjusted domestic after-tax profits of U.S. nonfinancial corportions averaged 4.25 percent of their gross domestic product, compared with a 7.75 percent average for 1947–69. The estimated 1977 ratio is below 4 percent. In this calculation by George Terborgh, based on Commerce Department data, the profits estimates were adjusted for capital consumption and inventory valuations to current replacement costs from the costs charged for income tax purposes (Terborgh 1977:5). When adjusted profits are related to net worth (with tangible assets restated at replacement costs), the 1970–77 average rate of return is 3.55 percent compared with 4.9 percent for the 1947–69 period. There was a similar drop in the before-tax profit rates.

A close relationship between profit rates and investment lies at the heart of both the neoclassical and flow-of-funds theories, and appears to be substantiated by various empirical investigations. Some economists subscribe to an accelerator model of investment behavior, claiming that in other models profits are a proxy for sales or output. I would argue that the reverse is true, and that when the movements of profits and sales diverge the profit rate is the more influential variable. Thus, in the recovery since April 1975 the sluggishness in growth of private fixed investment reflects the relatively low rates of return and uncertain prospects for the future.

The sluggish investment performance since 1975 has been all the more disturbing in view of various recent studies of capital requirements in the years ahead. Thus, the study by the Bureau of Economic Analysis (BEA) indicated that in order to meet the capital requirements of mandated social programs (environment, occupational safety and health, and greater energy independence) as well as to increase capital per worker at the rate of the previous decade, nonresidential structures and equipment outlays would have to rise to around 12 percent of GNP in the latter 1970s, compared with an average of 10.5 percent in the decade 1965–75. Since that study was completed the ratio has sagged to 9.5 percent in 1976, 9.8 percent in 1977, with a projected ratio of about 10 percent for 1978 based on the BEA survey of plant and equipment spending plans. This suggests, other things being equal, that policies to raise the ratio of saving and investment to GNP by at least 2 percent would be desirable in order to avoid increases in the real interest rate that would reduce the growth of capital and output per worker.

Economists have made a persuasive case that the U.S. tax system is biased against saving and investment—more so than is true of most other industrialized countries—and that reduction of the biases and creation of a more favorable climate for saving and investment would stimulate industry R&D spending as well as investment generally. In view of the projections of a "capital shortage" in the years ahead this is all the more important in the normative sense that the economic goals of our society, including continuation of past trends in productivity and real income per capita plus existing mandated social programs, cannot be achieved without devoting a larger fraction of GNP to capital formation.[2]

The theoretical case for greater capital formation has been made most forcefully by Martin Feldstein, President of the National Bureau of Economic Research. He points out that personal and corporate income taxes put a wedge between the national rate of return on capital and the net rate received by savers. He estimates that the latter rate, and thus the rate of time discount of future consumption, is less than half of the corresponding pretax average rate of return on private investment in the United States. As he puts it: "If the amount of future consumption that individuals require to forego a dollar's worth of present consumption is less than the rate at which investment produces future income from current capital investments we should save more" (Feldstein 1977). He also argues that the Social Security system reduces saving in the U.S.

Ture and Sanden explain the bias against saving and investment in the present U.S. tax system somewhat differently, stating:

". . . for the most part neither the part of income which is saved nor the return on such saving is excluded from the base of the income tax, the principal source of tax revenue. Since saving is the capitalized amount of the future income purchased by the saving, this characteristic of the income tax subjects the part of current income used to buy future income to a double tax, whereas the part of current income used to buy consumption goods is taxed only once" (Ture and Sanden 1977: 71).

Another way to put it is that income taxes reduce disposable income and thus impact both consumption and saving, but that since future income from the investments into which savings flow are also taxed, after-tax returns and thus the present values of investments are reduced, making saving and investment less attractive relative to consumption than would be the case with a neutral tax system.

Capital recovery allowances, which are not the full equivalent of expensing capital outlays, particularly in an inflationary environment when depreciation allowances are at original cost, ameliorate but do not eliminate the disproportionate burden on saving. So do certain tax "loopholes." On the other hand, some nonincome taxes accentuate antisaving bias. This is true of taxes on capital gains, which are basically capitalizations of expected increases in the earnings of assets. Since such earnings increases will be taxed as they accrue, taxing the capitalized value of such increases is a further layer of taxation on the same income stream. Estate, inheritance, and gift taxes are similar in their impact to capital gains taxes. Property taxes also add to the burden of saving, since they are the equivalent of income taxes on explicit or implicit income from the property. Furthermore, the provisions of the Tax Reform Act of 1969 limiting the maximum marginal rate on "earned " income to 50 percent in contrast to 70 percent on property income plainly serves to discourage investment.

In order to eliminate the antisaving bias of the U.S. tax system, radical reform would be necessary, involving two major measures:

1. The corporation income tax should be repealed, attributing corporate earnings to shareholders for inclusion in their taxable income—which, incidentally, would remove the differential treatment of corporations and unincorporated enterprises.
2. Current saving should be excluded from the base of the individual income tax while returns from investment and repayments of principal are fully taxed. Revenue losses could be made up by increasing tax rates on personal income less net saving or by a value-added tax that is essentially neutral with respect to saving decisions. Before specifying tax policy options for increasing after-tax profits, I want to stress the need to increase business earning power.

The basic cause of the decline in the profit rate that began in 1966 was the accelerating pace of price inflation. For one thing, most corporate managements apparently did not adopt pricing policies (to the extent they had discretion over prices) to reflect fully the impact of inflation on costs—particularly the replacement cost of fixed capital and inventories. More important, in my view, has been the use of macroeconomic policy to restrain inflation to the extent of holding price increases below the increase of unit costs—thus squeezing profit margins—in periods of high-level activity—particularly 1966, 1969, 1973, and also 1978, when rates of return again appear to be declining a bit. In addition, the wage-price freeze and subsequent controls from August 1971 to April 1974 not only limited profits growth, but distorted relative rates of return, which contributed to inadequate investment and capacity bottlenecks in 1973-74 in some basic industries. I also believe it was no accident that industry outlays for R&D have sagged in the 1970s, along with profit rate. Although R&D is expensed, when profits are sagging there is pressure to reduce expenses. More research is needed, however, on the relationship of current and prospective profit rates on R&D expenditure decisions.

TAX PROPOSALS

Enumeration of some of the more prominent tax proposals for stimulating private investment and saving follows.

1. Reducing effective corporate income tax rates by one or more of the following measures:

   a) Further acceleration of depreciation charges for tax purposes, or indexing depreciation to adjust from book depreciation of fixed assets at original cost to replacement costs based either on specific capital goods price indexes or on general price indexes, such as the private GNP deflator.

   b. Reduction of corporate income tax rates by decreasing the 22 percent normal tax, decreasing or graduating the present 26 percent surtax applicable to income above the $25,000 surtax exemption, increasing the surtax exemption, or by some combination of the alternatives. To encourage small business, an increase in the surtax exemption and a graduation of rates for increments of net income would be helpful.

   c) Elimination or reduction of the double taxation of corporate dividends. Here, too, there are alternative approaches, principally either to allow the corporation a deduction for its dividend distributions (as is done for interest payments), or to allow the shareholder a credit equivalent to the tax paid by the corporation with respect to the distributed earnings. The former approach is administratively simpler. Or, the corporate and personal income taxes could be completely integrated, with the shareholder paying personal income taxes on both dividends and his share of undistributed profits.

   d) Increase of the investment tax credit from 10 percent to, say, 15 percent. The advantage of the credit is that tax liabilities can be reduced by businesses, other things being equal, only by increasing investment. Most studies indicate that the credit does increase investment by somewhat more than the revenue loss. Businessmen claim that making the credit permanent would further increase its effectiveness.

2. Adjustment of the personal income tax.

   a) The Tax Reform Act of 1969 provided a maximum marginal rate on "earned" income. Extension of the maximum rate to property or capital income as well would encourage investment.

b) Reducing personal income taxes generally, as revenue requirements permit, and reducing the steepness of graduation of marginal rates, would also reduce antisaving bias. Changes in graduation would, however, have to be weighed against equity consideration.

c) Strengthening tax incentives for personal saving. There are a number of such incentives in existing law. Some provide tax exemption or deferral for income from capital, such as provisions relating to pension, profit-sharing, and stock bonus plans. Others give tax deferral to income that is saved. As discussed in the recent report of the Joint Committee on Taxation, some of the existing provisions could be broadened, or new provisions added (U.S. Congress 1977).

3. Revision of the capital gains tax.

A "rollover" treatment of capital gains, similar to that for owner-occupied residences, could be accorded to all assets by deferring the tax on gains so long as the proceeds from the sale of the assets were reinvested fully. Also, capital gains tax rates could be reduced, or an annual exemption of a specific amount provided. In addition, a more symmetrical treatment of capital gains and losses would be desirable to encourage greater willingness to undertake risky innovations.

With respect to the effectiveness of investment incentives involving a reduction in the corporate tax rate, quite a few econometric studies have been undertaken to answer the question, as recently reviewed by Visacher. Various analyses, such as those by Jorgenson and Hall, Bischoff, and Coen showed significant stimulative effects on investment of past increases in the investment tax credit, in particular, and of accelerated depreciation and reduction of the corporate tax rate. The effect of the latter was reduced, of course, by the fact that it lessened the tax-reducing effect of the other incentives on the implicit rental cost of capital.

As Christensen (1969) pointed out, however, the models showing strong effects of incentives were prepared in a partial equilibrium context. When the investment models are specified within a general equilibrium framework and tested in complete econometric models of the U.S. economy, the effects of the investment stimuli were found to be considerably less by Taubman and Wales, Klein and Taubman, Christensen, and others. As Harberger has noted, when tax incentives are analyzed in a general equilibrium framework, the effects attributed to them will vary significantly depending on the complementary policies pursued—particularly fiscal policy in financing the tax expenditures and associated monetary policies—as well as on related structural relations in the model, such as the interest sensitivity of saving (Harberger 1971). Also, as Lucas discovered, if it is assumed that tax changes are correctly anticipated by businessmen, the investment impact is substantially increased (Lucas 1975).

One important lesson from this discussion is, I believe, that tax incentives for investment (including R&D, discussed below) can be effective as long as the complementary macroeconomic policies are expansive and not offsetting. As Harberger wrote: "In the final analysis the long-run effects of investment incentives on output will stem from their influence on the amounts of basic resources (labor and capital) which are voluntarily supplied to the market. Ultimately it is how these tax stimuli affect the labor-leisure choice and the savings decision that determine their effect upon output" (Harberger 1971).

Finally, a few thoughts about federal nontax policies to encourage innovation and investment. Essential to vigorous investment growth is business confidence, as stressed by Arthur Burns (1977: 1), who attributes its sluggish recovery to date to the low level of corporate profits after inflation adjustments and lack of business confidence in the future as reflected in the stock markets. Certainly confidence has suffered many blows in recent years, and Burns does not view the multitude of policy initiatives since January 1977 (whose outcomes and impacts are uncertain), and the failure to date to deal with the inadequate profit rate as helping. Clear recognition of the key role of profits in our type of economy is needed and enactment of some of the types of measures suggested above would certainly be positively construed.

Regulatory reform to eliminate unnecessary regulations, and rationalize that which is retained on clear-cut cost-benefit principles, would also go a long way toward raising business confidence. In that connection it should be observed that product standards that are so stringent and costly as to slow down the introduction of new and improved products, as has been the case in the pharmaceutical industry since 1962, reduce the productivity effect and rates of return on product R&D. As far as regulation of public utilities and other natural monopolies is concerned, it is encouraging that in recent years regulation is being viewed less narrowly as merely a tool for controlling rates of return, and there is experimentation with using regulation positively, as a means of spurring more vigorous innovative activity and productivity advance in the regulated industries (Kendrick 1975).

PUBLIC SECTOR INVESTMENT

It is frequently advocated that once the full employment zone is reached, governments should run budget surpluses so as to supplement private saving in the financing of business investment. That is well and good, assuming private demand is strong enough to maintain full employment. But even more important for productivity growth is the appropriate allocation of government outlays between current services and investments, including the intangibles—R&D, education, training, health, safety, and mobility. As shown in Table 8-1, governments at all levels have devoted close to half of their revenues net of transfer payments to tangible and intangible investments. This is a higher fraction than is devoted to investments (including child-rearing) by the personal sector, which has averaged less than 40 percent in high-level years. Thus, the relative shift of national income since 1929 from the private to the public sector is one reason for the upward trend of the total investment ratio through 1966. But the business sector has consistently devoted more than its entire disposable income (gross cash flow) to investment. A major reason for the decline in the ratio of total gross investment to GNP after 1966 was the drop in the ratio of business cash flow to GNP 1966–69, a decline in the public investment ratio 1969–73, and the relative shift of gross income to persons after 1966.

It is important that governments continue to allocate a major portion of their net revenues to total investment. The minor part of such investments that is used to reduce unit real costs of government operations has the important payoff of making public monies go further by raising the productivity of the resources commanded by governments and thus reducing drain on other resources to pay for current operations. The major part of public outlays devoted to infrastructure and intangibles is important so long as social rate of return is at least equal to the rate of return on private investment. An important part of the return on public investment is its contribution to raising the productivity of private industry, thus increasing rates of return on private investments and innovational activity.

Of more direct relevance to our topic, it is highly important for scientific and technological progress that the federal government pursue a reasonably steady and predictable policy with respect to investment of public funds in support of R&D. The sharp cut-back of such support in the late 1960s and early 1970s was the primary reason for the substantial drop in the ratio of R&D expenditures to GNP and the bulge in the unemployment rates of scientists and engineers. I would hope that the new Science Adviser to the President and his Office of Science and Technology Policy would promote gradual increases in federal funding of R&D that are at least in line with the growth of potential GNP—and possibly somewhat faster if the estimated benefits warrant it. A steady, predictable R&D funding policy is important in view of the long lead-time required for planning the education of scientists and engineers.

Particularly important is steady, adequate support for basic research in order to keep up the flow of new knowledge into educational channels and into applied research, raising the productivity of both. Incidentally, the manner in which the findings of basic research enter the corpus of transmitted knowledge and their applications is an area requiring further research.

POLICIES TO PROMOTE R&D AND INVESTMENT

In this section, I turn to a discussion of some of the policy options for direct stimulation of private R&D expenditures and related activities. The case for special treatment of private R&D spending rests primarily on its characteristics of:

1. Inappropriability by the funding firm of all the benefits of its inventions because of externalities.
2. The uninsurable uncertainties of the outcomes of R&D.
3. Indivisibilities requiring R&D resources on an optimum scale larger than many firms can afford.

The theoretical arguments have been buttressed by research such as Mansfield's suggesting that social rates of return to R&D are far higher than—possibly even double—private rates of return. To the extent that the special characteristics of R&D differ by industry, by size of firm, and by type of project, a case can be made for selective grants or subsidies. We shall look at this after considering across-the-board incentives. The latter are obviously much more economical and convenient to administer, as they involve less bureaucratic judgment.

Business R&D outlays already enjoy an advantage over tangible fixed investment in that, since 1954, they may definitely be written off as an expense in the year in which they are incurred. The most frequently mentioned additional incentive is some form of tax credit, or equivalent cash payment to firms paying no tax, for business R&D outlays. Probably the most feasible plan would be to extend the present 10 percent tax credit on equipment purchases to include industrial R&D either as defined by the Financial Accounting Standards Board or as specifically defined for the purpose. An advantage of this approach is that there would be little or no interference by government with the private decisionmaking process. The tax purist would prefer to see a direct subsidy payment, which would have the same effect.

One objection to this approach is that public funds would tend to substitute in some degree for private. Judging from studies of the tangible investment tax credit, however, there would be a substantial positive effect. An alternative proposal, which would induce a larger increase in R&D outlays, would be to permit a larger tax credit on incremental R&D over and above the outlays of the previous year, or an average of several prior years. Even a 50 percent incremental R&D tax credit would cost the U.S. Treasury less than $1 billion, assuming a 10 percent increase in business R&D between 1978 and 1979. This compares with an almost $2 billion revenue loss from a 10 percent average credit on the $19 billion or so that business may spend on R&D in 1978.

A variant of the R&D tax credit proposal, whether average or incremental, would be to graduate the credit inversely to the size of the firm's R&D program up to some point. The rationale for graduation lies in the fact that uncertainties, indivisibilities, and even externalities tend to have a lessened negative impact on private R&D programs as they increase in size up to some point.

Another variant of the tax credit proposal, which I originated in a paper several years ago, would be to allow a larger credit to producers of capital goods and possibly of intermediate producers goods (Kendrick 1974a: 139–140). The rationale for this stems from *a priori* reasoning buttressed by Terleckyj's research findings that the productivity effects of indirect R&D performed by makers of producers' goods and purchased by user firms are even greater than the effects of their direct R&D outlays. Another justification for special incentives for capital goods producers is that to the extent that their relative productivity rises through process R&D and the product R&D of the firms from which they buy, the relative price of capital goods will tend to fall, which will stimulate tangible investment.

A related proposal is to allow accelerated depreciation of R&D plant and equipment outlays by business, or possibly a complete write-off for tax purposes in the year in which the costs are incurred. Alternatively, a larger investment tax credit could be granted for R&D facilities. Such measures would help increase the productivity of resources devoted to private R&D. By the same token, government grants to help modernize R&D facilities of universities and private nonprofit organizations would help improve the effectiveness of R&D activities in those sectors.

With respect to selective support of R&D, there have been proposals for creating a Federal Center for Industrial R&D, which would be authorized to disburse funds for R&D projects in the public interest that would not otherwise be undertaken because of major uncertainties high costs, or too great a fragmentation of a particular industy. In the latter case, the grants could be made on a matching basis to industry associations. Such arrangements for cooperative R&D might require special exemptions from the antitrust laws, however, governments of many other industrialized countries support such centers.

Governmental procurement policies can also be used to stimulate innovative activity by suppliers, as the ETIP experimental programs have demonstrated. Further institutionalization of such programs, particularly at the state and local levels, on a cooperative basis, is indicated.

During the past decade, federal government support for the gathering of domestic and foreign scientific and technological information has declined drastically. It is time again to increase informational services, particularly information from foreign countries whose R&D activities have increased relative to those in the United States. In that connection, the Internal Revenue Service should again allow full deduction of travel expenses to U.S. scientists who attend scientific meetings abroad. Special attention should be paid to gathering and disseminating information that would be of value to technologically lagging industries in this country. Informational services enhance the return to domestic R&D investments, as is evidenced by the fact that the National Technical Information Service (NTIS) is self-supporting.

Renewed support by the federal government to state technical service centers should be considered. These are of particular value to smaller firms. Evaluation of NSF's Innovation Center experiment may indicate the desirability of expanding the number of centers.

There are various other proposals for aiding small technical enterprises and "lone wolf" inventors, such as government guarantees of Small Business Investment Corporation loans to such enterprises, or the creation of a national research and development corporation on the British model, or tax incentives for shareholders of private corporations that invest in new or existing small technology-based companies.

Space precludes the discussions or enumeration of other proposals that have been made to encourage R&D and innovative activity. A useful compilation is contained in the document *U.S. Technology Policy,* published in March 1977 by NTIS for the Office of the Assistant Secretary for Science and Technology, U.S. Department of Commerce. Unfortunately, there has not been enough study and research with respect to the impact of the various policy options, although the policy studies that have been and are being supported by NSF are helpful and should be continued. But we shall never know enough to devise an optimal policy package for science and technology, or any other complex field. We must proceed to formulate a coherent set of policies on the basis of the best available knowledge at this time, presumably under the leadership of the Office of Science and Technology Policy, drawing on the best knowledge and advice available in NSF, the Commerce Department, and other agencies concerned.

Science and technology policy must, of course, be coordinated with related policies in order to promote the development of natural and human resources, the productivity of those resources, and their efficient economic utilization in order to attain the long-term objectives of our society. At present there is no single instrument of the federal government devoted to such coordination and formulation of consistent long-range policies. One is badly needed, since policies relating to science and technology, and the other major problem areas in our society, should not be made in isolation.

We assume that a combination of the policies outlined above increases the proportion of total R&D to GNP from the 2.2 percent of 1977 to 2.8 percent in 1990. This would result in a contribution to advances in knowledge of 0.9 percent, instead of the 0.6 projected assuming no relative increase. Furthermore, we would expect a 0.1 percent larger contribution from informal inventive and innovative activity, stimulated by the larger number of major inventions and innovations emerging from formal R&D programs. Also, the higher rate of tangible investment discussed in the previous section would accelerate the rate of diffusion of new embodied technology by an additional 0.1 percent. Altogether the positive program for economic progress discussed above could accelerate the rate of advance of productive knowledge by about one-half, from 0.9 to 1.4 percent.

CHANGES IN QUALITY OF LABOR

Projected increases in outlays for education and training and the associated real stocks of human capital should be accelerated somewhat by accelerated increases in stocks of tangible capital and of productive knowledge and know-how. Advances in technology generally upgrade the structure of demand for labor, increasing the requirements for more highly educated and trained personnel. Acceleration of technological advance, therefore, would tend to raise the prospective rates of return on higher education (which declined in the 1970s) and on training for skilled occupations, and thus to accelerate the growth of such investments by individuals and firms.

Various governmental initiatives are available to reinforce the trend toward higher levels of average education and training per worker in addition to increased public expenditures. There are bills before Congress to permit deduction from individual taxable income or to provide tax credits for some portion of tuition expenses. Expansion of loans, or loan guarantees from public funds for college or technical school expenses, has been advocated.[3] Expansion of subsidies to industry for training of youth and disadvantaged workers by the Employment and Training Administration of the U.S. Department of Labor would help increase employment as well as training. Expansion of continuing adult education programs is particularly important in view of accelerating technological advance and the gradual increase in the average age of the labor force projected for the decade ahead.

Finally, programs for further development and more rapid diffusion of educational technology would help increase the productivity of education and training. Major technological advances have been and are being made in the areas of computer-assisted instruction, programmed materials, closed-circuit TV, films, and other teaching aids. But diffusion has been slow in part because of the fragmented nature of the market. Possibly performance standards could be agreed on and centralized purchasing done through national associations of state and local governments and educational institutions at various levels. It is to be hoped that the Commissioner of Education in the Department of Health, Education and Welfare and the Administrator of Employment and Training in the Department of Labor are developing policies to enhance the productivity, as well as expand the volume, of resources devoted to education and training. In the high growth projection, we estimate that the policies noted in this section could result in a 0.1 percent larger contribution of education and training to growth in the 1980 decade.

With respect to health and vitality, the projection of a continued decline in the length of the average work week and work year suggests further minor gains from this source, according to Denison's analysis. So does the projection of continued increases of real health and safety outlays per capita. We do not envisage the possibility of further gains from this source in the high growth projection since the projected increases are already quite considerable. We would suggest, however, that intensification of health education and preventive medicine programs offer the cheapest route to additional gains.

Change in the age-sex mix of employment is not a useful policy objective. But increases in the ratio of actual to potential labor efficiency is. The main areas in which labor efficiency (under given technology) can be improved are those in which there are restrictive work practices, union work rules, or just plain lack of motivation and concern. It is here that quality of working life programs, job redesign, company productivity improvement programs, labor management productivity teams, productivity bargaining, incentive pay systems, and other programs designed to stimulate worker cooperation and efforts to cut unit real costs can play an important role (Kendrick 1977: Chapter 11). In response to the productivity slowdown of recent years there has been increased emphasis on such programs. The initial impetus came from the creation by executive order in 1970 of the National Commission on Productivity, reconstituted in 1975 by Congressional Act as the National Center for

Productivity and Quality of Working Life. Although this Center expired September 30, 1978, it has been replaced by a National Productivity Council, chaired by the director of the Office of Management and Budget. A number of quality of working life organizations have been formed in the private sector, as has the American Productivity Center in Houston, founded by C. Jackson Grayson in 1977. This organization is promoting productivity measurement and improvement at the company level in a succession of industries. If these efforts are continued and broadened they should have a cumulative impact on labor efficiency, specifically, and productivity, in general, in the decade ahead. Accordingly, we show a 0.1 percent positive contribution to growth from an increase in the ratio of actual to potential labor efficiency in our high projection.

It should also be noted that since fear of unemployment is a major cause of restrictive work rules and practices, maintenance of relatively full employment and provisions for job security by firms and other organizations (to the extent feasible) would also help increase labor efficiency.

CHANGES IN QUALITY OF LAND

Historically, the market system has been quite effective in promoting substitution of relatively more abundant and cheaper natural resources for those that were becoming relatively scarcer and therefore more expensive. Such substitutions have been further accelerated by price incentives (when allowed to operate) for search, discovery, and development of new resource supplies, and for research and development of alternative sources. Furthermore, a liberal international trade policy mitigates the effect on productivity of a declining average quality of domestic natural resources. I would recommend more complete reliance on market pricing of natural resources, and further liberalization of foreign trade policy, except where national security considerations dictate greater reliance on domestic resources even when costs are higher.

Possibly the effectiveness of the market-directed enterprise system could be enhanced by better projections of future requirements by firms and concerned government agencies. Nevertheless, we do not envisage any major offsets to the negative impact of declining average resources quality on productivity, especially in view of the accelerated growth projected in this section and the assumption of policies to promote greater energy independence. It is always possible, of course, that major new natural resource discoveries will be made, or that technological breakthroughs on new energy sources will come sooner than expected.

RESOURCE REALLOCATIONS

Relative shifts of labor and capital raised productivity in past periods, and are projected to continue to do so to a minor extent in the future. The tendency might be speeded up somewhat if competition and labor- and capital-mobility were increased. Certainly more vigorous enforcement of antitrust laws would help. So, too, would actions to reduce restrictions on entry by certain labor unions, professional associations, and other organizations. Better business and economic data would facilitate planning of adjustments. Improvement of programs to help retrain, relocate, and place displaced workers under the Comprehensive Employment and Training Act of 1973 could speed up mobility. Maintenance of high-level aggregate economic activity itself facilitates adjustments.

While I support these kinds of policies, I do not project a larger contribution to growth than is shown in the basic projection. Some increase in resource mobility would be required just to keep up with the faster pace of technological progress projected in our high growth model, and a faster shift to services has a negative weighting effect.

VOLUME-RELATED FACTORS

Given the faster rate of economic growth in the high growth projection, economies of scale would obviously contribute more than in the standard projection—0.5 compared with 0.35 percent. I am not projecting a higher rate of utilization of the higher productive capacity in 1990 than in the basic projection.

The rate of productivity is not only affected by the volume factors just described, but also by the variability of production over a period of time (Mohr forthcoming). So it is important from this point of view that fluctuations in real GNP, if they occur in the 1980 decade, be held to the small average amplitude of the post-World War II era up to 1973. The more severe 1973-75 contraction produced the first absolute decline in productivity in a quarter of a century, with unfavorable effects from which the economy has not yet fully recovered.

NET GOVERNMENT IMPACT

The relative increase in government employment will likely continue, all of it occurring at the state and local nonschool level. I do project that a vigorous program to enhance productivity in governments at all levels can add another 0.1 percent to the growth impact of government services to business.

Since 1973 the Bureau of Labor Statistics has been preparing and publishing labor productivity indexes, by functional groupings. These now cover outputs produced by 65 percent of federal government civilian employees in 245 organizational elements of 48 agencies. Just as important, the Joint Financial Management Improvement Program established by the Office of Management and Budget has been authorized to prepare annual reports analyzing the reasons for productivity changes and to prepare recommendations and plans for future productivity programs. The plans involve rationalization of internal agency programs for cost-reducing capital outlays, as well as creation of agency productivity committees to develop ideas for enhancing worker efficiency. The National Center for Productivity, which has strongly supported the federal productivity measurement and improvement programs, has been taking steps to encourage similar programs at the state and local level.

If these programs are continued and strengthened, it is not too much to expect that there should be some acceleration in government productivity growth in the decade ahead, with benefits to business and consumers (assuming government activities and outputs are the appropriate ones!).

With respect to increases in business costs imposed by governmental requirements and regulations—such as paperwork and conforming to standards—the basic projection already assumes some easing in the decade ahead. Further progress towards reducing paperwork, simplification of regulations, and application of strict cost-benefit principles in revising old standards and promulgating new ones as necessary, could further reduce the negative productivity impact of government requirements.

CONCLUSION

A growth rate close to 5 percent is not the most probable outcome for the decade ahead, and will not be achieved without broad public and official understanding of the benefits of such a rate and the kinds of measures necessary to stimulate productivity. If it is attained it will mean a rate of increase in real income per capita of about 3.5 percent a year, compared with 2.3 percent 1948-73. Increases in real labor compensation per hour would accelerate to about 4 percent. This would help reduce the impact of money wage-rate increases on unit costs, contributing to reduce inflation. It would help increase the international competitiveness of U.S. products, and thus contribute to improving the trade balance. Finally, it would increase the material strength of the nation and reduce the relative burden of outlays required for national security in an unsettled world.

Table 8–1. Total Gross Investment in Relation to Gross Product and
Sectoral Disposable Income, U.S. Domestic Economy
(Percentages, Selected Peak Years 1929–1973)

	1929	1948	1966	1973
Persons:				
DI/GNP	78.8	70.4	63.0	68.8
GI/DI	33.2	35.2	41.9	38.5
GI/GNP	26.1	24.8	26.4	26.5
Business:				
DI/GNP	10.0	10.2	12.5	9.3
GI/DI	124.4	123.8	102.4	128.0
GI/GNP	12.4	12.6	12.8	11.9
Governments:				
DI/GNP	10.4	18.7	24.2	21.7
GI/DI	44.3	28.6	46.3	46.5
GI/GNP	4.6	5.2	11.2	10.1
Total economy				
GI/GNP	43.1	42.7	50.5	48.5

Source: Kendrick (1976: 236–237).
Note: DI = disposable income of each sector
       GI   = total gross investment, tangible plus intangible
       GNP = gross national product or sum of sectoral disposable incomes

NOTES TO CHAPTER 8

1. Some of the following material has been drawn from parts of papers prepared by the author for the American Enterprise Institute, "Productivity and Economic Progress," and for the National Science Foundation in "Relationships Between R&D and Economic Growth Productivity" (Nov. 9, 1977).

2. See especially the study of capital requirements in 1980 prepared by the Bureau of Economic Analysis, summarized in the 1976 *Annual Report of the Council of Economic Advisers.*

3. See National Commission on Productivity (1971). In his *1978 Economic Report* President Carter has recommended loans and loan guarantees rather than tuition tax credits.

SUMMARY AND CONCLUSIONS:

SOME PARTIAL ANSWERS TO IMPORTANT QUESTIONS
Shlomo Maital and Noah M. Meltz

Problems related to the economy—energy, inflation, unemployment, balance of payments, poverty, the environment—often seem like a family of noisy children. All clamor for, and generally receive, due attention. In many ways, productivity has been an ignored middle child, despite its centrality to most of the other issues. Yet there is evidence of growing awareness that our productiveness, or lack of it, will have as much to do with our well-being as any other single variable. In his 1978 Economic Report, President Carter made brief mention of productivity, in the context of flagging business investment. Last year, in his 1979 Report, the "realities of slower productivity growth" were prominently featured in relation to job creation, living standards and inflation. And the current recession—and consequent glum statistics on output per person—has thrust the issue into the public eye even more.

The eight essays in this volume have addressed themselves to nearly all the key questions: Why should we be concerned about lagging productivity growth? What in fact is "productivity", and how should it best be measured? By how much has productivity declined? Is this decline cyclical in nature, related to the ebbs and flows of economic activity, or it is a secular departure from trend? What can be learned from Canada's experience, compared with that of the United States? What are the main sources of declining productivity growth? Does the possibility that people may work less hard today than they once did have something to do with it? What light can other disciplines shed on the problem? Is the problem of lagging productivity growth likely to improve, or become worse? What can be done to raise the level of productivity, and its rate of growth? What follows is an attempt to summarize and synthesize the contents of this book.

Why Should We Be Concerned about the Rate of Growth of Productivity?

Mark Twain once described one of his unforgettable characters as "fast rising from affluence to poverty". Do recent data on productivity indicate that the United States and Canada have embarked on a similar, fast "rise"? Are there solid reasons for us to be concerned?

Western economies have lately suffered the painful and repeated malady of stagflation—unacceptably high levels of both inflation and unemployment. A persuasive explanation of stagflation may be found, with productivity as the root cause, without the need for discarding Keynesian theory. "The main channel through which productivity change affects the economy," John Kendrick notes, "is its relationship to unit costs and prices". A slowdown in productivity growth can lead to higher inflation by accelerating the rise in unit costs. Moreover, wage bargains have been based on assumed productivity gains that no longer exist. When real wages rise faster than productivity growth can support, they become inconsistent with full employment; more unemployment results. Many collective agreements mention productivity growth rates that are twice those that prevail in practice.

Productivity growth also helps mediate social conflict, Albert Rees points out. The extra output made available by higher productivity creates a "social dividend" whose distribution "softens the clashes between competing groups". Absence of that dividend may express itself as inflation. When various segments of society express their aspirations for higher living standards by raising their money claims on available output, those claims in aggregate may exceed total output, with the result that prices rise. What is more, faced with the expectation of inflation, it may be perfectly rational for each individual or group of individuals to make such immoderate money claims, even though collectively the result is disastrous. This explains why a drop of 1 or 2 percent in the rate of productivity growth may lead to many times that amount of added inflation.

Not only is productivity growth "the main source of improvements in our standard of living" (Rees), it also appears to be the main source of economic growth in the major Western industrialized nations in the post-World War II period. Nishimizu and Hulten take note of the very basic, but heretofore ignored, point that productivity change itself generates additional capital accumulation. When this "indirect" contribution of productivity growth to aggregate output is added to its direct contribution, to create what the authors term a "dynamic residual," "productivity change . . . [accounts] for from more than one-half up to the entirety of the aggregate economic growth" in nine industrialized countries since World War II.

Why, then, should we be concerned? Because how well we live, how well we get along with one another, how well we do relative to other nations, are all related to productivity growth. It is a singularly pervasive determinant of nearly every aspect of economic performance.

There are, of course, many other legitimate economic goals besides growth. Have we explicitly favored these goals even when they came at the expense of growth? Filer poses this question provocatively:

If America desires to clean up its air, protect its workers from on-the-job hazards, and allow previously unemployed women with low levels of job experience to enter the labor force, who is to say that we are worse off achieving these goals at a cost of lower rates of productivity growth? There is no such thing as a free social cause.

Social causes are certainly not free; they are expensive. One of the key tasks of productivity research is to measure their cost in terms of lost output, an exceedingly complex problem at times. If we opt for ends that are inimical to growing productivity, we should know precisely what the economic price is. Indications are that it is high.

What Is Productivity? What Is the Best Way to Measure It?

"Productivity . . . is a ratio of output to one or more inputs" (Rees). There are many ways to define and measure the numerator of the ratio, that is, output, and the denominator, that is, input(s). Each of the three main methods is used in this volume. They are: output per man-hour, total factor productivity, and the production function method.

Output per man-hour is used by both Filer, and Ostry and Rao. It is the most common and intuitive measure of productivity, is based on reliable data, and, as Filer states, represents workers' actual command over goods and services. The major difficulty with this measure is, of course, that output is produced with capital, land, raw materials, and energy as well as with labor. Presumably, we would prefer a productivity measure that took this into account.

Total factor productivity, used by Kendrick, and Hulten and Nishimizu, divides output by a weighted average of labor and capital inputs, with weights defined as shares of each factor of production in gross output. Kendrick calls his variant total "tangible" factor productivity, because he uses gross stocks of tangible capital (land, structures and equipment, and inventories). The advantage of this measure is that it allows us to measure separately the contribution to output of improvements in *quality,* and increases in *quantity,* of labor and capital. Difficulties arise in choice of weights, particularly under conditions of factor market disequilibrium (Bruno 1968).

Output per man-hour, and total factor productivity, are easily reconciled, as Kendrick notes. Growth in total factor productivity equals growth in output per man-hour minus the contribution to output growth made by increasing capital per person; the latter is simply the rate of increase in capital per man-hour multiplied by capital's share in national income.

Production function approach is taken by Ostry and Rao to "explain" output, for thirty-five industries, as a function of capital, labor, energy, and materials—a so-called production function. Estimating the parameters of this function can reveal a great deal about the nature and magnitude of technical change, economies of scale, and the contribution of each individual factor of production to output. This approach is a generalization of total factor productivity, which rests on an assumed, implicit production function. The inclusion of energy and materials is an interesting innovation. It does, however, cause difficulties in interpretation; labor could come out more productive following greater use of energy, but this is not what we generally mean by higher productivity. Leaving out intermediate goods, though, is equally problematic. Nishimizu (1975) reasons that if higher productivity makes intermediate goods cheaper, ignoring this effect leads to underestimates in the importance of productivity growth in intermediate good producing sectors.

By How Much Has Productivity Growth Declined? Is This Decline Cyclical, Or Is It a Secular Departure From Trend?

It is exceedingly important to determine whether the lag in productivity growth is not a "statistical artifact," and to decide whether it is a temporary phenomenon related to the business cycle or a more or less permanent situation representing a firm departure from previous trends.

There is near unanimous agreement that the drop in productivity growth is indeed real. But how much of it stems from the fact that productivity normally stagnates during recession, and that the 1973-75 U.S. recession was a particularly deep one. Kendrick explains that the "high water mark" of total productivity growth for the United States was during 1948-66, when a 2.8 percent annual average increase was achieved. In the lastest period, 1966-78, the rate of productivity advance fell by one-half. For the last part of this period, 1973-78, he ascribes "almost half of the retardation [in productivity growth]" to the fact that "the economy had not yet fully recovered from the 1973-75 recession." This is consistent with the fact he notes that during the six postwar contractions in the United States, total factor productivity *fell* by nearly 0.5 percent yearly, on average. As the U.S. economy again dips into recession, this particular pattern seems to be faithfully repeating itself.

A dissenting position is adopted by Filer who claims that "the data do not reveal an unquestionable downturn in growth of output per labor-hour. The world may not be as bleak as we have been telling ourselves." He points out that the lowest growth rate of productivity, 1.7 percent, occurred in 1949, and the third highest, 4.5 percent, was in 1976. Moreover, Filer argues, if we exclude 1974 from our data, the average rate of growth in output per man-hour turns out to be 2.73 percent, exactly the same rate of growth as two decades earlier.

Apparently Canada did not experience a similar dip in productivity growth from 1966 on. Ostry and Rao cite figures showing that output per man-hour in all Canadian industries grew by just over 3 percent yearly for 1957-66 and 1967-73. Moreover, following the 1973-74 oil crisis, productivity gains returned, on average, to close to their previous values. This unusual divergence in Canadian and American experience—generally, Canada's economy follows that of the United States closely—stirred considerable interest and curiousity among contributors to this volume, and merits further investigation.

What Are Some of the Similarities, and Differences, in Canada's Productivity Experience, Compared to the United States?

If productivity growth was already slowing down in the United States by 1968, this was not true of Canada, as we have noted. Ostry and Rao show that Canada maintained strong productivity growth during 1967-73, based on "increased usage of capital" and "technological progress." In the recession years of 1974 and 1975, output per man-hour actually fell. They label this "in part . . . a cyclical phenomenon associated with the rate of labor hoarding," that is, with the retaining of workers even though the full amount of their labor is not needed, and point to evidence that "the rate of paid labor hoarding in manufacturing industries rose to levels three to five times above the 1961 to 1970 average". (Studies of U.S. experience suggest American firms may have used unemployment benefits to bankroll, in part, their own hoarding of labor). Meltz expresses some reservations about the labor hoarding theory.

Ostry and Rao hint that Canada's strong productivity showing prior to 1973 may have been related to higher capital formation in Canada, compared with the United States. It is not clear whether this also applies to the post-1975 period, when output per man-hour in Canada seemed to return to its former trend rate while in the United States it failed to do so. The reasons underlying this unusual divergence, could they be determined with precision, would shed much light on the determinants of productivity in both countries. One consequence has been that output per man-hour in Canada rose from less than two-thirds that of the United States (in 1960) to about three-quarters (in 1977). Japan has made even more striking gains, moving from 30 percent of U.S. productivity levels to virtual equality with Canada in the same time span. A recent paper by Jorgenson and Nishimizu (1978) showed that the level of *technology* in Japan pulled even with that of the United States between 1973 and 1974. Whatever the *causes* of lagging productivity in the United States—the subject we are about to turn to—the international *consequence,* should it persist, appears clear: weakening American industrial power, as other countries join West Germany, Denmark, Sweden, and Switzerland in exceeding U.S. per capita GNP.

What Are the Major Sources of Declining Productivity Growth? In Particular, Are People Perhaps Working Less Hard Than They Once Did?

In our efforts to "collar the culprit" for lagging productivity, the list of suspects is long and varied—slower technical change, decreased capital formation and consequent aging capital stock, decreased R&D spending, deteriorating quality of labor or management skills, or simply diminished effort per man-hour worked. Accurately identifying the cause or causes is very important, because it is a precondition for constructing the proper policies.

Kendrick and Filer each attack the problem quite differently and, not surprisingly, come up with different answers. (Anticipating this, Rees states from the outset that sources of productivity change are inter-related, hence "there is no unique way of partitioning productivity change" among them). Making use of Denison's growth-accounting approach (Denison, 1967, 1972), Kendrick finds that the 1.9 percent yearly drop in productivity growth for the United States can be apportioned roughly equally among four different causes: (1) slower growth in output, (2) slower technical change, (3) shifts of resources toward sectors where productivity gains are traditionally small, and (4) the negative effect of government regulation and the declining quality of land and natural resources.

Filer takes a multiple regression approach, with the change in output per man-hour as his dependent variable. He examines the early 1960s through the mid-1970s, and succeeds in explaining virtually all the variation in his dependent variable with only six factors. They are: (1) the rise in relative energy prices, (2) the rise in the price of capital goods, (3) changes in GNP, (4) the rising proportion of women in the workforce, (5) R&D spending (lagged both one and two years), and (6) time (entered in quadratic fashion).

Neither the Kendrick list nor the Filer list includes the favorite theory of the general public—the suggestion that we simply are not working as well or as hard as we did in the previous decade. Often, sluggish output per man-hour is taken *prima facie* as proof of this theory—as fallacious, in Rees' analogy, as inferring lower gasoline quality from diminished average miles per gallon. But many people would agree with the sociologist Amitai Etzioni that fundamental changes in the "work ethic," detrimental to productivity, have taken place:

If it is true that more and more workers are stoned on the job, would rather collect welfare than work, and, on the assembly line, are much more willing to allow it to break down—even to help it break down so that they can rest for a while—and if large numbers of people have begun to believe that hard work is unnecessary and even uncouth, the work ethic may indeed be waning. And *that* may be causing the productivity slowdown.

Leibenstein's X-efficiency theory provides the theoretical underpinnings for this explanation. He points out that the degree of effort (in contrast to the number of hours worked) on the part of employees, and indeed managers, is a variable, and that there is considerable latitude for workers in determining the nature, pace, quality, time patterns and length of each activity. Hence labor productivity will generally not be at its physical maximum. (Elsewhere, he has estimated the gap between maximal efficiency and actual output as about 20 percent, on average.) In his contribution to this volume, he focuses on the so-called "free rider" problem. Each worker (or manager) benefits in general from his firm's success. But if the firm has many employees, no single worker's contribution is significant in determining the firm's success or failure. Thus, "each worker is in a position where he would like to see workers in general do their jobs effectively, but he has no special motivation to do his particular job effectively." This is the so-called Prisoner's Dilemma, in which individualistic self-motivated behavior leads to collective ruin.

But, "not every force that lowers productivity contributes to the recent lag in productivity growth" (Rees). We must show that such forces have become more important. Perhaps it is "not unreasonable to postulate that the effort component of labor supply may have fallen off since 1970 in a way that it did not do prior to that date" (Filer). To shift from "not unreasonable" to "empirically demonstrable" requires us first to acknowledge, in Leibenstein's words, that "productivity depends on how work is organized, and on the motivational elements within the work place". From here, it is only a short step to searching beyond the borders of conventional economic theory for insights that other disciplines might contribute.

What Light Can Other Disciplines Shed on the Problem of Lagging Productivity?

If productivity depends on how work is organized, then experts on organizational behavior must have much to offer to the search for causes and cures. Organizational behavior seeks to understand why some firms are more effective and productive than others. According to Arnold, Evans, and House, while economics tries to isolate productivity-determining factors common to all firms, organizational behavior focuses on the "residual variance," that is, on ways in which firms *differ*. They accept as an article of faith the existence of X-inefficiency and seek to explain it. Their discipline, seen in this light, has a symbiotic or complementary relation to economics, rather than an adversary one.

Organizational effectiveness, they suggest, is primarily a "function of the degree of fit or congruence among the environment, the management practices, and the member preferences." They summarize for our benefit a vast body of literature on the effective use of information, goal-setting, the structure of rewards and incentives, implications of social learning theory, and self-regulation of labor. This is a valuable and necessary first step toward an even more difficult undertaking—showing that organizational effectiveness has declined in recent years (and, with it, productivity growth), and indicating in which specific areas this has occurred.

Is the Problem of Slow Productivity Growth Likely to Improve, or Become Worse?

The overall picture that emerges from these eight essays is both pessimistic and optimistic—pessimistic, because powerful forces are at work that continue to depress productivity growth (at least, in the United States), and optimistic, because a wide range of effective policies exist for surmounting the problem.

Kendrick forecasts that over the coming decade productivity growth for the United States will accelerate only modestly, to 1.8 percent annually (from 1.4 percent at present), still well below the 3 percent of the two postwar decades. More favorable age-sex mix of the labor force and, hopefully, a high level of employment will be offset by continued declines in the quality of natural resources, unfavorable sectoral shifts, and slower technical change.

If it is true that "more and more industries (are becoming) dominated by a relatively small number of very large firms" (Arnold, Evans, and House), then the amount of energy, effort, and motivation that people bring to their places of work will take on even more importance than it does at present. For, as Leibenstein argues, as firm sizes increases, firms become bureaucracies, and "the cash nexis between the demand for the products of effort and the supply of effort becomes attenuated," further aggravating the "free rider" problem. An alienated worker is not a productive one.

Filer notes the rise, over the past decade, in the proportion of workers who feel they are asked to do excessive amounts of work, and cites evidence of declining job satisfaction. Although the correlation between productivity and job satisfaction is uncertain (some studies show it to be negative), we cannot help but feel that continuing worker disaffection will be related to poor productivity performance, both as cause and as effect.

It is Kendrick's view that the proper combination of macroeconomic policies can restore the magical 3 percent productivity growth rate. We now turn to some of these remedies.

What Can Be Done to Raise the Level and Growth Rate, of Productivity?

In economic debate, policy implications follow analysis almost as inexorably as prescription follows diagnosis in medicine.

From the two papers on "remedies", it is clear that Canada and the United States differ both in the nature of their productivity problems and in their productivity objectives. While Canada's productivity growth rate exceeds that of the United States (though it is still well behind that of Western Europe), the *levels* of productivity of Canadian workers still trail those of American workers substantially. Hence, Daly addresses himself to measures which could close this gap.

As major causes of lower productivity in Canada Daly cites the higher degree of product diversity, tariff and non-tariff barriers to trade, relatively less technological innovation in Canada, a "greater gap between actual practice and best practice technology" in Canada than in the United States, and finally the fact that Canadian top management has less formal education, less formal training, and is generally less youthful than in the United States. (The counterintuitive Ostry and Rao finding of "constant or diminishing" returns to scale in Canadian manufacturing poses an interesting challenge to Daly's quite widely accepted view of the costs of product diversity.)

Daly urges policies that would correct the productivity-lowering factors that he lists. He also addresses the highly sensitive issue of economic nationalism, and presses the Ricardian argument that tariff barriers and policies that limit or check the operation of foreign subsidiaries in Canada primarily benefit small, elite, well-off groups. Daly is no less controversial in his views on the relation between capital intensity and productivity. He finds "no support for the view that further increases in the capital stock per person employed are needed to increase productivity levels in Canada," a view that, in general, runs counter to the thrust of Kendrick's prescriptions for the United States.

To regain the 2.8 percent annual growth rate of productivity experienced in the two decades prior to 1966, Kendrick devises a package of macroeconomic policies aimed, for the most part, at expanding capital formation. He proposes business tax reductions (mainly in the corporate income tax) that would raise the profitability of capital by about 2.5

percent, restoring it almost to mid-1960s levels, and other measures that would add 2 percent to the saving rate. Kendrick urges expansion of the investment tax credit to cover structures (as well as equipment), indexing depreciation allowances, reduction of double taxation of saving, and steps to boost R&D spending.

CONCLUSION

Joseph Pechman, Herbert Stein, and Albert Rees have all termed the slump in productivity growth "a mystery." Despite the best efforts of this book, there remain unanswered questions worthy of further investigation.

1. In spite of their great similarity, the American economy experienced a sharp decline in its productivity growth rate, while the Canadian economy did not. Was this difference due, for example, to the mix of industries in Canada, or are there some underlying factors that have helped Canada outstrip its southern neighbor? An industry by industry analysis could provide useful insights.

2. Several chapters stress the role of management. Additional micro-level research, or even "micro-micro" (according to Harvey Leibenstein, a "missing branch" of economics), could draw on the findings of organizational behavior and industrial engineering, and could assist, for instance, in developing training programs for managerial personnel.

3. Attitudes toward work merit much further research and analysis, not only as an interesting subject in itself but also in relation to the training of managers. If work attitudes have undergone important changes, the role of managers could become even more difficult and decisive.

4. How aware is the public of the importance of raising productivity? Is there a different perception of the role of productivity gains among workers in goods-producing industries (where, presumably, productivity rises are more visible) than among service workers? In the final analysis, attitudes and awareness of the public create the atmosphere within which public policy is shaped. Our present and future well being depend in large measure on the skill and energy we apply to our labor, and on how well we understand this simple truth.

BIBLIOGRAPHICAL REFERENCES

Abramovitz, M. 1977. "Rapid Growth Potential and Its Realization: The Experience of Capitalist Economics in the Postwar Period." Memorandum no. 211, Center for Research in Economic Growth, Stanford University.

Abramovitz, M. 1973. "U.S. Income, Saving and Wealth, 1929–1969." *Review of Income and Wealth* Series 19, no. 4. (December).

Abramovitz, M. 1956. "Resource and Output Trends in the U.S. since 1870." *American Economic Review* 46, no. 2. (May).

Abramovitz, M. and P. David. 1973. "Economic Growth in America: Historical Parables and Realities." Reprint no. 105, Stanford University, Center for Research in Economic Growth.

Aguilar, F.J. 1967. *Scanning the Business Environment.* New York: Macmillan.

Ahmad, S. 1966. "On the Theory of Induced Invention." *Economic Journal* 76.

Allen, J.A., J.M. Utterback, M.A. Sirbu, N.A. Ashford, and J.H. Holloman, 1978. "Government Influence on the Process of Innovation in Europe and Japan", *Research Policy* 7.

Allen, M.P. 1974. "The Structure of inter-organizational Elite Cooptation: Interlocking Corporate Directorates." *American Sociological Review* 39.

Allen, T.J. and S.I. Cohen. 1969. Information Flow in Research and Development Laboratories. *Administrative Science Quarterly* 14.

Argyris, C. 1965. *Organization and Innovation.* Homewood, Ill.: Irwin-Dorsey.

Arrow, K.J. 1962. "The Economic Implications of Learning by Doing." *Review of Economic Studies* 29.

Arrow, K.J., H. Chenery, H., B. Minhas, and R. Solow, 1961. "Capital-Labor Substitution and Economic Efficiency." *Review of Economics and Statistics.* 43, no. 3 (August).

Auer, L. 1970 *Regional Disparities of Productivity and Growth in Canada.* Ottawa: Minister of Supply and Services Canada.

Auer, L. 1970. *Canadian Agricultural Productivity.* Ottawa: Queen's Printer.

Aukrust, O. 1965. "Factors of Economic Development: A Review of Recent Research." *Productivity Measurement Review* (February).

Bacon, Robert and Walter Eltis. 1976. *Britain's Economic Problem—Too Few Producers.* London: Macmillan.

Bandura, A. 1977. *Social Learning Theory,* Englewood Cliffs, N.J.: Prentice-Hall.

Bandura, A. 1971a. *Psychological Modeling: Conflicting Theories.* Chicago: Aldine-Atherton.

Bandura, A. 1971b. "Vicarious and Self-Reinforcement Processes." In *The Nature of Reinforcement*, edited by R. Glaser. New York: Academic Press.

Berglas, E. 1965. "Investment and Technological Change." *Journal of Political Economy* 73, no. 2 (April).

Bergsman, Joel. 1974. "Commercial Policy, Allocative Efficiency, and 'X-Efficiency.'" *Quarterly Journal of Economics* 88 (August).

Berndt, E.R. and D.O. Wood. 1979. "Engineering and Econometric Interpretations of Energy-Capital Complementarity." *American Economic Review* (June).

Berndt, E. R. and D. O. Wood. 1975. "Technology, Prices and the Derived Demand for Energy." *Review of Economics and Statistics* 57, no. 3, (August).

Bodkin, R.G., E.P. Bond, G.R. Reuber, and T.R. Robinson. 1966. "Price Stability and High Employment: The Options for Canadian Economic Policy: An Econometric Study" (Economic Council of Canada, Special Study No. 5). Ottawa: Queen's Printer.

Bodkin, R.G. and L.R. Klein. 1967. "Nonlinear Estimation of Aggregate Production Functions." *Review of Economics and Statistics* 49.

Brechling, F. 1965. "The Relationship Between Output and Employment in British Manufacturing Industries." *Review of Economic Studies* 32, no. 3, (July).

Breton, Albert. 1974. *A Conceptual Basis for an Industrial Strategy.* Ottawa: Information Canada.

Breton, Albert. 1964. "The Economics of Nationalism." *Journal of Political Economy* 72, (August).

Brinner, R. 1978. *Technology, Labor and Economic Potential.* Lexington, Mass.: Data Resources Inc.

Britton, John and James M. Gilmour, assisted by Mark G. Murphy. 1978. *The Weakest Link—A Technological Perspective on Canadian Industrial Underdevelopment.* Ottawa: Science Council of Canada.

Brown, C. and J. Medoff. 1978. "Trade Unions in the Production Process." *Journal of Political Economy* 86, no. 3 (June).

Brown, M. 1966. *On the Theory and Measurement of Technical Change.* Cambridge: University Press.

Brown, M. and J.S. De Cani. 1963. "Technological Change and the Distribution of Income." *International Economic Review* 4, no. 3 (September).

Bruno, M. 1968. "Estimation of Factor Contribution to Growth Under Structural Design." *International Economic Review* 9, (February).

Bruno, M. 1962. *Interdependence, Resource Use and Structural Change in Israel.* Jerusalem: Bank of Israel.

Bucher, R. 1970. "Social Process and Power in a Medical School." In *Power in Organization*, edited by M. Zald. Nashville: University of Vanderbilt Press.

Buck, V.E. 1966. "A Model for Viewing the Organization as a System of Constraints." In *Approaches to Organizational Design* edited by J.D. Thompson. Pittsburgh, Penna.: University of Pittsburgh Press.

Burns, Arthur. 1977. "F.R.B. Burns Criticizes Carter Administration's Economic Policy." *The Washington Post*, (October 27), section A, p. 1.

Burns, T. and G.W. Stalker. 1961. *The Management of Innovation.* London: Tavistock.

Carroll, S.J. and H. Tosi. 1973. *Management by Objectives: Applications and Research.* New York: Macmillan.

Child, J. 1972a. "Organizational Structure and Strategies of Control: A Replication of the Aston Study." *Administrative Science Quarterly* 17.

Child, J. 1972b. "Organizational Structure, Environment and Performance: The Role of Strategic Choice." *Sociology* 6.

Child, J. and R. Mansfield. 1972. "Technology, Size and Organization Structure." *Sociology* 6.

Christensen, L. 1970. "Tax Policy and Investment Expenditures in a Model of General Equilibrium." *American Economic Review* 60 (May).

Christensen, L. and D.W. Jorgenson. 1973a. "Measuring Economic Performance in the Private Sector." In *The Measurement of Economic and Social Performance*, edited by Milton Moss. New York: Columbia University Press.

Christensen, L. and D.W. Jorgenson. 1973b. "U.S. Income, Saving and Wealth, 1929-69." *Review of Income and Wealth* 19 (December.)

Christensen, L. and D.W. Jorgenson. 1970. "U.S. Real Product and Real Factor Input, 1929-67." *Review of Income and Wealth* 16 (March).

Christensen, L. and D.W. Jorgenson. 1969. "The Measurement of U.S. Real Capital Input, 1929-67." *Review of Income and Wealth* 15 (December).

Christensen, L., D. Cummings, and D.W. Jorgenson. 1978. "Productivity Growth, 1947–73: An International Comparison." *The Impact of International Trade and Investment on Employment*, edited by William G. Dewald. Washington: Government Printing Office.

Christensen, L., D. Cummings, and D.W. Jorgenson. 1977. "Economic Growth, 1947–73: An International Comparison." in *New Developments in Productivity Measurement*, edited by J.W. Kendrick and B. Vaccara, Columbia University Press. New York.

Christensen, L., D.W. Jorgenson and L.J. Lau. 1973. "Transcendental Logarithmic Production Frontiers." *Review of Economics and Statistics* 55, no. 1, (February).

Clark, P.K. 1978. "Capital Formation and the Recent Productivity Slowdown." *Journal of Finance* 32, no. 3. (June).

Cline, W.R., N. Kawanabe, T.O.M. Kronjo, and T. Williams. 1978a. *Trade Negotiations in the Tokyo Round: A Quantitative Assessment.* Washington: The Brookings Institution.

Cline, W.R., N. Kawanabe, T.O.M. Kronjo, and T. Williams. 1978b. *Industry, Trade, and Commerce, A Structural Analysis of the Canadian Economy to 1990 with Quantitative Estimates of the Potential Impact of Tariff Reductions in the Tokyo Round of Tariff Negotiations,* Ottawa.

Council of Economic Advisers. 1976. *1976 Annual Report,* Washington.

Crozier, M. 1964. *The Bureaucratic Phenomenon.* Chicago: University of Chicago Press.

Cyert, R. and J.G. March. 1963. *A Behavioral Theory of the Firm,* Englewood Cliffs, N.J.: Prentice-Hall.

Dahl, R. 1957. "The Concept of Power." *Behavioral Science* 2.

Daly, D.J. Forthcoming a. "Corporate Strategies and Productivity Performance in Japan's Manufacturing Industries." In *Canadian Perspectives on Economic Relations with Japan,* edited by Keith A.J. Key. Montreal: Institute for Research on Public Policy.

Daly, D.J. Forthcoming b. "Mineral Resources in the Canadian Economy—Macroeconomic Implications." *Resources in Canada-United States Relations,* edited by Carl Beigie and William Diebold, Jr. Montreal: C.D. Howe Research Institute.

Daly, D.J. 1979a. "Missing Links in 'The Missing Link.'" *Canadian Public Policy* (Summer).

Daly, D.J. 1979b. "Size and Economies of Scale." *Perspectives on the Royal Commission on Corporate Concentration.* Montreal: Butterworth & Co.

Daly, D.J. 1978a. "Economies of Scale and Canadian Manufacturing." *Appropriate Scale for Canadian Manufacturing,* Ottawa: Science Council of Canada, 1978a.

Daly, D.J. 1978b. "Comment." In *The Impact of International Trade and Investment on Employment,* edited by William G. Dewald. Washington: Government Printing Office.

Daly, D.J. 1976. "Canada's Comparative Advantage." York University. Mimeo.

Daly, D.J. 1975. "The Empirical Applicability of the Alchian-Hirschleifer Modern Cost Theory." York University. Mimeo.

Daly, D.J. 1974. "New Approaches in the Development of Managers" and "Managerial Manpower in Canada." *Contemporary Issues in Canadian Personnel Administration. Toronto: Prentice-Hall.*

Daly, D.J. 1968. "Why Growth Rates Differ—A Summary and Appraisal." *International Review of Income and Wealth* (March).

Daly, D.J. and S. Globerman. 1976. *Tariff and Science Policies: Applications of a Model of Nationalism.* Toronto: University of Toronto Press.

Daly, D.J. and R. Peterson. 1973. "On Bridging the Gaps." *Management Science.*

Daly, Keith and A. Neef. 1978. "Productivity and Unit Labor Costs in 11 Industrial Countries, 1977." *Monthly Labor Review* (November).

David, P.A. and T. Van De Klundert. 1965. "Biased Efficiency Growth and Capital-Labor Substitution in the U.S., 1899–1960." *American Economic Review* 55, no. 3 (June).

Davis, R.C. 1951. *Fundamentals of Management.* New York: Harper & Row.

Dearborn, D.C. and R.A. Simon. 1958. "Selective Perception: A Note on the Departmental Identifications of Executives." *Sociometry* 21.

Denison, E.F. 1979. Statement, in: *Special Study on Economic Change,* Joint Economic Committee, U.S. Congress. Washington: Government Printing Office.

Denison, E.F. 1978. "Effects of Selected Changes in the Institutional and Human Environment Upon Output per Unit of Input." *Survey of Current Business* 58 (January).

Denison, E.F. 1974. "Accounting for U.S. Economic Growth 1929–1969." Washington: The Brookings Institution.

Denison, E.F. 1972. "Classification of Sources of Growth." *Review of Income and Wealth* Series 18, no. 1 (March).

Denison, E.F. 1969. "Some Major Issues in Productivity Analysis: An Examination of Estimates by Jorgenson and Griliches." *Survey of Current Business Part II* 49, no. 5 (May).

Denison, E.F. 1967a. "Why growth rates differ: Postwar Experience in Nine Western Countries." Washington: The Brookings Institution.

Denison, E.F. 1967b. "The Sources of Postwar Growth in the Nine Western Countries", *American Economic Review* Vol. 57.

Denison, E.F. 1964. "The Unimportance of the Embodied Question." *American Economic Review* 54, no. 2 (March).

Denison, E.F. 1962. "The Sources of Economic Growth in the United States and the Alternatives Before Us." New York: Committee for Economic Development.

Denison, E.F. and W. K. Chung. 1976. *How Japan's Economy Grew So Fast.* Washington: The Brookings Institution.

Denison, E.F. and Poullier. 1967. *Why Growth Rates Differ: Postwar Experience in Nine Western Countries.* Washington: The Brookings Institution.

Denny, M. and J.D. May. 1979. "Postwar Productivity in Canadian Manufacturing." *Canadian Journal of Economics* (February).

Denny, M. and J.D. May. 1978a. "Testing Productivity Models." Institute for Policy Analysis, University of Toronto.

Denny, M. and J.D. May. 1978b. "Factor-Augmenting Technical Progress and Productivity in Canadian Manufacturing." November, University of Newfoundland.

Diewert, W.E. 1977. "Aggregation Problems in the Measurement of Capital." Discussion paper no. 77–09, Department of Economics, University of British Columbia.

Diewert, W.E. 1976. "Exact and Superlative Index Numbers." *Journal of Econometrics* 4, no. 2 (May).

Diewert, W.E. 1969. "An Application of the Shephard Duality Theorem: A Generalized Leontief Production Function." University of Chicago, Center for Mathematical Studies in Business and Economics, Report 6921.

Domar, E. 1961. "On the Measurement of Technological Change." *Economic Journal* 71.

Domar, E. 1962. "On Total Productivity and All That." *Journal of Political Economy* 70.

Driver, M.J. and S. Streufort. 1969. "Integrative Complexity: An Approach to Individuals and Groups as Information Processing Systems." *Administrative Science Quarterly* 14.

Drucker, P. 1954. *Managing for Results.* New York: Harper & Row.

Duncan, R.B. 1972. Characteristics of Organizational Environments and Perceived Environmental Uncertainty." *Adminstrative Science Quarterly* 17.

Economic Council of Canada. 1978a. *Regulation Reference: A Preliminary Report to First Ministers,* November.

Economic Council of Canada. 1978b. *Fifteenth Annual Review: A Time for Reason.* Ottawa: Minister of Supply and Services.

Economic Council of Canada. 1975. *Looking Outward: A New Trade Strategy for Canada.* Ottawa: Information Canada.

Edwards, W. 1954. The Theory of Decision Making." *Psychological Bulletin* 51.

Emerson, R.M. 1962. "Power Dependence Relations." *American Sociological Review* 27.

Emery, F.E. adn E.L. Trist. 1965. "The Causal Texture of Organizational Environments." *Human Relations* 18.

Epstein, S. and N.P. Fenz. 1965. "Steepness of Approach and Avoidance Gradients in Humans as a Function of Experience: Theory and Experiment." *Journal of Experimental Psychology* 70.

Evans, M.G. and W. McQuillan. 1977. "A Longitudinal Analysis of the Context and Structure of a Large British Financial Institution." *Journal of Management Studies* 14.

Fabricant, S. 1959. *Basic Facts on Productivity Change.* New York: Columbia University Press.

Farrell, M.J. 1957. "The Measurement of Productive Efficiency." *Jour-*

nal of the Royal Statistical Society Series A (General) 120.

Feldstein, Martin S. 1977. "National Saving in the United States." *Capital for Productivity and Jobs.* Englewood Cliffs, N.J.: Prentice-Hall.

Ferguson, C. 1969. *The Neoclassical Theory of Production and Distribution.* Cambridge: Cambridge University Press.

Ferguson, C. 1965. "Time Series Production Functions and Technological Progress in American Manufacturing Industry." *Journal of Political Economy* 73, no. 2 (April).

Filley, A.C., R.J. House, and S. Kerr. 1976. *Managerial Process and Organizational Behavior.* Glenview, Ill.: Scott Foresman.

Filer, Randall K. 1978. *The Influence of Affective Human Capital on the Wage Equation.* Springfield, Va.: National Technical Information Service.

Fisher, I. *The Making of Index Numbers.* Boston: Houghton Mifflin.

Fleisher, L. 1969. "Conflict, Dissonance, and the Decision Sequence." *Dissertation Abstracts International* 30 (A-13): 1921.

Frank, James G. 1977. *Assessing Trends in Canada's Competitive Position: The Case of Canada and the United States.* Ottawa: The Conference Board in Canada.

Freedman, C. 1977. "Recent Growth in Productivity, Real Expenditure Per Capita and Real Income Per Capita: Accounting for the Differences." *Bank of Canada Review* (August).

Freeman, Richard B. 1976. *The Overeducated American.* New York: Academic Press.

French, J.R.P. and B. Raven. 1959. "The Bases of Social Power." In *Studies in Social Power,* edited by D. Cartwright. Ann Arbor: Institute for Social Research, University of Michigan.

Frohn, J. "Estimation of CES Production Functions with Neutral Technical Change for Industrial Sectors in the Federal Republic of Germany 1958–1968." *Review of Income and Wealth* 2.

Gallman, Robert. 1972. "Changes in Total U.S. Agricultural Productivity in the Nineteenth Century." *Agricultural History* 46, no. 1 (January).

Gerard, H.B. 1967. "Choice Difficulty, Dissonance, and the Decision Sequence." *Journal of Personality* 35.

Gilmour, J. 1978. "Industrialization and Technological Backwardness: The Canadian Dilemma." *Canadian Public Policy* (Winter).

Globerman, S. 1978. "Canadian Science Policy and Technological Sovereignty." *Canadian Public Policy* (Winter).

Goldsmith, R.W. 1957. *A Study of Saving in the United States.* Princeton: Princeton University Press.

Gollop, F. and D.W. Jorgenson. 1977. "U.S. Productivity Growth by Industry, 1947–1973." In *New Developments in Productivity Meas-*

urement, edited by J.W. Kendrick and B. Vaccara. New York: Columbia University Press.

Goodman, P. 1968. "The Measurement of an Individual's Organization Map." *Administrative Science Quarterly* 13.

Gordon, M.J. 1978. "A World Scale National Corporation Industrial Strategy." *Canadian Public Policy* (Winter).

Gordon, M.J. 1974. "Canadian Manufacturing: A Strategy for Development." *The Business Quarterly* (Winter).

Gordon, Walter L. 1978. *What Is Happening to Canada.* Toronto: McClelland and Stewart.

Gorecki, Paul K. 1977. *Economies of Scale and Efficient Plant Size,* Research Monograph 1, Research Branch, Bureau of Competition Policy, Department of Consumer and Corporate Affairs.

Gorecki, Paul K. 1976. *Economies of Scale and Efficient Plant Size in Canadian Manufacturing Industries.* Ottawa: Bureau of Competition Policy, Department of Consumer and Corporate Affairs.

Government of Canada. 1972. *Foreign Direct Investment in Canada.* Ottawa: Information Canada.

Gregory, R.G. and D.N. James. 1973. "Do New Factories Embody Best Practice Technology." *Economic Journal* 83.

Griffin, James M. and Paul R. Gregory. 1976. "An Intercountry Translog Model of Energy Substitution Responses." *American Economic Review* 66, no. 5 (December).

Griliches, Z. 1967. "Production Functions in Manufacturing: Some Preliminary Results." In *The Theory and Empirical Analysis of Production.* New York: National Bureau of Economic Research.Griliches, Z. 1964. "Notes on the Measurement of Price and Quality Changes." In *Models of Income Determination.* Princeton: Princeton University Press.

Griliches, Z. and D. Jorgenson. 1967. "The Explanation of Productivity Change." *Review of Economic Studies* 34, no. 99. (July).

Griliches, Z. and D. Jorgenson. 1966. "Sources of Measured Productivity Change: Capital Input." *American Economic Review* 56, no. 2 (May).

Griliches, Z. and V. Ringstad. 1971. *Economies of Scale and the Form of the Production Function: An Econometric Study of Norwegian Manufacturing Establishment Data.* Amsterdam: North-Holland.

Grinyer, P.H. and D. Norburn. 1975. "Planning for Exisiting Markets: Perceptions of Executives and Financial Performance." *Journal of the Royal Statistical Society* Series A, 138, no. 1.

Hall, R.F. and D.W. Jorgenson. 1967. "Tax Policy and Investment Behavior." *American Economic Review* 57 (June).

Hall, R.H. 1963. "The Concept of Bureaucracy: An Empirical Assessment." *American Journal of Sociology* 69.

Harberger, Arnold. 1971. "Tax Policy and Investment Expenditures: Discussion." *Tax Incentives and Capital Spending.* Washington: The Brookings Institution.

Harberger, A. 1959. "The Fundamentals of Economic Progress in Under-developed Countries: Using the Resources at Hand More Effectively." *American Economic Review* 49.

Harvey, O.J., D.E. Hunt, and H. Schroder. *Conceptual Systems and Personality Organization.* New York: Wiley.

Hickman, B.G. and R.M. Coen. 1976. *An Annual Growth Model of the U.S. Economy.* Amsterdam: North-Holland.

Hickson, D.J., C.R. Hinings, C.A. Lee, R.E. Schneck, and J.M. Pennings. "A Strategic Contingencies Theory of Intra-Organizational Power." *Administrative Science Quarterly* 16.

Hickson, D.J., D.S. Pugh, and D.C. Pheysey. 1969. "Operation Technology and Organization Structure: An Empirical Reappraisal." *Administrative Science Quarterly* 14.

Hinings, C.R., D.J. Hickson, J.M. Pennings, and R.E. Schneck, 1974. "Structural Conditions of Intra-Organizational Power." *Administrative Science Quarterly* 19.

House, R.J. 1971. "A Path-goal Theory of Leader Effectiveness." *Administrative Science Quarterly* 16.

House, R.J. and M.L. Baetz. 1979. "Leadership: Some Empirical Generalizations and New Research Direction." In *Research in Organizational Behavior,* edited by B. Staw. Greenwich, Conn.: JAI Press.

Hudson, E.A. and D.W. Jorgenson. 1978. "Energy Prices and the U.S. Economy, 1972–76" *Data Resources U.S. Review* (September).

Hudson, E.A. and D.W. Jorgenson. 1974. "U.S. Energy Policy and Economic Growth, 1975-2000." *The Bell Journal of Economics and Management Science* (Autumn)

Hufbauer, G.C. 1966. *Synthetic Materials and the Theory of International Trade.* Cambridge: Harvard University Press.

Hulten, C.R. 1979. "On the Importance of Productivity Change." *American Economic Review* 69, 19.

Hulten, C.R. 1975. "Technical Change and the Reproductibility of Capital." *American Economic Review* 69. 19.

Jamieson, B.D. 1973. "Behavioral Problems with Management by Objectives." *Journal of the Academy of Management* 16.

Janis, I.L. 1959. "Decisional Conflicts: A Theoretical Analysis." *Journal of Conflict Resolution* 3.

Janis, I.L. and L. Mann. 1977. *Decision Making: A Psychological Analysis of Conflict, Choice, and Commitment.* New York: The Free Press.

Janis, I.L. and L. Mann. 1968. "A Conflict-Theory Approach to Attitude

Change and Decision Making." In *Psychological Foundations of Attitudes,* edited by A. Greenwald, T. Brock, and T. Ostrom. New York: Academic Press.

Johnson, Harry G. 1965. "A Theoretical Model of Economic Nationalism in New and Developing States." *Political Science Quarterly* .

Johnston, J. 1975. "A Macro Model of Inflation." *Economic Journal* 85 (June).

Johnston, J. 1972. *Econometric Methods.* New York: McGraw-Hill.

Jones, E.E. and C.A. Johnson. 1973. "Delay of Consequences and the Riskiness of Decisions." *Journal of Personality* 42.

Jorgenson, D.W. 1973. "The Economic Theory of Replacement and Depreciation." In *Econometrics and Economic Theory,* edited by W. Sellekaerts. New York: Macmillan.

Jorgenson, D.W. 1965. "Anticipations and Investment Behavior." In *The Brookings Quarterly Econometric Model of the United States,* edited by J.S. Duesenberry *et al.,* Chicago: Rand McNally.

Jorgenson, D.W. and Z. Griliches. 1967. "The Explanation of Productivity Change." *Review of Economic Studies* 34.

Jorgenson, D.W. and L.J. Lau. 1977. *Duality and Technology.* Amsterdam: North-Holland.

Jorgenson, D.W. and L.J. Lau. 1971. "Conjugate Duality and the Transcendental Logarithmic Production Function." *Econometrica* 39, no. 4.

Kaldor, Nicholas. 1957. "A Model of Economic Growth." *Economic Journal* (December).

Kelman, H.C. 1958. "Compliance, Identification, and Internalization: Three Processes of Attitude Change." *Journal of Conflict Resolution* 2.

Kendrick, J. Forthcoming. "Productivity." *Encyclopedia of American Economic History.* New York: Scribner's Sons.

Kendrick, J. 1978. "Sources of Productivity Growth and of the Recent Slow-Down." George Washington University. Mimeo.

Kendrick, J. 1977. *Understanding Production. An Introduction to the Dynamics of Productivity Change.* Baltimore: Johns Hopkins University Press.

Kendrick, J.W. 1976. *The Formation and Stocks of Total Capital.* New York: National Bureau of Economic Research.

Kendrick, J.W. 1975. "Efficiency Incentives and Cost Factors in Public Utility Automatic Revenue Adjustment Clauses." *Bell Journal of Economics and Management Science* (Spring).

Kendrick, J. 1974a. "Productivity and Business." In *Labor, Technology, and Productivity in the Seventies.* New York: New York University Press.

Kendrick, J. 1974b. *Postwar Productivity Trends in the United States, 1948–1969.* New York: National Bureau of Economic Research.

Kendrick, J. 1961. "Productivity Trends in the United States." Princeton: Princeton University Press.

Kendrick, J. and E. Grossman. 1980. *Trends and Cycles in Productivity in the United States.* Baltimore: Johns Hopkins University Press.

Kendrick, J. and R. Sato. 1963. "Factor Prices, Productivity and Economic Growth." *American Economic Review* 53.

Kennedy, C. 1964. "Induced Bias in Innovation and the Theory of Distribution." *Economic Journal* 74.

Kerr, S. 1975. "On the Folly of Rewarding A, While Hoping for B." *Academy of Management Journal* 18.

Klein, L.R. and R.S. Preston. 1967. "Some New Results in the Measurement of Capacity Utilization." *American Economic Review* 57.

Kloek, T. 1966. *Indexcijfers: enige methodologisch aspecten.* The Hague: Pasmans.

Kravis, Irving B. 1976. "A Survey of International Comparisons of Productivity." *Economic Journal* (March).

Kravis, Irving B., Alan Heston, and Robert Summers. 1978a. *International Comparisons of Real Product and Purchasing Power.* Baltimore: The Johns Hopkins University Press.

Kravis, Irving B., Alan Heston, and Robert Summers. 1978b. "Real GDP Per Capita for More than One Hundred Countries." *Economic Journal* 88 (June).

Kravis, Irving B., Zoltan, Kenessy, Alan Heston, and Robert Summers. 1975. *A System of International Comparisons of Gross Product and Purchasing Power.* Baltimore: The John Hopkins University Press.

Kuh, E. 1965. "Cyclical and Secular Labour Productivity in the United States Manufacturing." *Review of Economics and Statistics* 47.

Kunreuther, H. and P. Slovic. 1978. "Economics, Psychology, and Protective Behavior." *American Economic Review* 68.

Kuriloff, A.H. 1966. *Reality in Management.* New York: McGraw-Hill.

Landsberger, H.A. 1961. "The Horizontal Dimension in Bureaucracy." *Adminstrative Science Quarterly* 6.

Latham, G.P. and J.J. Baldes. "The Practical Significance of Locke's Theory of Goal Setting." *Journal of Applied Psychology* 60.

Latham, G.P. and G.A. Yukl. 1975. "A Review of Research on the Application of Goal Setting in Organizations." *Academy of Management Journal* 18, no. 4.

Lave, L. 1966. *Technological Change: Its Conception and Measurement.* Englewood Cliffs, N.J.: Prentice-Hall.

Lawler, E.E., III, 1976. "Control Systems in Organization." In *Handbook of Industrial and Organizational Psychology,* edited by M.D. Dunnette. Chicago, Ill: Rand McNally.

Lawler, E.E., III, and J.G. Rhode. 1976. *Information and Control in Organizations.* Santa Monica, Calif.: Goodyear.

Lawrence, P.R. and J.W. Lorsch. 1967. *Organization and Environment.* Boston, Mass.: Divison of Research, Harvard Business School.

Leibenstein, Harvey. 1976. *Beyond Economic Man: A New Foundation for Microeconomics.* Cambridge: Harvard University Press.

Leibenstein, Harvey. 1975. *General X-Efficiency Theory and Economic Development.* Oxford: Oxford University Press.

Leibenstein, Harvey. 1966. "Allocative Efficency vs. X-Efficiency." *American Economic Review* 56.

Leibenstein, Harvey. 1969. "Organizational or Frictional Equilibria, X-Efficiency, and the Rate of Innovation." *Quarterly Journal of Economics* 83, no. 4.

Leibenstein, Harvey. 1960. *Economic Theory and Organizational Analysis.* New York: Harper & Row.

Lermer, G. 1973. "Evidence from Trade Data Regarding the Rationalization of Canadian Industry." *Canadian Journal of Economics* 6.

Levhari, E., E. Kleiman, and N. Halevi. 1966. "The Relationship between Two Measures of Total Productivity." *Review of Economics and Statistics* 48, no. 3 (August).

Levinson, H. 1970. "Management by Whose Objectives?" *Harvard Business Review* 48, no. 4.

Levitt, Kari. 1970. *Silent Surrender: The Multinational Corporation in Canada.* Toronto: Macmillan.

Lindblom, C.E. 1959. "The Science of Muddling Through." *Public Administration Review* 19.

List, W. 1978. "A Plant Where Job Frustration Isn't Allowed on the Payroll." *Toronto Globe & Mail* (June 19).

Locke, E.A. 1968. "Toward a Theory of Task Motivation and Incentives. *Organizational Behavior and Human Performance* 3.

Lucas, R.E., Jr. 1975. "Econometric Policy Evaluation: A Critique." *The Phillips Curve and Labor Markets.* Amsterdam: North-Holland.

MacCharles, Donald C. 1978. "The Cost of Administrative Organizations in Canadian Secondary Manufacturing Industries." Ph.D. dissertation, University of Toronto.

MacCrimmon, K.R. and D.N. Taylor. 1976. "Decision Making and Problem Solving. In *Handbook of Industrial and Organizational Psychology,* edited by M.D. Dunnette. Chicago: Rand McNally.

Machlup, F. 1967. "Theories of the Firm: Marginalist, Behavioral, Managerial." *American Economic Review* 57.

Malinvaud, E. 1961. "The Analogy Between Atemporal and Intertemporal Theories of Resource Allocation." *Review of Economic Studies* 28.

Malinvaud, E. 1953. "Capital Accumulation and Efficient Allocation of Resources." *Econometrica* 21.

Mann, L, I.L. Janis, and R. Chaplin. 1969. "The Effects of Anticipation of Forthcoming Information on Predecisional Processes. *Journal of Personality and Social Psychology* 1.

Mansfield, E. 1968. *The Economics of Technological Change.* New York: W.W. Norton.

Manz, C.C and H. Sims. 1979. "Self-Management: A Substitute for Leadership." Unpublished paper, Pennsylvania State University.

March, J.G. and H.A. Simon. 1958. *Organizations.* New York: Wiley.

Mark, J.A. 1978. "Productivity Trends and Prospects." Statement before the Joint Economic Committee, *United States Congress, June 8.*

McCarthy, M. 1978. "The U.S. Productivity Growth Recession: History and Prospects for the Future." *Journal of Finance* 32, no. 3 (June).

McCarthy, M. 1965. "Embodied and Disembodied Technological Progress in the CES Production Function." *Review of Economics and Statistics* 47.

McMillan, C.J. Forthcoming. "Human Resource Policies, Labor Markets and Unions: Canada-Japan Comparisons." *Canadian Perspective on Economic Relations with Japan,* edited by Keith A.J. Hay. Montreal: Institute for Research in Public Policy.

Meadows, E. 1978. "A Close-Up Look at the Productivity Lag." *Fortune* (December).

Meltz, Noah M. 1965. *Changes in the Occupational Composition of the Canadian Labour Force 1931-1961.* Ottawa: Queen's Printer.

Miller, D.W. and M.K. Starr. 1967. *The Structure of Human Decisions.* Englewood Cliffs, N.J.: Prentice-Hall.

Miller, G.A. 1956. "The Magical Number Seven, Plus or Minus Two." *Psychological Review* 63.

Mills, Edwin S. 1978. *The Economics of Environmental Quality.* New York: W.W. Norton.

Mintzberg, H. 1973. *The Nature of Managerial Work.* New York: Harper & Row.

Mischel, W. 1973. "Toward a Cognitive Social Learning Reconceptualization of Personality," *Psychological Review* 80.

Mischel, W. and B. Moore. 1973. "Effects of Attention to Symbolically Presented Rewards upon Self-Control." *Journal of Personality and Social Psychology* 28.

Mitchell, E. 1968. "Explaining the International Pattern of Labor Productivity and Wages: A Production Model with Two Labor Inputs." *Review of Economics and Statistics* 50, no. 4 (November).

Mohr, Michael. In process. "Labor Productivity and the Business Cycle." In *New Directions in Productivity Measurement and Analysis* New York: National Bureau of Economic Research.

Montgomery, D.B. and C.B. Weinberg. 1977. "Strategic Intelligence Systems." Research report #392, Stanford Graduate School of Business.

Mussa, Michael. 1974. "Tariffs and the Distribution of Income: The Importance of Factor Specificity, Substitutability, and Intensity in the Short and Long Run." *Journal of Political Economy* 82:1191–1204.

Nadiri, M. I. 1972. "International Studies of Factor Inputs and Total Factor Productivity: A Brief Survey." *Review of Income Wealth* 2.

Nadiri, M. I., 1970. "Some Approaches to the Theory and Measurement of Total Factor Productivity: A Survey." Journal of Economic Literature, (December).

National Academy of Sciences, Panel to Review Productivity Statistics. Forthcoming. *Measurement and Interpretation of Change.*

National Commission on Productivity. 1971. *Education and Economic Growth* (June).

Nelson, R., M. Peck, and E. Kalachek. 1967. *Technology, Economic Growth and Public Policy.* Washington: The Brookings Institution.

New York Stock Exchange. 1979. "Reaching a Higher Standard of Living." New York: Office of Economic Research.

Nisbett, R. and L. Ross. 1979. *Human Inference.* Englewood Cliffs, N.J.: Prentice-Hall.

Nishimizu, M. 1978. "U.S. and Japanese Economic Growth, 1952–1974: An International Comparison." *Economic Journal* 88.

Nishimizu, M. and C.R. Hulten. 1978. "The Sources of Japanese Economic Growth: 1955–1974." *Review of Economics and Statistics* 60, no. 3 (August).

Nishimizu, M. 1975. "Total Factor Production Analysis: A Disaggregated Study of the Post-War Japanese Economy with Explicit Consideration of Intermediate Inputs, and Comparison with the United States." Ph.D. dissertation, Johns Hopkins University.

Nordhaus, W.D. 1972. "The Recent Productivity Slowdown." *Brookings Papers on Economic Activity* 3.

Nordhaus, W.D. and J. Tobin. 1973. "Is Growth Obsolete?" In *The Measurement of Economic and Social Performance,* edited by Milton Moss. New York: Columbia University Press.

Norsworthy, J.R. and L.J. Fulco. 1978. "Productivity and Costs During Recession and Recovery." *Monthly Labor Review* (August).

Norsworthy, J.R. and L.J. Fulco. 1974. "Productivity and Costs in the Private Economy, 1973." *Monthly Labour Review,* (June).

Norsworthy, J.R. and M.J. Harper. 1979. "The Role of Capital Formation in the Recent Slowdown in Productivity Growth." Working paper 87, U.S. Department of Labor, Bureau of Labor Statistics.

Odiorne, G. 1965. *Management by Objectives.* New York: Pitman.

Ohkawa, K. and H. Rosovsky. 1973. *Japanese Economic Growth.* Stanford: Stanford University Press.

Okun, A. 1962. "Potential GNP: Its Measurement and Significance," American Statistical Association, Bus.

O'Reilly, C.A., III and K.H. Roberts. 1977. "Task Group Structure, Communication, and Effectiveness in Three Organizations." *Journal of Applied Psychology* 62.

O'Reilly, C.A., III. and K.H. Roberts. 1974. "Information Filtration in Organizations: Three Experiments." *Organizational Behavior and Human Performance* 11.

Organization for Economic Cooperation and Development. 1978. *Main Economic Indicators.* (May)

Ozawa, T. 1974. *Japan's Technological Challenge to the West, 1950–1974.* Cambridge: M.I.T. Press.

Pack, Howard. 1971. *Structural Change and Economic Policy in Israel.* New Haven: Yale University Press.

Palda, Kristian S. 1979. *The Science Council's Weakest Link: A Critique of the Science Council's Technocratic Industrial Strategy for Canada.* Vancouver: The Fraser Institute.

Parsons, T. 1960. *Structure and Process in Modern Societies.* New York: Free Press.

Patrick, H. 1977. "The Future of the Japanese Economy: Output and Labor Productivity." *The Journal of Japanese Studies* 3, no. 2.

Patrick, H. and H. Rosovsky. 1976. *Asia's New Giant.* Washington: The Brookings Institution.

Pennings, J.M. and P.S. Goodman. 1977. "Toward a Workable Framework." In *New Perspectives on Organizational Effectiveness,* edited by P.S. Goodman and J.M. Pennings. San Francisco: Jossey-Bass.

Perrow, C. 1970. "Departmental Power and Perspectives in Industrial Firms." In *Power in Organizations,* edited by M. Zald. Nashville: Vanderbilt University Press.

Perry, G.L. 1971. "Labour Force Structure, Potential Output and Productivity." *Brookings Papers on Economic Activity* 3.

Pettigrew, A.M. 1971. *The Politics of Organization Decision-Making.* London: Tavistock.

Pfeffer, J. 1973. "Size, Composition and Function of Hospital Boards of Directors: A Study of Organization-Environment Linkage." *Administrative Science Quarterly* 18.

Pfeffer, J. 1972a. "Size and Composition of Corporate Boards of Directors: The Organization and Its Environment." *Administrative Science Quarterly* 17.

Pfeffer, J. 1972b. "Merger as a Response to Organizational Interdependence." *Administrative Science Quarterly* 17.

Pfeffer, J. and H. Leblebici. 1973. "Executive Recruitment and the Development of Interfirm Organizations." *Administrative Science Quarterly* 18.

Pfeffer, J. and A. Leong. 1977. "Resource Allocation in United Funds: An Examination of Power and Dependence. *Social Forces* 55.

Pfeffer, J. and P. Nowack. 1976. "Joint Ventures and Interorganizational Interdependence. *Administrative Science Quarterly* 21.

Pfeffer, J. and G.R. Salancik. 1978. *The External Control of Organizations: A Resource Dependence Perspective.* New York: Harper & Row.

Porter, L.W. and K.H. Roberts. 1976. "Communication in Organizations. In *Handbook of Industrial and Organizational Psychology,* edited by M.D. Dunnette. Chicago: Rand McNally.

Preston, R.S. 1967. "Simultaneous Estimation of Industry Production Functions." University of Pennsylvania, Ph.D. dissertation.

Quinn, Robert P. and Graham L. Staines. 1979. *The 1977 Quality of Employment Survey.* Ann Arbor: Institute for Social Research, The University of Michigan.

Rao, P.S. Forthcoming. "An Econometric Analysis of Labour Productivity in Canadian Industries: Some Further Results." Discussion paper, Economic Council of Canada.

Rao, P.S. 1978. "An Econometric Analysis of Labour Productivity in Canadian Industries." Discussion paper 125, Economic Council of Canada.

Reid, Frank and Noah M. Meltz. 1979. "Causes of Shifts in the Unemployment-Vacancy Relationship: An Empirical Analysis for Canada." *Review of Economics and Statistics* 61.

Reuber, G.L. 1970. "Wage Adjustments in Canadian Industry, 1954–66" *Review of Economic Studies* 37.

Ronan, W.W., G.P. Latham, and S.B. Kinne, III. 1978. "Effects of Goal Setting and Supervision on Worker Behavior in Industrial Situations." *Journal of Applied Psychology* 58, no. 3.

Rotstein, Abraham. 1974. *The Precarious Homestead: Essays on Economics, Technology and Nationalism.* Toronto: Clarke-Irwin.

Runkel, P.J. 1956. "Cognitive similarity in facilitating communication. *Sociometry* 19.

Safarian, A.E. 1969. *The Performance of Foreign-Owned Firms in Canada.* Montreal: Private Planning Association of Canada.

Safarian, A.E. 1966. *Foreign Ownership of Canadian Industry.* Toronto: McGraw-Hill.

Sahota, G. 1966. "The Sources of Measured Productivity Growth: United States Fertilizer Mineral Industries, 1936–1960." *Review of Economics and Statistics* 48, no. 2 (May).

Salancik, G.R. and J. Pfeffer. 1974. "The Bases and Use of Power in Organizational Decision Making: The Case of a University." *Administrative Science Quarterly* 19.

Salancik, G.R., J. Pfeffer, and J.P. Kelley. In press. "A Contingency Model of Influence in Organizational Decision Making." *Pacific Sociology Review.*

Salter, W. 1960. *Productivity and Technical Change.* London: Cambridge University Press.

Scherer, F.M., A. Beckenstein, E. Kaufer, and R.D. Murphy. 1975. *The Economics of Multi-Plant Operation: An International Comparisons Study.* Cambridge: Harvard University Press.

Science Council of Canada. 1979. *Forging the Links: A Technology Policy for Canada.* Ottawa: Minister of Supply and Services.

Selznick, P. 1949. *TVA and the Grass Roots.* Berkeley and Los Angeles: University of California Press.

Siedule, T. and K. Newton. 1979. "Tentative Measure of Labour Hoarding, 1961–1977." Discussion paper 128, Economic Council of Canada.

Simon, H.A. 1978. "Rationality as Process and as Product of Thought." *American Economic Review* 68.

Simon, H.A. 1976a. *Administrative Behavior,* 3rd ed. New York: The Free Press.

Simon, H.A. 1976b. "From Substantive to Procedural Rationality. In *Method and Appraisal in Economics,* edited by S.J. Latsis. Cambridge: Cambridge University Press.

Simon, H.A. 1964. "On the Concept of Organizational Goal." *Adminstrative Science Quarterly* 9.

Simon, H.A. 1957. *Models of Man.* New York: Wiley.

Solow, R. 1964. "Capital, Labor, and Income in Manufacturing." In *The Behavior of Income Shares; Selected Theoretical and Empirical Issues.* Princeton: Princeton University Press.

Solow, R. 1957. "Technical Change and the Aggregate Production Function." *Review of Economics and Statistics* 39.

Star, S. 1974. "Accounting for the Growth of Output." *American Economic Review* (March).

Statistics Canada. *Historical Labour Force Statistics, 1979.* Catalogue 71–201.

Statistics Canada 1978a. *Aggregate Productivity Measures, 1946–77.* Catalogue 14–201.

Statistics Canada. 1978b. *Corporations and Labour Unions Returns Act, Report for 1975,* Catalogue 61–210. Ottawa: 1978b.

Statistics Canada. *Quarterly Review of Job Vacancies, Second Quarter 1978.* Catalogue 71–002.

Statistics Canada. *National Income and Expenditure Accounts, 1926-74.* Catalogue 13-53.

Statistics Canada. *Domestic and Foreign Control of Manufacturing Establishments in Canada, 1969-70.* Catalogue 31-401.

Statistics Canada. *The Labour Force, March 1974.* Catalogue 71-001.

Stedry, A.C. and E. Kay. 1966. "The Effects of Goal Difficulty on Performance." *Behavioral Science* 11.

Stigler, G. 1961. "Economic Problems in Measuring Change in Productivity." In *Output, Input, and Productivity Measurement.* Princeton: Princeton University Press.

Strauss, G. 1964. "Tactics of Lateral Relationships: The Purchasing Agent." *Administrative Science Quarterly* 7.

Streufort, S., P. Suedfeld, and M.J. Driver. 1965. "Conceptual Structure, Information Search and Information Utilization." *Journal of Personality and Social Psychology* 2.

Taylor, L.D., S.J. Turnovsky, and T.A. Wilson. 1972. *The Inflationary Process in North American Manufacturing.* Institute for the Quantitative Analysis of Social and Economic Policy, University of Toronto.

Tedeschi, J.T., B.R. Schlenker, and S. Linkskold. 1972. "The Exercise of Power and Influence: The Source of Influence." In *The Social Influence Processes,* edited by J.T. Tedeschi. Chicago: Aldine.

Terborgh, George. 1977. *Corporate Earning Power in the Seventies: A Disaster.* Washington: Machinery and Allied Products Institute.

Theil, H. 1965. "The Information Approach to Demand Analysis." *Econometrica* 33, no. 1.

Thompson, J.D. 1967. *Organizations in Action.* New York: McGraw-Hill.

Thorsen, C.E. and M.J. Mahoney. 1974. *Behavioral Self-Control.* New York: Holt, Rinehart & Winston.

Thurow, L. 1968. "Disequilibrium and the Marginal Productivity of Capital and Labor." *Review of Economics and Statistics* 50, no. 1 (February).

Tornqvist, L. 1936. "The Bank of Finland's Consumption Price Index." *Bank of Finland Monthly Bulletin,* no. 10.

Triandis, H.C. 1960. "Cognitive Similarity and Communication in a Dyad. *Human Relations* 13.

Ture, Norman B. and Kenneth Sanden. 1977. *The Effects of Tax Policy on Capital Formation.* New York: Financial Executives Research Foundation.

Tversky, A. and D. Kahneman, 1974. "Judgement under Uncertainty: Heuristics and Biases." *Science* 185.

Umstot, D.D., C.H. Bell, Jr., and T.R. Mitchell. 1976. "Effects of Job Enrichment and Task Goals on Satisfaction and Productivity: Implication For Job Design." *Journal of Applied Psychology* 61, no. 4.

U.S. Congress. Joint Committee on Taxation. 1977. "Tax Policy and Capital Formation," report prepared for the House Ways and Means Committee Task Force on Capital Formation (April).

U.S. Department of Labor. 1974. *Job Satisfaction: Is There a Trend?.* Manpower research monograph 30.

Visacher, Michael. "The Effect of Tax Incentives on Investment Behavior." *Tax Policies for R & D and Technological Innovation.* Pittsburgh: Graduate School of Industrial Administration, Carnegie-Mellon University.

Vroom, V.H. 1974. "A New Look at Managerial Decision-making." In *Organizational Psychology,* edited by D.A. Kolb, I.M. Rubin, and J.M. McIntyre. 2nd ed., Englewood Cliffs, N.J.: Prentice-Hall.

Vroom, V.H. 1964. "Some Psychological Aspects of Organizational Control." In *New Perspectives in Organizational Research,* edited by W.W. Cooper, H.J. Leavitt, and M.W. Shelly, III. New York: Wiley.

Wall, J.L. 1974. "What the Competition is Doing: Your Need to Know." *Harvard Business Review* 52, no. 6.

Walters, D. 1979. "Productivity: Changing Concepts." In *Shaping the Future: Canada in a Global Society,* edited by W. Baker. Ottawa: University of Ottawa.

Walters, D. 1968. *Canadian Income Levels and Growth: An International Perspective.* Ottawa: Queen's Printer.

Walton, R. 1977. "Work Innovations at Topeka: After Six Years." *Journal of Applied Behavioral Science* 13.

Watanabe, T. "Improvement of Labor Quality and Economic Growth: Japan's Postwar Experience." *Economic Development and Cultural Change* 21.

Watkins, Mel. 1978. "The Economics of Nationalism and the Nationality of Economics: Critique of Neoclassical Theorizing." *Canadian Journal of Economics* Supplement (November).

West, E.C. 1971. *Canada-United States Price and Productivity Differences in Manufacturing Industires.* Ottawa: Information Canada.

Wonnacott, Ronald J. 1975a. *Canada's Trade Options.* Ottawa: Information Canada.

Wonnacott, Ronald J. 1975b. "Industrial Strategy: A Canadian Substitute for Trade Liberalization?" *Canadian Journal of Economics* (November).

Woodward, J. 1958. *Management and Technology.* London: Her Majesty's Stationary Office.

Yukizawa, Kenzo. 1977. "Relative Productivity in American and Japanese Industry and Its Change, 1958–1972." Paper presented to the International Economic Association Congress, Tokyo, Japan, September.

Zajonc, R.B. and D.M. Wolfe. 1966. "Cognitive Consequences of a Person's Position in a Formal Organization." *Human Relations* 19.

Zand, D. 1972. "Trust and Managerial Problem Solving." *Administrative Science Quarterly* 17.

Zander, A. and T.T. Newcombe, Jr. 1967. "Group Levels of Aspiration in United Fund Campaigns." *Journal of Personality and Social Psychology* 6.

Index

Administrator of Employment and Training, 260
Alberta, productivity growth, 56
American Productivity Center, 261
Arab oil embargo, 111. *See also* Energy
AVRO Arrow, 244

Bank of Canada, Research Department, 62
Behavior: bureaucratic, 173; maximizing, 137-139, 148, 202-207, 210-213; nonmaximizing, 202-204, 209; rational, 139-144; satisficing, 139-140
Bounded rationality, 139-142
Bureau of Economic Analysis (BEA), 249-250
Bureau of Labor Statistics (BLS), 31, 32, 33, 262
Burns, Arthur, 254
Business confidence, 254
Business cycle: effect on productivity, 117, 241, 262, 268-269; and labor hoarding, 269

Canada. *See* Productivity, Canada
Canada-U.S. automotive agreement, 233-234, 243-245
Candide model, 59-62
CANSIM, 61
Capacity utilization, 13, 16, 49, 62
Capital, projected requirements, 249-250

Capital formation, 35, 86, 101-102; and economic growth, 93, 98-99, 250; and productivity, 6, 50, 86-88, 266, 269
Capital inputs. *See* Factors of production
Capital stock, 52, 226-228, 230; average age of, 25-26; measurement of, 31-32, 33, 35; per person in Canada, 226-230
Capital-labor ratio, 47, 241; and productivity, 30, 50-51. *See also* Factors of production
Capital-output ratio, 213-215
Carter, Jimmy, Economic Report of the President, 265
Clean Air Act, 118-119
Cobb-Douglas production function, 64, 114, 124-126
Collective bargaining, 5, 192
Commerce Department, 249; Office of the Assistant Secretary for Science and Technology, 258-259
Commissioner of Education, 260
Comparative advantage, 229-231, 237, 244
Compensation. *See* Labor compensation
Comprehensive Employment and Training Act of 1973, 262
Congressional Joint Economic Committee, 242
Construction Division, Statistics Canada, 61

Construction sector, productivity growth of, 46
Control systems. *See* Management control systems
Conventions: as decision elements, 207-209; and lexicographic preference ordering, 209-212
Costs, 9-10, 17-19, 21; unit capital, 18-19; unit labor, 17-19, 231; unit, and plant size, 232
Council of Economic Advisors, 11, 29, 241
Council on Wage and Price Stability, 32

Decisionmaking, 134, 136-139, 143-148; behavioral analysis of, 136-148; conflict theory of, 143-148, 187-193; economic theory of, 137-139, 141, 148, 195-197; and information, 141, 148-163; method of, 142-143, 189 and organizational effectiveness, 148; participatory, 164-165; and productivity, 164-165, 187-191, 192
Demographic changes in labor force. *See* Labor force, demographic changes
Denison, Edward F., 24, 225; reference to estimates of, 25, 27, 28, 29, 30, 217. *See also* Growth accounting
Department of Commerce, 10, 249, 258
Department of Health, Education and Welfare, Commissioner of Education, 260
Department of Labor, 121, 194; Administrator of Employment and Training, 260; Bureau of Labor Statistics, 31-33, 262; Employment and Training Administration, 260
Dynamic residual. *See* Residual, dynamic

Earnings. *See* Labor compensation
Economic Council of Canada, 39, 54, 58, 103
Economic growth, 103-108; and productivity growth, 30, 86, 98-99, 266; rate of, 14
Economies of scale, 28, 80, 102, 218, 273; constant or diminishing, 49-50; and economic growth, 28, 262; and productivity, 10, 13, 117, 233, 262

Education, 5, 230, 260; and quality of labor, 27, 259-261. *See also* Labor, quality of
Efficiency, 166-171. *See also* Productivity
Effort, as discretionary variable, 200-204, 210-216, 271; as game-theoretic problem, 204-207, 215. *See also* Labor, quality of
Employment, 78; and productivity, 21, 59, 247
Employment and Training Administration, 260
Energy, 32; price of, 51-52, 62, 78; and productivity, 35, 43, 51-53, 78, 111, 117
Environment of the firm, 134, 151-152, 166-171
Environmental movement, effect on productivity growth, 118-119, 187, 193
Environmental Protection Agency (EPA), 118-119, 125
Establishment Survey, Statistics Canada, 59
ETIP, 257

Factors of production: efficiency of, 91, 93; and productivity growth, 41-46, 50-51, 56, 125, 226-228; quality of, 118, 226; rate of substitution between, 10, 25, 32, 117; utilization of, 199. *See also* Labor, quality of; Natural resources, quality of
Farm sector: productivity growth of, 13, 16
Federal Center for Industrial R&D, 257
Feedback in decisionmaking, 164-165, 172, 174, 180, 183-184
Feldstein, Martin, President of the National Bureau of Economic Research, 250
Financial Accounting Standards Board, 256
Firm: Neoclassical theory of, 132-134, 137-138, 200, 218, 219; organizational behavior theory of, 133, 194; X-efficiency theory of, 217
First Ministers, 54
Fisherian rate of technical change, 99, 106-107
Foreign ownership, 232, 234-235, 236, 238-239

Free rider problem, 199, 205, 215; and labor productivity, 202-203, 215, 272. *See also* X-efficiency

Game-theoretic problem: of convention, 207-209; of effort determination, 204-207, 215
General Agreement on Tariffs and Trade (GATT), 233-235, 243-244
General Review of the Manufacturing Industries of Canada, 62
Goals: of economic actors, 137, 140, 148, 179, 200-201, 204; of government policies, 223-224; organizational, 149-150, 173, 174, 184
Goal-setting process, 134, 165; and productivity, 164-165, 190-193, 217. *See also* Management by objectives
Government policies, 235-239; and adjustment to lower tariffs, 235-236; and productivity growth, 29-30, 37, 80, 216, 231-239, 247-263, 273-274; and research and development, 244-245, 256-259
Gross National Product, 11, 24-25, 29; maximization of, 223-224; measurement of, 16, 223; and social welfare, 29. *See also* Productivity
Growth accounting, 4, 10, 225, 228-229; error in, 49; and international trade, 228-231; method of, 113-115; results of, 115-118; *See also* Residual

Hecksher-Ohlin-Samuelson theory of trade, 219, 229
Help Wanted Index, as measure of demand for labor, 78
Hicks, John R., induced innovation hypothesis, 214
Hicks-neutral technical change, 48, 49, 64, 88
Hours of work, 4, 60-61, 122; decline in, 29-30, 119-120, 260
Human capital, 27, 117. *See also* Labor, quality of

Industrial democracy, 193
Industrial psychology, 132
Industry mix, 126
Industry Productivity Division, Statistics Canada, 61
Inflation, 9-10, 109, 251; and productivity, 2, 17-19, 266

Information, 141, 142, 148, 150-163, 172-175, 183-185, 197; accessibility of, 151-152, 162-163; bias of, 158-163; communication of, 152-157, 162-163; distortion of, 153, 156-157, 162-163; and power, 160-162; weighting the importance of, 157-163
Intertemporal theory of production, 85-91
Investment: and business confidence, 254; and economic growth, 249-250; public sector, 255-256; and tax policy, 248-255. *See also* Capital formation

Job enrichment, 165
Job satisfaction, 120-123, 165
Joint Committee on Taxation, 253
Joint Financial Management Improvement Program, 263

Kendall tau coefficient, 113
Kennedy Round, 50, 233-234, 243-244
KLEM production function, 48, 63-67
Knowledge, advances in, 5-6, 25-26. *See also* Research and development; Technical change
Korean War, 113

Labor: demand for, 27, 259; quality of, and education, 4, 27, 119, 226, 230, 259-260, 273; quality of, effort component of, 3, 4, 119-122, 260, 270-273; quality of, measurement of, 5, 120; quality of, and motivation, 260; quality of, and productivity growth, 27, 118-119, 125, 247, 259-261; quality of, and health of safety, 260; quality of, and government policies, 248, 259-261; quality of, and training, 27, 230, 259-260, 273; restrictive work practices of, 260. *See also* Effort
Labor compensation, 18-19, 231
Labor efficiency, 29-30
Labor force: age-sex composition of, 27, 54, 117, 119, 125, 247, 260; demographic changes in, 4-5, 121-122, 125; and productivity growth, 24, 49, 51, 54, 80, 125
Labor hoarding, 43, 77-78, 269
Labor mobility, 28, 235

Labor productivity. See Productivity, labor
Labor unions, 5, 206–207, 213, 260, 262
Labor utilization, 16
Labour Division, Statistics Canada, 59
Labour Force Survey Division, Statistics Canada, 59
Lexicographic preference ordering, 209–212
Locke, E. A., theory of goal-setting, 164

Malinvaud intertemporal production frontier, 85–86
Malinvaud-type intertemporal technology, 86
Management by objectives (MBO), 165
Management control systems, 134, 171–175; and data validity, 172; extrinsic, 172–174, 175, 195; intrinsic, 174–175, 195; and self-regulation, 178–180, 181, 183–185. See also Reward systems
Management practices: and individual productivity, 175, 181–185; and motivation, 134–136, 165, 175
Manufacturing sector, 43–44, 77, 231, 232–234, 236–239
Mark Zero model of productivity growth, 107
Mark I model of productivity growth, 106
Mark II model of productivity growth, 106
Mark III model of productivity growth, 106–107
Monetary incentives, 165
Motivation, 135–137, 200–204, 215, 217; extrinsic, 172–174; intrinsic, 174–175; and productivity, 194, 260, 271; and social learning theory, 175–176, 178–180

National Bureau of Economic Research, 250
National Center for Productivity, 263
National Center for Productivity and Quality of Working Life, 260–261
National Commission on Productivity, 260
National Productivity Council, 261
National Research Council, Technical Information Service, 237–238
National Technical Information Service, 258

Natural resources, quality of, 30, 229–230, 261; and productivity growth, 27, 78, 247, 261–262
Neoclassical growth theory, 99
New York Stock Exchange, 109
NSF Innovation Center, 258

OPEC, 39, 43, 51
Occupational Safety and Health Act (OSHA), 118–119, 125–126
Office of Management and Budget, 261; Joint Financial Management Improvement Program, 263
Office of Science and Technology Policy, 255, 258
Office of the Assistant Secretary for Science and Technology, 258
Ontario Economic Council, 103
Ontario Ministry of Labour, 103
Organizational behavior, 271–272; and economic theory, 132–134; and productivity, 194, 196, 271–272
Organizational effectiveness, 135–136, 147–148, 169–171; and decision-making practices, 136–137; and goals, 149; and information flow, 162–163; and motivation, 136–137
Organizational efficiency, 166–167
Organizational goals, 132, 138–139, 140, 149–150, 164–166
Organizational structure, 134, 166–167, 169–171, 183–184, 195
Output/capital ratio, 17–19

Pollution laws, 126
Price deflator, 17–19
Prices, 17, 19, 32–33, 125, 231; input, 116–117; and productivity growth, 17, 19, 21
Primary sector, 44, 76, 78, 229
Prince Edward Island, productivity growth, 56
Prisoner's Dilemma, 204–207, 209, 213, 271
Product diversity, 232, 234, 238. See also Specialization
Production, intertemporal theory of, 85–91; neoclassical theory of, 88–91
Production function, 37, 48–49, 63–67, 203, 267–268
Productivity, Canada, 41–50, 68–80, 223–225, 240–242, 269; Canada–United States Comparisons, 41, 47–48, 56, 80, 218, 225–231, 233–234, 238, 240, 243, 269–270; of capital, 19; construction sector,

13-17 *passim*, 46; definition of, 1,
40, 110, 190, 267-268; farm sector,
12-17 *passim*, 27-28; growth, 15,
125-126, 228, 240-241; growth,
analysis of, 114-123, 247; growth,
projections of, 247, 272; growth,
sources of, 4-6, 10, 24-30, 33, 35,
40-42, 49-56, 111, 113, 114, 215,
228, 247; by industry, 12-17,
19-23, 33, 41-50, 77-79; labor, 3,
10, 17, 29-30, 40, 76-79, 109-111,
113, 260-261; labor definition of,
110; labor, and demographic change,
121-122; labor, growth of, 110-111,
113, 114-123; labor, measurement
of, 111, 119-120, 125; lag in growth
of, 2-6, 30, 117-118, 125, 187-190,
193, 196, 243, 268-270; lag in
growth of, causes of, 57, 118-123,
269-272; manufacturing sector,
12-17 *passim*, 43-44, 49-56, 77-79,
231, 232; measurement of, 3, 4,
13, 40, 63-75, 111, 113, 115-118,
119-120, 125, 223-224; measurement of, service sector, 44, 46;
partial ratios, 19; primary sector,
12-17 *passim*, 27-28, 44, 230;
service sector, 12-17 *passim*, 44, 46;
share-weighted, 33, 35-36; single
input, 3; and social conflict, 2, 266;
statistics, meaning of, 3; total factor,
25, 93, 98, 224-225, 267; total
factor, estimation of, 33, 63-67;
total tangible factor (TFP), 10-17,
33; United States, 4, 11-17, 110-
114, 268
Productivity Section, Statistics
Canada, 60
Profit, 17, 254; margin, 248, 251-252;
and productivity growth, 19, 218-
219; taxation of, 248-251
Profit maximization, 132, 138-139,
140

Quality of Employment Surveys,
120-122
Quality of labor. *See* Labor,
quality of
Quality of land. *See* Natural resources, quality of
Quality of Working life, 260-261

Ramsay utility function, 99
Rationality: assumption of 137, 139,
143-144; bounded, 140-142;
selective, 201-202; substantive vs.

procedural, 140-141.
See also Behavior
Regional problems, 56-57
Regulation, 27-28, 53-54, 118-119,
125-126, 263. *See also* Government policies
Regulatory reform, 254-255
Research, interdisciplinary, 131-132,
220, 271-272
Research and Development (R&D),
25, 125, 236-238, 252; and govern-
ment policies, 237-238, 244-245;
and productivity growth, 6, 25,
54-55, 115-116, 125, 248,
256-259; and taxation policy,
237-238, 248, 249, 256-257.
See also Technical change
Residual, 29-30, 33, 35, 54; analysis
of, 5-6, 113-114; dynamic, 86,
90-93, 98-99, 107, 266. *See also*
Productivity, total factor
Resource reallocations, 28, 30, 262
Restrictive work rules, 5, 30, 260,
261
Reward systems, 134, 179-180
Ricardian tradition of trade theory,
229
Roles, 135
Rules, 211

Satisficing, 139-140
Science Advisor to the President, 255
Science Council of Canada, 243,
244-245
Service sector, 44, 46
Small Business Investment Corpora-
tion, 258
Social conflict, 2, 266
Social Learning Theory (SLT),
175-176, 195; and motivation, 176,
178-180; and productivity, 181-185
Social security system, U.S., 250
Social trends, 30, 120-121, 193
Solow-type model of growth,
103-106
Specialization, 28, 50, 233-234, 237
Stagflation, 265-266
Standard of living, 2, 109-110, 266
Statistics Canada: Construction Divi-
sion, 61; Establishment Survey, 59;
Industry Product Division, 61;
Labour Division, 59; Labour Force
Survey, 59; Productivity Section, 60
Strike activity, 79
Subjective expected utility model
(SEU), 139

Survey Research Center, University of Michigan, 120-121

Tariff policy, 50, 218-219, 232-236, 243, 273
Tastes, change in, 21
Tax policy, 247-255, 273; reform of, 251-254
Tax Reform Act of 1969, 251, 252
Technical change, 49, 53, 101-102, 236; speed of adoption of, 236-238, 239; resistance to, 214-215; and productivity growth, 50-51, 242, 247
Technical Information Service, 237-238
Total tangible factor productivity (TFP). *See* Productivity, total tangible factor
Trade policy, 229, 261

Training, 27, 230, 259-260. *See also* Labor, quality of

Uncertainty, 167-171, 183
Unemployment, 24, 261; technological, 213-214
United States. *See* Productivity, United States
University of Michigan, Survey Research Center, 30, 120-121
Utility maximization, 138, 148, 212

Vietnam War, 122

Wages. *See* Labor compensation; Standard of living
Welfare, social, 2-3, 109, 223-224

X-efficiency, 199-204, 215, 218, 237, 271
X-inefficiency, 133, 196-197, 200, 219, 272

About the Editors

Shlomo Maital is associate professor of economics, Faculty of Industrial Engineering, Technion-Israel Institute of Technology, in Haifa, Israel. During 1977-80 he was a visiting lecturer in the economics department and Woodrow Wilson School of Public & International Affairs, Princeton University.

He has published scholarly articles on public finance, macroeconomics and the history of economic thought in *Econometrica, The American Economic Review, Economica, Public Finance, Journal of Public Economics, Journal of Econometrics, and The Economic Journal.*

Professor Maital's current research interest lies in applying psychology to understanding economic behavior. His book on this subject will be published in 1982.

Noah M. Meltz is a professor of economics and director of the Center for Industrial Relations, University of Toronto. He received his B. Comm. from the University of Toronto and an A.M. and Ph.D. from Princeton University. Professor Meltz was an economist with the Canada Department of Labor before joining the University of Toronto in 1964.

Labor market analysis is Professor Meltz's main area of research interest. He has conducted studies of historical occupational trends in Canada, as well as projections of future manpower requirements. His recent studies have dealt with the role of Canada Employment Centers in the labor market, the relationship between vacancies and unemployment in the post-war period, the occupational structure of earnings in Canada, work-sharing and job-sharing, and an economic analysis of shortages of tool and die makers.

Professor Meltz is a consultant to the Canada Department of Employment and Immigration, Economic Council of Canada, the Ontario Ministry of Labor, the Ontario Economic Council, and the Israel Central Bureau of Statistics. He is the past president of the Canadian Industrial Relations Association.

Participants

Hugh Arnold, Management Studies, University of Toronto
Orley Ashenfelter, Industrial Relations Section, Princeton University
Tassos Belessiotis, Ontario Economic Council
Ron Crowley, Central Analytical Services, Department of Labour
  (Canada)
D.J. Daly, Administrative Studies, York University
Edward Denison, Bureau of Economic Analysis, U.S. Department of
  Commerce
Arthur Donner, Research Securities of Canada Ltd.
Martin Evans, Management Studies, University of Toronto
Randall Filer, Department of Economics, Brandeis University
Robert House, Management Studies, University of Toronto
John W. Kendrick, Department of Economics, The George Washington
  University
John B. Kervin, Centre for Industrial Relations, University of Toronto
Harvey Leibenstein, Harvard University
Shlomo Maital, Woodrow Wilson School of Public & International
  Affairs, Princeton University, and Technion—Israel Institute of Tech-
  nology
Noah Meltz, Centre for Industrial Relations, University of Toronto
Mark Mueller, Department of Labour (Canada)
Mieko Nishimizu, Woodrow Wilson School of Public & International
  Affairs, Princeton University
John Norsworthy, Bureau of Labor Statistics, U.S. Department of Labor
Sylvia Ostry, O.E.C.D.
P.S. Rao, Economic Council of Canada
Al Rees, Sloan Foundation
Frank Reid, Centre for Industrial Relations, University of Toronto
John Sawyer, Institute for Policy Analysis, University of Toronto
Farid Siddiqui, Research Branch, Ontario Ministry of Labour
Gerald Swartz, Research Branch, Ontario Ministry of Labour
Lorie Tarshis, Ontario Economic Council
John Vanderkamp, Department of Economics, University of Guelph
Leonard Waverman, Institute for Policy Analysis, University of Toronto